UML &
Data
Modeling:
A Reconciliation

David C. Hay

Foreword by Sridhar Iyengar

Published by:
Technics Publications, LLC
966 Woodmere Drive
Westfield, NJ 07090 U.S.A.
www.technicspub.com
Edited by Carol Lehn
Cover design by Mark Brye

Cover Origami:
Designed by Tomako Fusé
Folded by David C. Hay
Photographed by Włodzimersz Kurniewicz

Copyright © 2011 by David C. Hay
ISBN, print ed.   978-1-9355041-9-1
Printing (4 5 6 7 8 9)
Library of Congress Control Number: 2011938560

ATTENTION SCHOOLS AND BUSINESSES: Technics Publications books are available at quantity discounts with bulk purchase for educational, business, or sales promotional use. For information, please write to Technics Publications, 966 Woodmere Drive, Westfield, NJ 07090, or email Steve Hoberman, President of Technics Publications, at me@stevehoberman.com.

Dedicated in memory of my college roommate and life-long friend:

Mark Rumsey MacHogan
1947-2010

Table of Contents

Foreword

By Sridhar Iyengar

I had the interesting experience of initially meeting David Hay in the late 1990s a couple of years after Unified Modeling Language (UML) became an Object Management Group (OMG) standard. I was giving a talk at the DAMA Data Warehouse Conference on the topic of modeling and metadata management using UML and a related standard at OMG called the Meta Object Facility (MOF). The audience was interested to learn about UML but somewhat skeptical because the use of Peter Chen's E/R modeling notation was well known and established in the data modeling community. There was one particular attendee (you guessed right - it was David!) who was a little more vocal than the rest and challenged me when I asserted that UML and its notation was not just for object modelers but could also help data modelers. I thoroughly enjoyed the debate but confess I was a bit irritated because the flow of my talk was interrupted a bit!

What followed back and forth at this conference and again in a couple of follow on conferences was an indication of how widespread the 'impedance mismatch' was that existed between the community of data modelers/data architects and object modelers/object architects. There were several debates during talks and also after talks during cocktails on this clash of data/object modelers and I challenged the audience to be more open minded about UML in part because there was a lot more to UML than just simple structural modeling of objects.

I was extremely pleased to see David join the effort at OMG in establishing a new Information modeling and Metadata Management standard. David was determined to do something that others had tried but given up too soon. He really wanted to bridge the data modeling and object/UML modeling community not just by using the UML notation in a superficial manner, but also by addressing concerns that data architects and data modelers actually faced in their daily work – concerns about structure and semantics, as well as notation and methodology familiar to data modelers. I have followed the debates on OMG mailing lists where David over the years has earned the respect of his object modeling colleagues (he clearly already did this in the data modeling community years ago) and ultimately influenced the standard and along the way finished this much needed book – a practical handbook.

David has pulled off the impossible – balancing the need to keep the notation familiar enough to data modelers but acknowledge the audience already familiar with UML – and explaining not just the notation, but also the best practices in data modeling as he leads the reader using practical and simple to understand examples. In that sense, David is 'with the reader' in his/her journey to use the UML notation (with or without UML tools) effectively for data modeling and architecture. The author's experience, pragmatism and a community building expertise are well demonstrated in this book. He has even included a historical background of the two communities involved. (We are both showing our years of experience and gray hair!)

This book comes at a time when data modelers, object modelers and semantic web modelers are all beginning to realize the value of modeling and architecture. My hope is that this book brings those communities together, because in this world of big data and deep analytics, and the need to understand both structured and unstructured data – attention to design and architecture is key to building resilient data intensive systems for the mobile and connected world. We are realizing more and more that the value we derive is not just from the programs that run on various devices and servers, but from the underlying data. The better we understand the data, the more we can gain from the designing, using and analyzing internet scale data systems.

David – You have done it! Thanks for taking on the this very important work of bridging data modelers and UML modelers, extending the state of the art and for writing about this important notation and technique that will guide data modelers for years to come.

I hope you learn and gain as much from reading this book as I did. Enjoy!

Sridhar Iyengar, an IBM Distinguished Engineer, serves on the OMG Board of Directors and is working on the development and integration of Architecture, Business and IT Modeling standards. He leads the technical strategy for Software Tools & Methods Research at the IBM TJ Watson Research Center. Sridhar is also a member of the IBM Software Group Architecture Board Steering Committee helping drive software tools direction across IBM.

Preface

Since Leibniz there has perhaps been no man who has had a full command of all the intellectual activity of his day. Since that time, science has been increasingly the task of specialists, in fields which show a tendency to grow progressively narrower. A century ago there may have been no Leibniz, but there was a Gauss, a Faraday, and a Darwin. Today there are few scholars who can call themselves mathematicians or physicists or biologists without restriction.

A man may be a topologist or an acoustician or a coleopterist. He will be filled with the jargon of his field, and will know all its literature and all its ramifications, but, more frequently than not, he will regard the next subject as something belonging to his colleague three doors down the corridor, and will consider any interest in it on his own part as an unwarrantable breach of privacy.

- Norbert Wiener, *Cybernetics*; 1948.[1]

This book is about two "camps" in the information management world that each represent large bodies of specialized knowledge. Those in each camp suffer from the specialization phenomenon described above by Dr. Wiener. Each seems to be seriously unenlightened about the other.

Data modeling or object modeling? Whose side are you on? Why are there sides? What's going on here?

After a decade of various people's trying to represent data structures graphically, the entity/relationship version of the data model was formalized in 1976,[2] and variations on it have followed. The Unified

---

[1] Norbert Wiener. 1948, 1961. *Cybernetics: of Control and Communication in the Animal and the Machine, second edition.* (Cambridge, MA, The MIT Press). 2.

[2] Peter Chen. 1977. "The Entity-Relationship Approach to Logical Data Base Design". The Q.E.D. Monograph *Series: Data Management.* Wellesley, MA: Q.E.D. Information Sciences, Inc. This is based on his article, "The Entity-Relationship Model: Towards a

Modeling Language (UML) was officially released a little over twenty years later, in 1997.[3] Its adherents claim that UML's "Class Model" is the rightful successor to the data model. Others are not convinced.

The fact of the matter is that the intellectual underpinnings and the orientation of UML's object-oriented model are very different from those of the data modelers' entity/relationship model. There appears to be a kind of intellectual "impedance mismatch" between the two approaches.[*] This is partially *technological*, as object-oriented programmers attempt to save persistent object data in relational databases—which have significantly different structures from them.[4] It's also a *cultural* mismatch, however, coming from significant differences in world views about systems development.[5] UML, after all, was originally intended to support object-oriented *design*, while data (entity/relationship) modeling was intended to support the *analysis* of business structures. These are very different things.

Unified View of Data", ACM Transactions on Database Systems, Vol. 1, No. 1, (March 1976), pages 9-36.

[3]   Object Management Group (OMG). 1997. "UML Specification version 1.1". (OMG document ad/97-08-11). Published at http://www.omg.org/cgi-bin/doc?ad/97-08-11.

[*]   The analogy is derived from electrical engineering, where the term "impedance matching" refers to the use of a transformer to make the load (impedance) required on a target device (such as a loudspeaker) match the load produced on a source device (such as an amplifier). This is described in (among other places): American Radio Relay League, 1958. *The Radio Amateur's Handbook: The Standard Manual of Amateur Radio Communication.* (Concord, New Hampshire: The Rumford Press).

[4]   Ted Neward. 2006. "The Vietnam of Computer Science", *The Blog Ride: Ted Neward's Technical Blog.* June 26, 2006. Retrieved from http://blogs.tedneward.com/2006/06/26/The+Vietnam+Of+Computer+Science.aspx, 7/10/2011.

[5]   Scot Ambler. 2009 "The Cultural Impedance Mismatch", The Data Administration Newsletter. August 1, 2009. Available at: http://www.tdan.com/view-articles/11066.

In 1960, my father observed that up until about 1949, he knew everything there was to know about radio technology. Never again would he be able to say that.

In 1969, when I began my career in information technology, the body of knowledge I looked forward to mastering seemed pretty formidable. I had learned Fortran in college, but now I would have to master Basic and COBOL. And then there was IBM's Job Control Language, which was required if I was to use the operating system. This was *too much!*

Little did I know…

What ultimately happened was that a very large proportion of what is to be known *now* in this industry concerns things that *did not exist* in 1969. Each of the two "camps" being alluded to in this book is responsible for a profoundly huge body of relatively new knowledge. Each body of knowledge and its associated disciplines have come into existence only in the last 40 years—but each is immense. Maintaining mastery of either is sufficiently challenging that it is easy to ignore those in other—even adjacent—disciplines.

Moreover, the interaction of the two disciplines has also followed Dr. Wiener's prediction:

"These specialized fields are continually growing and invading new territory. The result is like what occurred when the Oregon country was being invaded simultaneously by the United States settlers, the British, the Mexicans, and the Russians—an inextricable tangle of exploration, nomenclature, and laws."[6]

We all, however, ignore those adjacent disciplines at our peril. It behooves data modelers to learn enough about object-oriented design to understand the implications of the assertions made in their models. It would also benefit object-oriented designers to understand enough about the challenges of data and database administration to be able to make sense out of the data-oriented specifications (and problems) they have to respond to.

More significantly, both groups are encouraged at least to understand the differences between their worlds if they are to fully understand how business requirements can become system requirements.

---

[6]   Norbert Wiener. 1948, 1961. *Op. cit.* 2.

Oh, and did I mention that the Semantic Web is lurking out there? You understand, don't you, that this is an entirely *new* body of knowledge–that will change everything yet again.

The assignment today is to try to reconcile the object-oriented and the data groups. On the one hand, it is for data modelers to learn how to use a new technique–a sub-set of the UML notation–to produce the business-oriented entity/relationship models they know. On the other hand, it is for object-oriented UML modelers to improve their knowledge of a technique they already know, in order to expand their understanding just what a data model could be. Moreover, after reading this book, both groups should have a better understanding of just what makes a "good" business data model.

David C. Hay
Houston, Texas

Acknowledgements

After 20 years as a data modeling bigot, and 5 of those being UML's worst critic, I must thank Dagna Gaythorpe and DAMA International for signing me up to work with the Object Management Group, in order to work with them on the Information Metadata Model (IMM). I must admit that I felt a little like a KGB agent in the CIA the first time I attended an OMG meeting, but all were most friendly and helpful, so the experience turned out to be profound and extremely valuable.

This of course leads me to offer my true thanks to the OMG IMM team for finally forcing me to really understand what UML is all about, and why it is like it is.

In particular, I want to thank Jim Logan, Ken Hussey, and Pete Rivet for helping me come to grips with the different thought processes that are behind UML. Learning a new language—especially when it means learning a new culture and a new way of looking at the world—is difficult, and I really appreciate their patience.

I only hope that I have represented that point of view fairly.

My gratitude also goes to my mentors in the data modeling world: Richard Barker, Cliff Longman, and Mike Lynott. They are the ones who introduced me to the conceptual ("semantic") way of looking at the world. Meeting them as an adult finally showed me what I wanted to do when I grew up.

In particular, Mike has put in a great deal of effort editing and helping to shape this book.

Thanks also to Bob Seiner, publisher of *The Data Administration Newsletter*, for publishing a series of four articles in 2008, "UML as a Data Modeling Notation". These articles served as the seeds for this book.

Much appreciation goes to the people who read the manuscript and provided useful comments and suggestions: Roland Berg, Harry Ellis, William Frank, Allan Kolber, Kent Graziano, Frank Palmeri, and Russell Searle.

Thanks also must go to my Publisher, Steve Hoberman and Editor Carol Lehn-Dodson for helping put this whole work together.

And as always, my greatest appreciation goes to my wife, Jola for her patience, and to my children Bob and Pamela for their inspiration.

Chapter 1: Introductions

This book has two audiences:

- Data modelers (both analysts and database designers) who are convinced that UML has nothing to do with them; and

- UML experts who don't realize that architectural data modeling really *is* different from object modeling (and that the differences are important).

Your author's objective is to finally bring these groups together in peace.

The easy part of the book (for all audiences) is to understand the notation required for this joint approach. More difficult is the change in attitude required in each case. The objective here is to become successful architectural entity/relationship modelers—who happen to use the UML notation. The idea is to provide *all* modelers with guidance on how to produce a high quality entity/relationship model to describe the underlying data architecture for an organization. The notation we will be using happens to be the Unified Modeling Language Class Diagram.

The Structure of the Book

This book is in four parts:

- *Chapter One: Introductions* – Separate Introductions for data modelers and UML modelers, along with an introduction for all.

- *Chapter Two: UML and Architectural Models* – A detailed description of the underlying issues between UML Class notation and conceptual entity/relationship models.

- *Chapter Three: How to Draw a Data Model in UML* – A systematic description of the steps and best practices for making the entity/relationship model using (a slightly modified version of) the UML notation. Specifically, how to create a model to be a powerful tool, to support both the definition of requirements and the systems development process overall.

- *Chapter Four: An Example* – An excerpt of the model presented in the companion book to this one. This shows both the mechanics of using UML, as well as demonstrating best practices for presentation.

- *Appendix A* – A brief summary of the approach.

- *Appendix B* – A history of modeling in the information technology industry, including the divergent paths that led to the current impasse.

This chapter contains three introductions: one directed to each of the communities involved, followed by one describing the nature of the issues that have traditionally separated the two groups. This third introduction, for both audiences, includes a bit of history, plus a description of an architectural framework to put the various points of view in context.

All of this is in preparation for the heart of the effort: how to use a modified version of the Unified Modeling Language (UML) to produce an effective business-oriented conceptual entity/relationship model.

Observations

Before proceeding, three observations should be kept in mind:

- There are better and worse data modelers.

- There are better and worse UML modelers.

- Neither "community" is as homogeneous as the previous paragraphs would suggest.

Introduction for Data Modelers

Premise: A class model in UML is not the same thing as an entity/relationship model.

The Unified Modeling Language (UML) began as a collection of elements to support object-oriented design. It was derived from an assortment of existing approaches and, as a result, it is not a single notation. Rather, it is an array of notations for modeling elements as diverse as classes, behaviors, events, and others.

By the time *object (class) models* appeared in the early 1990s, the use of models to support the discovery of system requirements for business was already highly developed. Both *data flow diagrams* and entity/relationship data models were nearly 20 years old. Modeling in that context (whether it was data flows, processes, events, or data structures) clearly distinguished between modeling the nature of the business and modeling the systems that would support that business.

Then, in 1990, Peter Coad and Edward Yourdon coined the term *"object-oriented analysis"* to describe a merging of the "semantic data modeling" approach (as they described entity/relationship modeling) with object-oriented programming concepts such as services and messages.[7] They claimed that semantic data modeling did not provide adequately for inheritance, and asserted that classification structure and assembly structure were not adequately treated.[*] In their view, object-oriented analysis would address both of these shortcomings.

To their credit, they still viewed the assignment as one of addressing the *problem space* (the business) rather than the *solution space* (the computer and its programs). To them an "object" was "an encapsulation of Attributes and exclusive Services; an abstraction of *something in the problem space*, with some number of instances in the problem space." (Emphasis added.)[8]

Unfortunately, over the successive years, the connections with the problem space became more distant. By the time UML came into existence, the aspect of analyzing the world outside the computer appears to have been lost.

In 1999, the "three amigos" of UML (James Rumbaugh, Ivar Jacobson, and Grady Booch), defined an *object* as a "discrete entity with a well-defined boundary and identity that encapsulates state and behavior; an instance of a class".[9] A *class*, in turn, is "the descriptor for a set of

---

[7] Peter Coad and Edward Yourdon. 1990. *Object-Oriented Analysis* (Englewood Cliffs, NJ: Yourdon Press).

[*] As it happens, they were wrong on both counts. Semantic data modeling does account for inheritance through sub-types and super-types. And classification and assembly structures can be represented as well.

[8] Ibid. page 31.

[9] James Rumbaugh, Ivar Jacobson, and Grady Booch. 1999. *The Unified Modeling Language Reference Manual.* Reading, Massachusetts: Addison-Wesley. 30.

objects that share the same attributes, operations, methods, relationships, and behavior."[10] Note that there are no constraints in either of these definitions as to what kinds of objects or classes are of interest. *Anything* is an object.

To the extent that the term "object-oriented analysis" continued to be used, it placed much more emphasis on the "object-oriented" than on the "analysis".

The entity/relationship modeling world uses classes in a similar way to those in UML, but it has a much narrower definition of what constitutes a class. First of all, an "entity" (in the entity/relationship world), unlike an "object" (in the object-oriented world), is not concerned with operations, methods, or behavior. Those belong to the world of "process modeling." An entity/relationship model is only concerned with the *structure* of data. Second, an *entity class*♣ in an entity/relationship model is not just a class of any "discrete entities with a well-defined boundaries and identities". It is limited to what Richard Barker calls classes of things or objects "of significance, whether real or imagined, about which information needs to be known or held."[11]

The entity/relationship orientation being addressed in this book is concerned only with those entities that are of interest to a business, while traditional UML encompasses any objects and classes that one can come

---

[10]   Ibid.p.185.

♣   When he first developed the technique of data modeling, Dr. Chen referred to an "entity" as a thing in the world and an "entity type" as the definition of a class of such things. It was an entity type that was represented by a box on the diagram. Over time, however, people became careless and used the word "entity" to refer to the entity type boxes. With the advent of object-orientation, with its clearer distinction between "objects" and "classes", it became apparent that discipline should be re-introduced to the data modeling world. In the interests of this, and to recognize the common structures of the two worlds, entity types will herein be referred to as **entity classes**.

[11]   Richard Barker, 1990, *CASE*Method: Entity Relationship Modeling* (Wokingham, England: Addison-Wesley).

up with. Indeed, according to James Martin and James Odell, an "object type" (that is, a "class") is simply "a concept".[12]

Any concept.

This includes computer elements and artifacts in addition to those of interest to the business.

Does this mean that the UML class diagram *notation* cannot be used to produce conceptual entity/relationship diagrams? Of course it doesn't. The data model entities to be discussed here are certainly a subset of the objects defined by the three amigos.

The problem for data modelers (whether business modelers or database designers) is that UML is *here*. Whatever its flaws, it is widely recognized as a standard. The general public sees no difference between a UML class model and any kind of entity/relationship data model. We can proclaim that UML is fundamentally different from data modeling and has nothing to do with database design—but none of this prevents clients and hiring managers from asking whether you know how to model with UML.

Your author has been one of the most vocal opponents of UML's approach to class models over the years, primarily on aesthetic grounds, but also because of its design orientation.[13] In more recent years, however, he has "gone over to the dark side" and has been working on a project for the Object Management Group (OMG), the creators of UML. That OMG project (***Information Metadata Management*** or ***IMM***) is initiated to produce a set of metamodels that would describe entity/relationship modeling itself, as well as relational database design, XML Schema design, and others. It was necessary in this project to produce what are essentially "conceptual" entity/relationship models—even for such technologically bound subjects as relational database and XML Schema design—but since it is the OMG, it was considered politic to use UML Class notation.

Ok, it's true. It *can* be done. To be sure, the tools for manipulating UML are significantly more complex to use, because UML (even the class

---

[12]   James Martin and James Odell, 1995, Object-Oriented Method: A Foundation (Englewood Cliffs, NJ: PTR Prentice Hall).

[13]   Among others, see David Hay, 1999, "UML Misses the Boat." East Coast Oracle Users' Group: ECO 99 (Conference Proceedings / HTML File). Apr 1, 1999. Available at http://essentialstrategies.com/publications/objects/umleco.htm.

models) includes annotations specific to object-oriented design, which are unneeded in an entity/relationship model. With patience, however, an appropriate sub-set of the notation can be lifted and used. It is a matter of learning how to turn off the object-oriented options in the tool.

Numerous software programs are available for drawing UML diagrams. Your author has only used one tool, MagicDraw, offered by NoMagic, Inc. This one he found to be quite adaptable to his requirements. At first it looked as though there were some logical obstacles that prevented conceptual entity/relationship modeling from being done at all.

It turned out, however, that in each case (in MagicDraw, at least), there was always a "secret handshake"[*] that made the required step possible.

It is important to realize the three premises behind the approach described in this book:

1) Only entity classes that *pertain to the business at hand*[♦] will be treated.

2) Only a *subset* of the *notation* used in UML can be used to represent the semantics of a business or other domain.

3) The *meaning* of one symbol is subtly–if fundamentally–different from that used in the object-oriented world. In particular, in UML, "roleName" means something very different from the entity/relationship modeler's idea of a role name.

With these slightly different meanings, a diagram using these subsets carries exactly the same semantics as a corresponding diagram using the

---

[*] Translation for non-Americans: back in the 19th Century, private clubs would only admit people who revealed their membership by shaking hands in a particular way. To get in, you "just had to know the secret handshake". Much software is the same way. To get access to a particular feature, "you just have to know…".

[♦] "Business at hand" refers to the subject being modeled, which might be a business to be sure, but it might also be a microbiology lab or a space shuttle. The key is that we are interested in describing the "problem space", not the "solution space." For convenience in this book the term will be "business", even though the subject matter could well be other than commercial. In other cases the non-committal "domain" will be used.

Information Engineering, Barker/Ellis, or any other entity/relationship notation.

This book shows you how to do it. It will take familiar concepts and show you how to represent them using the UML class notation. The notation is not (dare we say it?) pretty. But it is viable.

Note, however, that issues with UML modeling notwithstanding, people even within the data modeling community have very different ideas about what constitutes a "good" data model. Be advised, therefore, that this book does reflect the prejudices of your author. He has been doing data modeling for over twenty years, now, and learned from the beginning to address it as a semantic, not a technical discipline.

This book will reflect that history and those prejudices.

Thus, even as the book will show UML modelers how to expand their horizons to use their notation in a new way, it will also introduce you, as data modelers, to a new notation. Moreover, you should also be able to improve your skills for producing accurate and coherent models of a business or governmental domain—whatever notation you finally adopt.

Introduction for UML Modelers

Premise: An entity/relationship model is not the same thing as a class model in UML.

Data modelers come in at least two varieties. Some (***database modelers***) view data modeling as a prelude to database design, and, in fact, include many relational design concepts (such as "foreign keys") in their data models. Using ERwin as a modeling tool, with its emphasis on database design techniques, is particularly conducive to that way of thinking. The second group (***business concept modelers***) views data modeling as a way to describe the language of a business without regard for the technology that might one day capture and manage its data. Their assignment is to understand the nature of the organization well enough that system requirements described by business clients can be put in a proper context. This group tends to view the world a bit more abstractly and is concerned with accurately describing the business, without addressing such things as database performance.

The first group creates what are here called *logical data models,*[*] while the second group creates what will here be called *conceptual data models.*[♥]

Both of these groups find UML to be at least annoying, if not threatening to their world views. The *database* modelers are up against the fact that the *object-oriented approach* to data is dramatically different from the *relational database approach.* Most significantly, object-orientation makes extensive use of sub-typing (*inheritance*), while this cannot be directly represented in a purely relational database.

Moreover, while the database modeler views a database as a corporate resource and is concerned with controlling access to the data and their definitions, the object-oriented developer is concerned with designing data (object) structures as a part of program design. As used by an object-oriented designer, a class in UML refers to a piece of program code that describes a set of attributes and behaviors—with objects in that class coming into existence and going out of existence as needed. There are no formal structures for controlling the definitions of classes, and any data security measures must be programmed explicitly. Thus, to an object-oriented designer and programmer, the disciplines and security constraints being invoked by the database administrator are a hindrance to the rapid development of systems.

From the point of view of the *business concept* modelers, **UML class models** are different from **entity/relationship models** (conceptual ones, at least) because the object-oriented community is *not constrained* in specifying what constitutes a class. Pretty much anything (including elements of the technology itself) can be an *object.* These then are collected into a UML *class.* In the conceptual entity/relationship world,

---

[*]   Words and phrases highlighted with bold italics are defined further in "Appendix I: Glossary".

[♥]   For an industry that is all about getting the business to clean up its vocabulary to describe its world coherently and consistently, the data modeling business has its own problem with language. There are at least two definitions extant for both "conceptual modeling" and "logical modeling" These discrepancies will be disposed of shortly. For the moment, the definitions presented here will have to do.

on the other hand, an entity can *only* be something of significance to the business, about which it wishes to hold information.[*]

Among other things, the business modeler's objective in creating a model is to present it to an audience of business experts who know nothing about modeling, but who know enough about their business to determine whether the model accurately describes it or not. For this reason, *aesthetics* is important. The viewer must be able to understand what is being asserted by the model. UML, on the other hand, was not developed with an eye towards the aesthetic implications of the notation.

Moreover, from the point of view of both groups of data modelers, a *relationship* is treated very differently from an object-oriented designer's *association*. In the former case, a relationship is a *structure* connecting two entity classes together. It is complete, like a bridge, with two ends. Both must be present and named. The object-oriented designer, on the other hand, sees an association as consisting of two (or more) *paths*. In this case, what is important is not the structure itself, but what processing is either required or possible to get from one side to the other.

As it happens, this particular discrepancy has technological origins: In a relational database management system, once an association is created between two classes (and implemented with two tables), it is equally "navigable" in both directions. In object-oriented programs, code must be written to go in each direction between two classes.

This book will mostly make use of familiar UML, although it will have to bend it a little to create the equivalent of a conceptual entity/relationship diagram.

But it is important to realize three things about using UML to do conceptual entity/relationship modeling:

1) Only entity classes that *pertain to the business at hand*[♥] will be treated.

---

[*]   In fact, some data modelers are a bit casual in the way they define entities, so it is to be hoped that they too can benefit from this book.

[♥]   "Business at hand" refers to the subject being modeled, which might be a business or a microbiology lab or a Space Shuttle. The key is that we are interested in describing the "problem space", not the "solution space." For convenience in this book, the term will be "business", even though the subject matter could well be other than

2) Only a *subset* of the *notation* normally used in UML can be used to represent the semantics of a business or other domain.

3) The *meaning* of some symbols is subtly–and fundamentally–different from their meaning as used in the object-oriented world. In particular, in UML, "role name" means something very different from the entity/relationship modeler's idea of a relationship name.

Note, however, that issues with UML modeling twists notwithstanding, people even within the data modeling community have very different ideas about what constitutes a "good" object model. In the face of that, be advised that the book you are viewing reflects the prejudices of your author. He has been doing data modeling for over twenty years, now, and learned from the beginning to address it as a semantic, not a technical discipline–with special emphasis on the word "discipline".

This book will reflect that history and those prejudices.

So, even as the book will show data modelers how to expand their horizons to use UML, perhaps it will also introduce you to using UML in a new way as well—to produce more business-oriented models.

Combined Introduction

The approach to modeling in this book is predicated on an understanding of both the history and the current perspectives of the two communities. The history is presented in more detail in Appendix B, but a few words about it are worth mentioning here. The current perspectives of the two communities are best understood in terms originally laid out by John Zachman in his "Framework for Information Architecture" and refined by your author. This "combined introduction" addresses both of these points.

Historical Threads

The history describes the concepts that have driven the information processing industry and how they are interrelated in complex ways. Each person who created a ground-breaking concept at any time was undoubtedly well-read and knew a lot about what had gone before—in

commercial. In other cases, the non-committal "organization" will be used.

various areas of interest. But even so, that person's readings and exposure to ideas were invariably selective, reflecting his or her personal biases and interests.

Appendix B contains an extensive history of the information technology industry. What is striking about that are the three main threads:

- **Data Processing** – The origins of computers and programming

- **Object-oriented Development** – The advent of object-oriented programming and the changes that it brought to the whole development process.

- **Data Architecture** – Recognition of an enterprise's data as an asset as significant as money, human resources, and capital equipment and the effect of this on how data are managed.

The stream that is "Object-oriented Development" is noteworthy for being dominated by the technology of computer programming. Both the languages themselves and the way people organized programs were the domain of people whose lives were dominated by the task of producing working, effective, and powerful program code. Data are seen by these people as elements to be manipulated by programs. Even the insight of object-orientation–organize the programs around data rather than processes–did not change the fundamental fact that programs are themselves "processes".

The stream that is here labeled "Data Architecture" is noteworthy for not being dominated by technology at all. While database technologies have formed a large part of the history of this field, the focus of this industry is less on the technology than on how the data are gathered, processed, and–most significantly–*used* in the business. Data are treated as resources to be managed, manipulated, and controlled. Technology's role is to make this possible. Who produces data? What transportation and translation occurs before they get to their ultimate consumers? Who has the right to modify data structures? Who has the right to have access to the data? These are among the questions addressed by data management. Programs are written to support the actors that manipulate data themselves, but it is the organization and security of those data that are most important to the enterprise.

Architectural Framework

The current perspectives of the two communities are best understood by looking at the world in terms of an *Architectural Framework*.

In 1980, John Zachman published his "Framework for Information Systems Architecture",[14] wherein he tried to establish a comprehensive set of categories for understanding the body of knowledge that is information's role in an enterprise. His great insight was to recognize that, in the development of information systems, different participants have very different views of the effort. In particular, he identified six different *perspectives* or *views*. In 2003, your author modified the terms for the central three of those.[15] He did not, however, change the fact that, fundamentally, there are two overall categories: views of the business, and views of the technology. Specifically, the perspectives are:

Views of the Business

1. **Scope (planner's view):** This defines the enterprise's direction and business purpose. This is necessary in order to establish the context for any system-development effort. It includes definitions of the boundaries of system-development or other development projects.

2. **Enterprise model (owner's view):** This defines–in business terms–the nature of the business, including its structure, processes, organization, and so forth.

3. **Model of fundamental concepts (essential view):** This row (called the "information-system designer's view" in Mr. Zachman's original version), defines the business described in Row Two, but in more rigorous terms. Note that to arrive at this view, it is necessary to examine the underlying essence (fundamental structures) of the business owners' views of the enterprise.

Views of Technology

4. **Technology model (designer's view):** This row (called the "builders' view" in Mr. Zachman's version) is the first

---

[14]   John Zachman, 1987, "A framework for information systems architecture", IBM Systems Journal, Vol. 26, No. 3. (IBM Publication G321-5298)

[15]   David Hay, 2003. *Requirements Analysis: From Business Views to Architecture*. Englewood Cliffs, NJ: Prentice Hall PTR.

perspective that deals with technology. It describes how technology may be used to address the information-processing needs identified in the previous rows. Here, object-oriented databases are chosen over relational ones (or vice versa), kinds of languages are selected, an approach to structuring programs is selected, user interface techniques are identified, and so forth.

5. ***Detailed representations (builder's view):*** This row (called the "sub-contractor's view" in Mr. Zachman's version) sees the details of a particular language, database storage specifications, networks, and so forth, from the view of the person actually building new systems.

6. ***Functioning system:*** Finally, a new view is presented to the organization in the form of a new system.

The original version of the Framework then addressed, for each of these "rows", the dimensions of what each row views: data (what), activities and functions (how), and locations (where).

For purposes of this discussion, we are concerned only with the first column: data (and, to a lesser degree activities) and the middle three viewers: business owner, architect, and designer. The groups we are discussing in this book are shown in the graphic representation of the Architecture Framework shown in Figure 1-1.

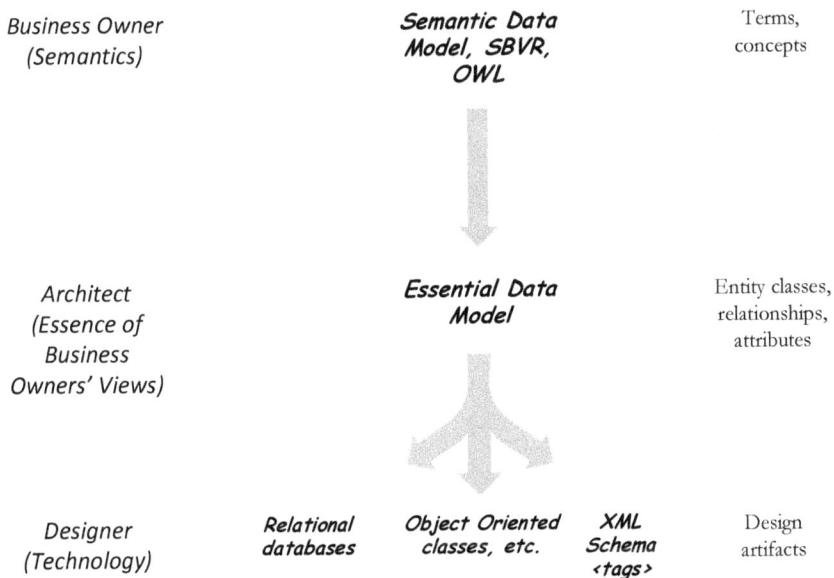

Business Owner (Semantics)	***Semantic Data Model, SBVR, OWL***	Terms, concepts
Architect (Essence of Business Owners' Views)	***Essential Data Model***	Entity classes, relationships, attributes
Designer (Technology)	*Relational databases* ***Object Oriented classes, etc.*** *XML Schema ‹tags›*	Design artifacts

Figure 1-1: The Players and Their Artifacts

A particularly powerful tool for describing the nature and structure of a business is the entity/relationship diagram. Among other things, the technique can be used to produce a "conceptual data model". Unfortunately, in our industry, there are several definitions for "conceptual data model", as will be discussed in more detail in Chapter Two. For our purposes, there are two kinds that are of interest: the **semantic data model** and the **architectural data model.** Either is a drawing of things or objects of significance to a business, along with relationships among them. Also, in either case, the model can be used to allow business people to see clearly what things about the business the analyst may have misunderstood. Finding such misunderstandings during a modeling session (and correcting them, of course) is vastly cheaper than finding them embodied in a system that was subsequently built at great expense. This, among other things, provides a very good basis for the data management objective of managing a company's data as a corporate resource.

Business Owner's View

The business owner's view (the "Row Two" model) can be supported, to some degree, by a semantic data model, where entity classes represent only the concrete things seen by business people in their terms. It is not, however, very effective at representing the different terms people use for the same things, or for representing different things that may have the same name. Because of the often conflicting ways different people describe their worlds, therefore, it is often better to use something like the semantic language, **Web Ontology Language** (**OWL**), or the English (or other natural) language descriptions that constitute the Object Management Group's approach to semantics and business rules, *The Semantics of Business Vocabulary and Business Rules.*

The Web Ontology Language (OWL) is actually one of a succession of languages developed for the **Semantic Web**–an extension of the World Wide Web that addresses the structure of data, not just of web sites.♥ The idea is that sentences can be expressed in a structured way, where each of the terms is reference to an identified object on the world-wide web. The structure of the sentences is defined in terms of the **Resource**

♥   For the best introduction to the Semantic Web and the OWL, see Dan Allemang and Jim Hendler. 2009. *Semantic Web for the Working Ontologist: Effective Modeling in RDFS and OWL.* (Boston: Morgan Kaufmann).

Definition Framework, an approach that reduces all language to subjects, predicates, and objects. Thus, the sentence that "a **Pension Plan** (is) BasedOn a **Component of Legislation**" is an RDF expression, with the terms "Pension Plan" "BasedOn" and "Component of Legislation" all identified as terms on the world-wide web. Ideally, by using the same **Unique Reference Identifier** (**URI**) all occurrences of a term would refer to the same definition, although people are not required to use the same URI for a term, so this is not guaranteed. The **Web Ontology Language** (OWL) takes this further to provide semantics for making inferences from the basic sentences.

This is a relatively new way of setting out to define a business, which specifically makes it possible to capture exactly the language used by any business person, and provides a way to make the definitions consistent.

The Object Management Group (OMG) published a different approach to business semantics in 2008, *The Semantics of Business Vocabulary and Business Rules* (SBVR).♠ This also attempts to provide structure to language for expressing rules. Here, without using the World Wide Web, each term is also carefully defined, as well as the propositions that link them together. For example, in the context of a rental care agency, a *Branch* is defined as a **Rental Organization unit** that has *rental responsibility*. This is the definition of "Branch", in terms of "Rental Organization", a term that is defined elsewhere, and *rental responsibility*, a predicate that is defined elsewhere.

Architect's View

A more powerful way to use the entity/relationship approach is to describe the architect's view ("Row Three"). This *Essential Data Model* is specifically concerned with identifying the language that describes what

---

♠   To learn about SBVR there are two sources: 1) The source document is "Semantics of Business Vocabulary and Business Rules". 2008. Object Management Group. *http://www.omg.org/spec/SBVR/1.0/pdf*. The descriptions here are dense, but it is thorough and logically approached. And there is a Case Study. 2) A more accessible approach is to preview Graham Witt's forthcoming book on the subject in a series of articles at http://www.brcommunity.com/b461.php.

is *fundamental* to the enterprise as a whole. That is, the model captures its *essence*. Here, an entity is a fundamental "thing of significance to the organization", and an entity class is a collection of such things. A relationship associates a hypothetical instance of an entity class with one or more hypothetical instances of another entity class. This has traditionally been addressed using one of several data modeling approaches and notations.

This model is translatable into English sentences understandable to the business, but it is constrained to language that describes fundamental concepts, not just the more concrete elements that are part of a business' everyday life.

Designer's View

This architectural model can then be converted to a ***logical data model*** that more closely reflects the technology of database management. This is the "Row Four" model, of which there are numerous kinds: This can be relational tables and columns, object-oriented classes, XML Schema tags, or whatever.

Each of the elements shown on the figure has a different view of the world. Not only does the architect see the world differently from the designers, but object-oriented designers see the world quite differently from the relational database designers.

The Unified Modeling Language (UML) was originally designed to support object-oriented design. This is why it was not widely accepted either by architectural modelers or relational database designers.

Summary

This chapter sets the stage for the rest of the book, acknowledging that there are two very different communities in this industry—the object oriented and the data oriented—whose misunderstanding of each other has caused difficulties on several fronts. Actually, there are three communities: the object-oriented developers, the data-oriented analysts, and data oriented developers. The distinctions are actually three-way:

- Those who support data management and define system requirements on behalf of those who run the business or the government agency.

- Those who design and implement databases either to support operational systems or to support analytical "data warehouses".

- Those who design object-oriented software.

In the context of the Zachman Framework for enterprise architecture, the first group consists of the "architects" who produce models describing the fundamental things of significance to the business and the relationships among them.

The second and third groups consist of designers, each making use of a particular data manipulation and management technology. The second and third group's views are different from each other, and both have different views than the first.

It is the first group that represents the reference point for this book. It is architect's models that we are going to learn how to create here. The notation that the object-oriented group is accustomed to using will be the basis for the modeling approach, but the concerns of the other two groups will very much be reflected in the result.

Chapter 2:
UML and Essential Data Models

The next two chapters cover similar ground. The difference is that Chapter Three offers step by step instructions for creating a conceptual entity/relationship model, while this chapter sets the stage by describing the philosophical differences between the two approaches. Among other things, here we describe the differences between architecture and design, as well as the differences between traditional data models and object models.

Impedance Mismatch

The Unified Modeling Language was introduced as the unification of multiple languages for describing not only object classes, but also processing, events, use cases, and other artifacts of the system development process. While the various notations are expected to describe the business that is paying the bills for systems projects, it is clear that the objective of the class model was to support object-oriented systems design. This becomes apparent as we try to use the notation to describe business concepts without regard for technology.

Even so, the class diagram is closely enough related to the more business-oriented entity/relationship model, that the approach described in this book is possible. The design perspective, however, is sufficiently different from the architectural perspective that the differences must be made explicit to proceed.

First, it must be recognized that the underlying structure of a relational database is vastly different from the underlying structure of object-oriented code, and the problems associated with translating one to the other have led to the adoption of the term, *impedance mismatch* to describe those problems.

The term "impedance mismatch" is borrowed from electrical engineering. In electrical engineering, the term "impedance matching" refers to the use of a transformer to make the load (impedance) required on a target device (such as a loudspeaker) match the load produced on a source device (such as an amplifier).[16] In the information technology industry, the expression was originally coined to describe the problems associated with converting between object-oriented classes, with their hierarchical structures, and relational structures that are limited to simple two-dimensional tables.[17]

That a conversion is required to go from one mode of thinking to another would not be particularly noteworthy, except that there are emotions surrounding the "world views" of the communities represented by each technology. Scott Ambler went further than this, however, when he coined the term "cultural impedance mismatch" to describe the divergence of attitudes between the object-oriented community and the data community,[18] This included both the "architects" and "designers" in the data world, vs. the "designers" in the object-oriented world.

Appendix B contains your author's view of the history of the information technology's last 50 years or so. It does so in terms of three streams:

- **Data Processing (~1960 - 1985)** – This takes us from large mainframe computers using Assembly Language, through Fortran and COBOL, and then on to PL/1 and Pascal. During the same period, the original "object-oriented" languages, Simula and SmallTalk, came into use to support process control computers. In the 1960s also, the seeds of rebellion against the monolithic mainframe computer center appeared in the form of computer time-sharing, allowing remote, interactive use of computers. Then in the late 1970s, minicomputers became common, and in 1980 everything changed with the arrival of the commercially viable personal computer, and the early 1980s saw the launch of the Internet, linking the world's computers together. Also by the early 1980s, structured programming and structured design had become popular approaches to program design.

---

[16]   American Radio Relay League, 1958. *The Radio Amateur's Handbook: The Standard Manual of Amateur Radio Communication.* (Concord, New Hampshire: The Rumford Press). 42.

[17]   Ted Neward. 2006. "The Vietnam of Computer Science". *The Blog Ride: Ted Neward's Technical Blog.* Retrieved 8/6/2001 from http://blogs.tedneward.com/2006/06/26/The+Vietnam+Of+Computer+Science.aspx

[18]   Scott Ambler, 2009, "The Cultural Impedance Mismatch", *The Data Administration Newsletter*, August 1, 2009. Available at: http://www.tdan.com/view-articles/11066.

- *Object-oriented Development (~1980 – present)* – In response to the advent of the personal computer's graphic user interfaces, the object-oriented languages of SmallTalk and C++ took on more significance. All of these languages were particularly well suited for manipulating the "real time" interactive objects that appear on a modern computer screen. Java came along in 1995, and was particularly suitable for animating web pages on the newly emerging World Wide Web. From all of this grew object-oriented design and object modeling, ultimately resulting in UML.

- *Data Architecture (1970 – Present)* – During the 1960s, people began to try to assemble data into databases. It was Dr. Codd's introduction of relational theory in 1970 that changed all that. Over the next 20 years, the industry moved to accepting relational databases as the standard. In parallel with that were more sophisticated techniques for defining system requirements: data modeling and structured systems analysis, along with other modeling tools and techniques. During this period, companies came to understand that data and information are corporate assets to be managed—even more than the hardware and software that produces them. Data management became an important profession.

The stream that is "Object-oriented Development" is noteworthy for being dominated by the technology of computer programming. Both the languages themselves and the way people organized programs were the domain of people whose lives were dominated by the task of producing working, effective, and powerful program code. Data are seen by these people as elements to be manipulated by programs. Even the insight of object-orientation—organize the programs around data, rather than processes—did not change the fundamental fact that programs are "processes".

The stream that is here labeled "Data Architecture" is noteworthy for not being dominated by technology at all. While database technologies have formed a large part of the history of this field, the focus of this stream is less on the technology than on how the data are gathered, processed, and—most significantly—*used* in the business. Data are treated as resources to be managed, manipulated, and controlled. Technology's role is to make that possible. Who produces data? What transportation and translation occurs before they get to their ultimate consumers? Who has the right to modify data structures? Who has the right to have access to the data? These are among the questions addressed by data management. Programs are written to support the actors that manipulate data themselves, but it is the retention and security of those data that are most important.

These two points of view are far from incompatible. Indeed, both are required in order to build useful systems. The problem is that the body of knowledge for each has become complex enough to discourage those in the other camp from mastering it. Hence misunderstandings abound.

This mismatch has several aspects, some philosophical and some technological. Each of these will be addressed in detail later in this chapter. But first:

Note that there are "impedance mismatches" among *three* groups, not just two. In addition to the object-oriented design world, the data world itself consists of two groups: those concerned primarily with the technical aspects of designing databases and squeezing them onto real computers, and those concerned with the business dimensions of managing the information derived from those data. The latter group produces the data models that support both database design and object-oriented program design, but these are different from both design approaches. The object-oriented designer and the relational database designer have issues to resolve between themselves, as well.

Figure 2-1 reproduces Figure 1-1 from Chapter 1, to show again the different players (and the different kinds of models) involved with creating systems. The parties we are concerned with here are the architects, the relational database designers, and the object-oriented designers. Note that their products are circled on the Figure.

The following sections in this chapter will first address the relationship between architectural entity/relationship modeling and object-oriented design (which is the primary concern of this book), and then address the relationships between object-oriented design and relational database design.

Business
Owners
(Semantics)

*Semantic Data
Model, SBVR,
OWL*

Terms,
concepts

Architects
(Essence of
Business
Owners' Views)

*Essential Data
Model*

Entity classes,
relationships,
attributes

Designers
(Technology)

*Relational
Databases*

*Object Oriented
classes, etc.*

*XML
Schema
‹tags›*

Design
artifacts

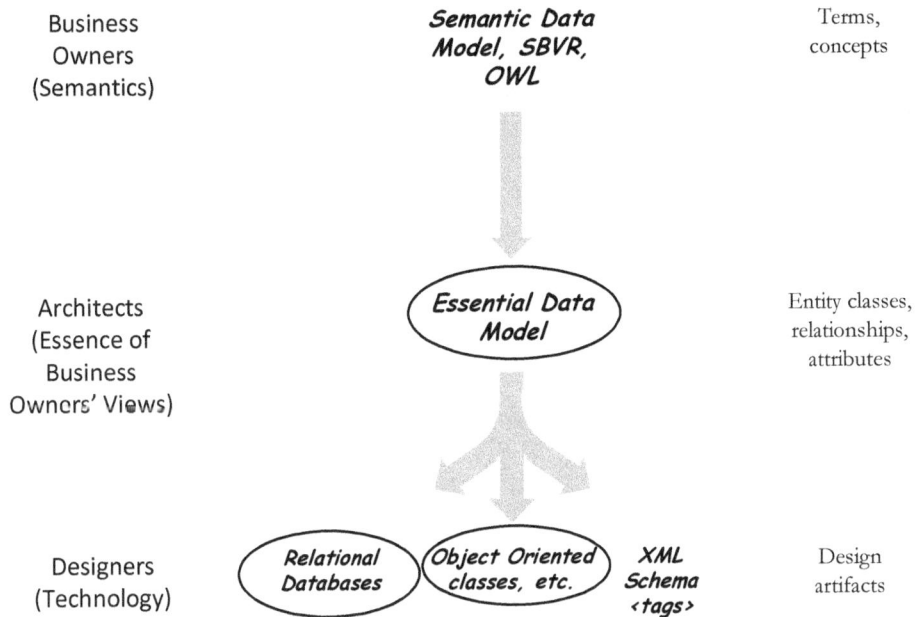

Figure 2-1: The Artifacts

Architecture vs. Object-oriented Design

This section addresses the specific differences between the data architecture described by entity/relationship models and object-oriented design as exhibited by UML models.

Limiting Objects to Business Objects

The only kind of class of interest in the architectural model is a collection of instances of things that Richard Barker describes as being "of significance to the enterprise"[19] (or to the government agency, academic area, or other domain). This sub-set of all the classes in the world consists of what are called here *entity classes*. As described in the last chapter, (see footnote about Dr. Chen on page12), the term "entity class" is an attempt to return some discipline to the vocabulary of entity/relationship modelers, as well as a gentle attempt to connect data modeling with the world of object orientation.

As was also pointed out in the previous chapter, according to the "three amigos" of UML, an *object* in the UML world is a "discrete entity with a well-defined boundary and identity, that encapsulates state and behavior; an

---

[19]   Richard Barker, 1990, *Op. cit.*

instance of a class".[20] A *class*, in turn, is "the descriptor for a set of objects that share the same attributes, operations, methods, relationship, and behavior."[21] Aside from being slightly circular, there is nothing wrong with these definitions from the entity/relationship point of view—as far as they go. The problem is that there are no constraints in either of these definitions as to what kinds of objects or classes are of interest. *Anything* can be an object. It could be something tangible in the world. It could be a concept. It could be something manipulated by a computer program, such as a cursor, or a data file. According to James Martin and James Odell, an "object type" (that is, a "class") is simply "a concept"[22]

Any concept.

In creating an entity/relationship model, we are only concerned with classes that represent things of significance in the domain being modeled.♠

Behavior

One area of concern that generates the greatest discussion is that of *behavior*. It is, however, the easiest to address: object-oriented object models represent it; data models don't.

Object-orientation bundles together, along with the program code that defines each class, references to the pieces of code that process events affecting objects in that class. That is, when you define a class, you define not only its attributes and roles, you also define the processing required to create, manipulate, and destroy instances of that class. The definition of a class is a combination of its structure *and* its behavior.[23]

This is not done in the data world—at least not in data models. It is true that relational databases may include stored procedures that are thus integrated into a database. But they do not come up during the modeling of a business'

[20]   James Rumbaugh, *et. al.* 1999. *Op. cit.*

[21]   James Rumbaugh, *et. al.* 1999. *Op. cit.*

[22]   James Martin and James Odell. 1995, *Op. cit.*

♠   Again, this domain could be an enterprise (or a significant part of one), a government agency, or an area of academic interest. But it is a subject area, not concerned with any technology that might be used to accommodate it.

[23]   Meilir Page-Jones, 2000, Fundamentals of Object-Oriented Design in UML (New York: Dorset House).

data. Data modelers are interested first and foremost in capturing the *structure* of data. Separately, analysts address the processes involved with manipulating them. Data modelers are particularly adamant on this point because the subject of their models is limited to classes of things of interest to the business. To describe the behavior of these real-world classes is much more complicated than simply identifying the computer programs that create and update data describing them.

In fact, analysts have several modeling approaches to choose from for represent business processes—the "behavior" of the enterprise. The simplest, and one that should be done along with a data model, is the *function hierarchy*. This does not describe processing as such, but it does describe what the enterprise being analyzed *does*. That is, beginning with its *mission*, the ongoing operational activity of the enterprise.[24] This is then composed of 7 or 8 or 9 principal *functions* are identified. A function describes something the enterprise does in support of the mission. This is independent of any mechanisms that might be involved. Each of these functions is similarly described in terms of 7 or 8 or 9 principal sub-functions required to carry it out. This goes on, exploding successive levels of functions until reaching the most atomic functions that cannot be meaningfully sub-divided.

The *business process model* is descended from the *data flow diagram*. This is, in fact, one of the kinds of UML diagrams available as well. It presents *business processes* and the flow of data among them. This model can be linked to the entity/relationship model in two ways: First, the **CRUD Matrix** simply associates each entity class with the business processes that (C)reate, (R)etrieve, (U)pdate, or (D)elete instances of that entity class. A second approach, which works for data flow diagrams at least, is to map the *data stores* (places and forms where data pause in traversing the model) to the data model entity classes. Each data store can be considered a SQL-like "view" of the data model, or a *virtual entity class* being defined in terms of sets of *basic entity classes* and relationships from the data model. This is analogous to the way "views" might be defined from tables and columns in a relational database.

One modeling technique (also available as a UML technique) consists of creating a diagram to describe the "behavior" of either a part of the business or a particular entity class. The *state/transition diagram* portrays each *state*

---

[24]   Object Management Group (OMG). 2010. "The Business Motivation Model Version 1.1". (OMG Document formal/2010-05-01). Available at http://www.omg.org/spec/BMM/1.1/PDF/. 13.

(the particular condition that someone or something is in at a specific time) and each *event* (something that happens) that moves the part of the business or entity class from one state to another. Note that any reference to an activity here describes events, rather than processes.

A variation on the state/transition diagram is the *entity life history*, a modeling technique that describes the events affecting an entity class in sequence, without explicitly describing the states involved. This is more a picture of the structure of the events.[25]

In the physical database design world, there is a bit more intimacy between data structures and processing with the introduction of *stored procedures*— bits of program code that do become part of a database. But from the point of *conceptual* data modelers, behavior is not an issue.

Relationships and Associations

What in entity/relationship modeling is called a "relationship", in UML is called an "association". These are clearly analogous concepts, but they are viewed in fundamentally different ways.

Traditionally, in both communities, the naming of each end of an association/relationship has not been very well disciplined—when it is done at all. UML does have a specific approach to naming roles (association ends), but often the roles are not labeled at all. Data modelers have a different approach, but they also often neglect to label relationship names as well.♥

As for entity/relationship modelers, except for books by Graeme Simsion and Graham Witt,[26] Richard Barker[27], and your author,[28] entity/relationship literature provides no rules at all for naming roles, beyond casually referring

[25]   For more information about this and all of the techniques described above, see David C. Hay, 2003, *Requirements Analysis: From Business Views to Architecture*. (Upper Saddle River, NJ: Prentice Hall PTR).

♥   That is, when entity/relationship modelers don't label relationships, they are not using one approach, but when UML modelers don't label relationships, they are not using a different approach.

[26]   G.C. Simsion, and Graham C. Witt, 2005, *Data Modeling Essentials*. Third Edition (Boston: Morgan Kaufmann).

[27]   Richard Barker, 1990, *Op. Cit.*

[28]   David C. Hay, 1995, *Data Model Patterns: Conventions of Thought* (New York: Dorset House).

to "verb phrases". The authors mentioned do provide structured approaches that are similar to each other. While they are not identical, the objective of all three works is, for each relationship, to create two assertions about the *structure* of the business (or other modeled domain). This is in the form of **subject** (the first entity class), **predicate** (the relationship name), and **object** (the second entity class). The term "predicate" simply means "what is affirmed or denied of the subject".[29] Note that the relationship in each direction is a whole unit. Each combination of the three elements is uniquely named—once in each direction.

This book will describe the version developed by Harry Ellis and Richard Barker that your author used in his previous books.

Taking a completely different approach, UML literature is very specific about how to use the **role name** (the association name at one end) simply to *label* the second class. "A role name is … used to navigate from an object to neighboring related objects. Each class "sees" the associations attached to it and can use them to find objects related to one of its instances."[30] Consequently, for the object-oriented modelers who do label association role names, these are nouns, labeling the second class for the benefit of programs navigating from the first class.

That is, rather than being a *structure*, linking two entity classes, the object-oriented designer using UML sees an association as a *path*, calling for *program code* to address navigation from one side to the other. Thus, a "rolename" (in the UML language) is a *label* for the second class to be used solely for the purpose of navigation. Note, however, that this association "property" of the first class does not actually include the second class—only its label. The concept of "predicate" does not exist in object-oriented design. The following sections elaborate on these points.

This difference traces to the underlying languages used to retrieve data: The data-oriented world uses SQL and other **declarative languages** to describe the relationship and its classes as a unit. The object-oriented world uses **procedural languages**, which describe the processes required to retrieve and process the data. This is a fundamental difference in world view between the developers in the two technologies.

More detailed descriptions of each point of view follow in the next two sections.

---

[29]   *DK Illustrated Oxford Dictionary*, 1998. (New York: Oxford University Press). 642.

[30]   James Rumbaugh, *et. al.* 1999. *Op. cit.* 414.

Entity/Relationship Predicates

In general, entity/relationship modeling books acknowledge that relationships can be named with a "verb phrase", creating a semantic structure of subject/predicate/object. Specification about what such a verb phrase might consist of varies from author to author. It can be as simple as "has", or "is related to", or it can be as specific as "lives at" or "is assigned to".

This author, however, endorses the Barker-Ellis approach. It adds a semantic discipline to the structure of these verb phrases. Specifically, in all cases, the verb is "to be". This has the effect that this part of the predicate can be used to specify the relationship's minimum cardinality—in the form "may be" or "must be". ("May be" and "must be", in grammar, are called *verbal auxiliaries*.[31])

The field of logic actually has a word for what remains of the predicate: the *copula*. This is "a part of the verb *be* connecting a subject and predicate".[32] Expanding the definition cited above, then, a *predicate* is more completely described as "what is affirmed or denied about the subject by means of a *copula*".[33] That is, the copula is the *preposition* (not a verb) that describes the content of the assertion being made.

Figure 2-2 shows a model using the Barker-Ellis notation. In this case, each relationship can be expressed as two ordinary English sentences:

- Each **Order** <u>may be</u> *composed of* <u>one or more</u> **Line Items**.

- Each **Line Item** <u>must be</u> *part of* <u>one and only one</u> **Order**.

That is, reading the relationship name in each direction, you get two strong assertions about the nature of the domain being modeled. The role names "part of" and "composed of" are the parts of the predicates that in logic are the **copulas** referred to above.

---

[31] Merriam Webster, "Must". Retrieved on September 28, 2010 from http://www.merriam-webster.com/dictionary/must.

[32] *DK Illustrated Oxford Dictionary*, 1998. *Op. cit.* 187.

[33] *Ibid.* 642.

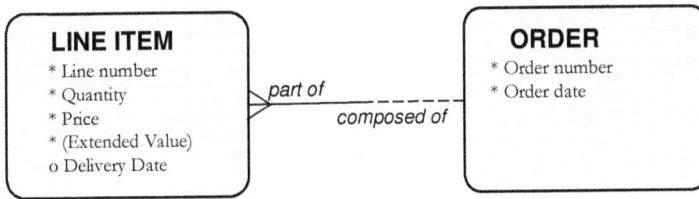

LINE ITEM
* Line number
* Quantity
* Price
* (Extended Value)
o Delivery Date

part of
composed of

ORDER
* Order number
* Order date

*Figure 2-2: Barker-Ellis Predicates**

The sentences are constructed from the elements in the drawing according to the following template:

> Each
>
> <subject entity class>
>
> must be   …if the line next to the subject entity class is solid
>
> (or)
>
> may be   …if the line next to the subject entity class is dashed
>
> <predicate copula>♥
>
> One or more   …if the object entity class has a "crow's foot" (>)
> next to it
>
> (or)
>
> exactly one   …if the object entity class does not have a "crow's
> foot" (>) next to it.
>
> <object entity class>

The first entity class, then, is the **subject** of the assertion, and the second entity class is the **object**. The predicate "verb phrase", then, consists of the "verbal auxiliaries" ("must be" or "may be"), a prepositional phrase copula

---

*   All Barker-Ellis models in this book were produced by the data modeling tool, Oracle Designer. In that tool, all entity class names can only be shown as all upper case characters.

♥   Ok, the <relationship name>…

("composed of" or "part of", in this case), plus an auxiliary phrase describing the maximum cardinality ("one and only one" or "one or more"). ♦

This means the heart of a relationship is the predicate copula—which is (nearly) always a prepositional phrase. ♣ This is appropriate, since the preposition is the part of speech that describes relationships. You may recall Grover in the children's television program, "Sesame Street", who loved prepositions. His favorite words were "in", "above", "around", and so forth.

We can think of predicate prepositions here, then, as "Grover Words".

If the modeler is successful, these relationship sentences appear self-evident to the viewer. These are perfectly normal, non technical sentences. Not only do they sound like conventional English ♠, they are also strong sentences, such that if the assertions are, in fact, wrong, one cannot simply let them go. One has to disagree with them.

The entity/relationship-oriented reader will recognize that not all in that community follow the constrained naming conventions described here. Without this discipline in constructing "verb phrases", however, modelers are forced to come up with something like "An **Order** *has* zero, one or more **Line Items**" or "A **Person** *drives* zero, one, or more **Cars**". This is *not* conventional business English. Alternatively, the copula might be added, but it only gets concatenated into something like "a **Project Assignment** is *of* one and only one **Person**" and "a **Project Assignment** is *the basis for* zero, one, or

---

♦   Note that on the diagram, the role name is closer to the subject entity class. This facilitates reading this sentence, since the "must be/may be" designation is closest to that entity class. When we get to the UML version, it will be at the other end. See full description of this on page 3-69.)

♣   Ok, it can also be either a gerund or an infinitive, but the idea is the same.

♠   By the way, your author has used this in Spanish, and a Quebecois colleague has used French, which suggests that it should work with any western language. Moreover, his book, *Requirements Analysis: From Business Rules to Architecture* has been translated into Chinese, and he is told that the relationship names translate very well–at least in one direction. (Apparently the backwards syntax gets a little clumsy in Chinese.)

more **Time Sheet Entries**". The problem here is that "is" does not convey optionality.♥

In addition, without using the structure described here, it is very easy to simply use a phrase like "has" or "is related to". These are quite meaningless as relationship names. For any relationship, these are "true" statements. For the sentences to be effective, however, if they are *not* true, this must be obvious to the observer.

Note, however, that coming up with disciplined but self-evident role names is *very difficult*. To do so means that you really understand the nature of the relationship, and that you are good at manipulating language. This requires considerable analytic skill to understand the true nature of the relationship, as well as the linguistic skill to come up with the right words.♦ You know you are successful, however, if the resulting sentence seems self-evident to the reader, or, if it is untrue, this also is evident.

Unfortunately, many modelers don't have the inclination or the ability to do so. The final product suffers.♠

Specifying Role Names in UML

On the face of it, conversion to UML should be very easy. The UML entity/relationship **Relationship Name** seems to take the same form as UML

♥ I know, I know: "It depends upon what the meaning of the word 'is' is." – William J. Clinton. December 22, 2007. (I don't think he was talking about this kind of Copula, though.)

♦ If you went into the computer science curriculum because you had trouble in English class, this may not be the career for you.

♠ As an indication of how important it can be to use the right role name, the editors of the Hitchhiker's Guide to the Universe were once "sued by the families of those who had died as a result of taking the entry on the planet Tral literally (it said 'Ravenous Bugblatter Beasts often make a very good meal *for* visiting tourists' instead of 'Ravenous Bugblatter Beasts often make a very good meal *of* visiting tourists')." [Douglas Adams. 1982. *The Restaurant at the End of the Universe*. (New York: Pocket Books). 37-38.]

Association Name. In Figure 2-3, translating the cardinality symbols to UML, we can read the relationship:

- Each **Order** may be *composed of* one or more **Line Items**.

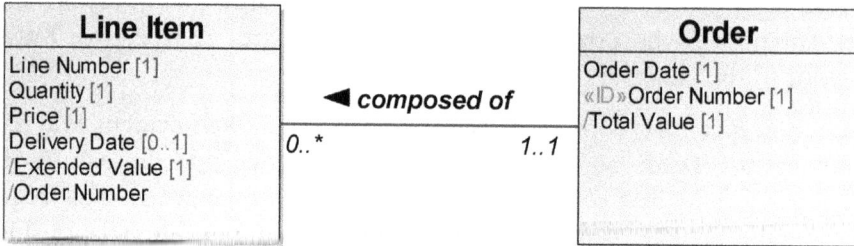

Figure 2-3: UML Associations

The problem, however, is that the relationship name can only be specified in one direction. In UML, you can have one or the other, but not both. This constraint makes that approach unworkable.

Ah, but there is a solution–*rolenames*. In each direction, an entity class is playing a role with respect to the other entity class. The UML concept of "Role Name", therefore, would seem to do the trick. This would permit us to have something like what is shown in Figure 2-4.

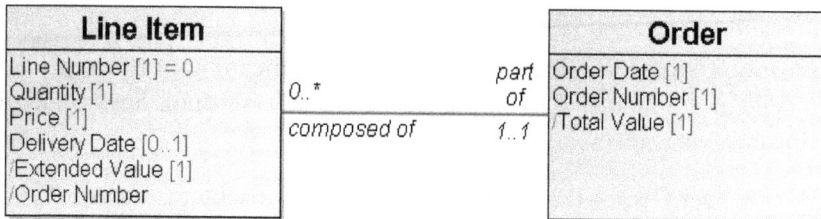

Figure 2-4: Role Names in UML

The relationship portrayed in Figure 2-4, then, can show cardinality and optionality with UML's graphics♥ and the Barker-Ellis language, as follows:

♥ We have already made one departure from UML syntax. In a business-oriented model, to be read by non-technical people, relationship names contain spaces between words. Also, by convention, they are entirely lower case. This is discussed further below (pages 39 and 69).

Each

<Subject Entity Class>

must be ...if the second entity class has "**1**.." next to it

(or)

may be ... if the second entity class has "**0**.." next to it

<Predicate Copula>♣

one or more ...if the second entity class has "..*****" next to it

(or)

one and only one ... if the second entity class has "..**1**" next to it.

<Object Entity Class>

   .

Thus, in Figure 2-4, the role reading from right to left produces the sentence:

- Each **Order** may be *composed of* one or more **Line Items**.

From left to right, it reads:

- Each **Line Item** must be *part of* one and only one **Order**.

These are exactly the sentences we had in the Barker-Ellis version.♠

A Fundamental Change to UML

If we are to take over UML as a data modeling notation, we have to acknowledge that we are making a *fundamental change* in the meaning of one of its elements:

♣   ...that is, <relationship name>

♠   Note that the position of the role names has been reversed from that of the entity/relationship model in Figure 2-3. This is because instead of the optionality half-line being a dashed or solid line next to the first entity class, the "must be"/ "may be" symbol is now described by the symbols "..1" and "..0". This is closer to the second entity class, thereby making the sentence more intuitive.

> *As defined originally, a UML role name is **not** a predicate. For an architectural model, this is a change.*

In entity/relationship modeling, properties of the subject entity class include both attributes and relationship predicates. By definition, each property that is a relationship *includes the other entity class.*

That is, a relationship in an entity/relationship model describes a combination of subject entity class, predicate, and object entity class as a set. And, yes, this *set* is a property of the subject entity class.

Figure 2-5 shows a model fragment using an entity/relationship interpretation for a sample UML drawing, where each **Order** must be *from* one and only one **Party** and must be *to* one and only one (other) **Party**. That is, each **Party** may be *a customer in* one or more **Orders** and each **Party** may be *a vendor in* one or more **Orders.**[*]

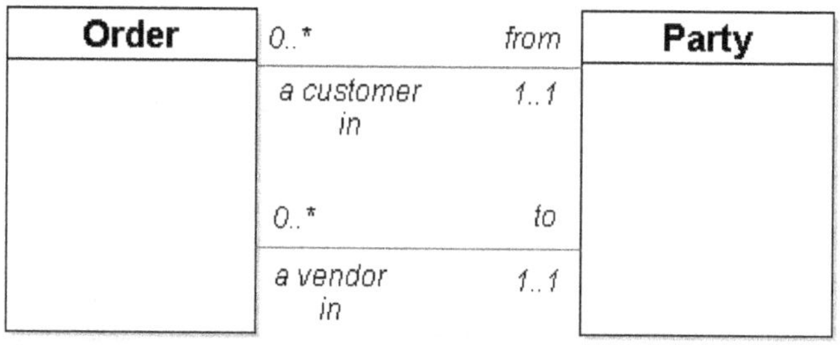

Figure 2-5: Predicates in the Entity/Relationship Version

The association that is a property of a UML class, on the other hand, is *not* the same as an entity class's relationship.

Properties of UML classes also include both attributes and associations. But in this case, a relationship property does *not include the other entity class.*

Figure 2-6 shows how UML would see these relationships. The Class **Order** still has the two association properties "from" and "to", but without knowledge of the classes the properties are related to.

---

[*]   A business rule, outside this model, may assert that the same **Party** may not be both a customer in and a vendor in the same **Order.**

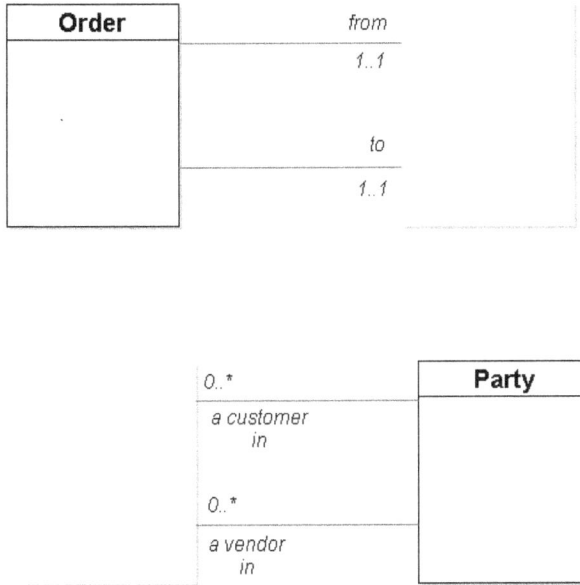

Figure 2-6: The UML View

In UML, the property of a subject class is simply the association *plus the label for the object class*. This is the description of a *path* to be taken by a program from a subject class to an object class. There is no concept of a **predicate** in a standard UML model.

Since the object class itself is *not* part of the property all that is available to a program is the label for that class—its **role name**. The closest you could come to the semantic statement is something like "Each **Order** must have a property *from*, that labels another class." In addition, from the other direction, "Each **Order** must have a property *to*, that labels another class." Note that there is no way to recognize that both associations are with the same entity class.

Similarly, going the other direction, we see that each **Party** may have the property *a customer in* and the property *a vendor in*, but there is no way to tell that both properties are referring to the same class.

Among other things, this means that the role name itself may not be duplicated. This is unrealistic, since it is not out of the question to have two relationships with the same name from a subject entity class—with different object classes. This is particularly common when using the "XOR" constraint. This is a UML feature that happens to be also useful in the entity/relationship version of our diagrams. In the case of Figure 2-7, this asserts that "Each **Line Item** must be either *for* one **Service** or *for* one

Product. From the perspective of **Line Item**, there are two properties that have the same name.

The MagicDraw Tool is adamant about enforcing this, but that's only if the association is *owned by* ("property of") the subject class. To fix it, make sure that each Role Name is owned by the relationship, not the subject class. (Unfortunately, the class is the default, so you have to go through and change them all manually.) Then, if you have two relationships that share a role name, it isn't an issue. *"for"* is a property of each association separately, so there is no conflict.

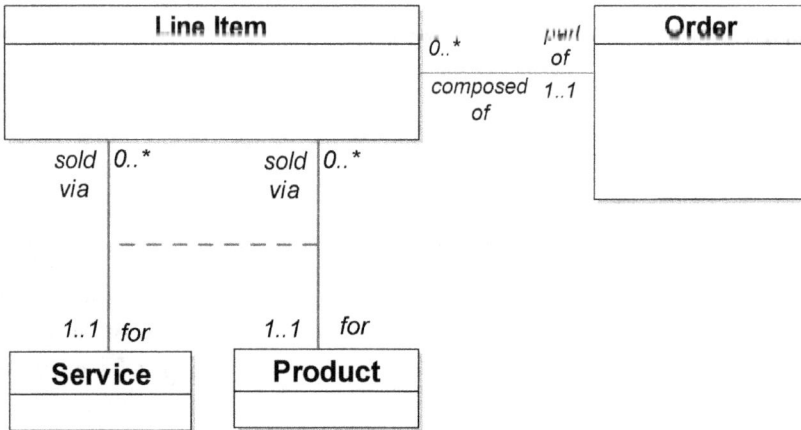

Figure 2-7: Duplicate Role Names

Figure 2-8 shows how UML modelers have to deal with our example, where each **Order** has as a property an association with something that *plays the role of* **customer**. Each **Order** also has as a property another association with something that *plays the role of* **vendor**.

Going the other direction, each **Party** has a property that is an association with something that may *play the role of* **purchase order** one or more times, plus a property that is an association with something that may play *the role of sales order* one or more times.

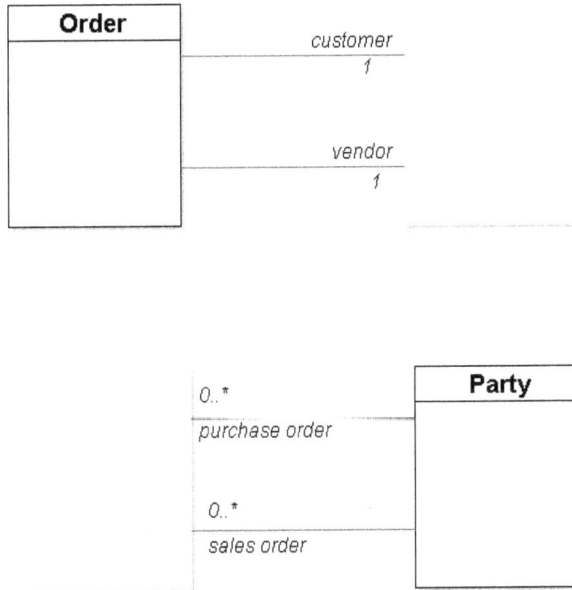

Figure 2-8: Roles in the Object-Oriented Version

But of course in neither case to we get to see what exactly it is that is playing those roles.

This explains why it is common for UML modelers to simply reproduce the object class name as the role name.

The origin of this problem is UML's roots in object-oriented *design*. Object oriented programming languages—Java, for example—are organized in terms of "namespaces". A ***namespace*** is a collection of objects, with the constraint that no namespace can contain another namespace. By convention, each entity class defines a namespace. Hence the namespace describing the class **Order** in the example cannot also contain the class **Party**. The only way to characterize the property of **Order** that is one of its associations with **Party**–is to label it with the *role* played by **Party**. Thus, all that can be said is that each **Order** must be related to one **Party** that plays the role of being a *customer*. Each **Party**, on the other hand may be related to one or more **Orders**, each one of which plays the role of being a **Purchase Order**.

This is fundamentally incompatible with the entity/relationship interpretation. If we are to adapt UML to represent entity/relationship models, then the interpretation of ***rolename*** has to become that of a ***predicate***. The implications of this are described below.

One Solution: Stereotypes

UML has a facility for extending its basic syntax called the *stereotype*. This is a particular annotation that can be added to a diagram to portray a new category of meaning.[34] In this case, one solution that would appeal to the UML community would be to simply recognize that a predicate is different from a role and use a stereotype to make the distinction. This would mean that every relationship name in this ostensibly entity/relationship model would be labeled with something like <<predicate>> (or an abbreviation thereof).

This is not acceptable to the entity/relationship community. The whole point of an entity/relationship diagram is for it to be simple enough that it can be communicated to a non-technical audience. Any modeling term appearing on the diagram would be a technical-sounding distraction and, therefore, completely unacceptable. There is one possible solution, though: when conceptual entity/relationship models are translated into default object-oriented designs, stereotypes could be added to those models. This would look something like Figure 2-9. Presumably, this would be more acceptable to that community.

But that's pretty convoluted even for object-oriented developers.

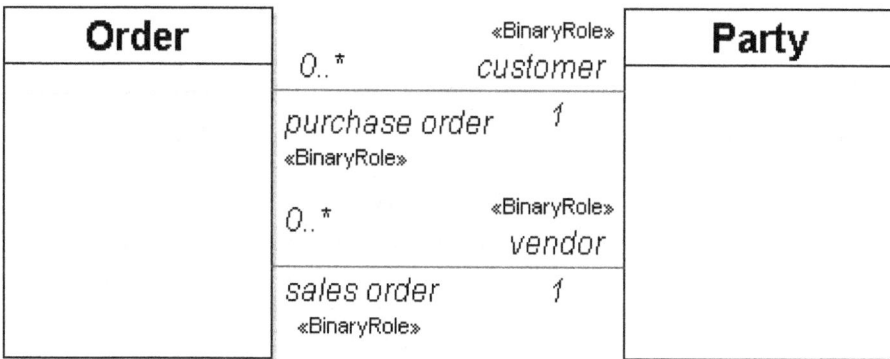

Figure 2-9: Role Stereotypes

Second Solution: Conversion

A better alternative would be simply to recognize that an architectural entity/relationship model is *not the same* as an object-oriented design model.

---

[34]   James Rumbaugh, *et. al.* 1999. *Op. cit.* P. 449.

The diagram and its purpose should be clearly communicated. In such a diagram, the names at the ends of relationships would be understood to be predicates, with the expectation that they each are part of a complete sentence assembled not only from that predicate itself but also from the cardinality constraints and both entity class names.

In the data modeling world, it is already assumed that the entity/relationship model is *not the same thing* as a database design model, and that a conversion is required to go from one to the other. In this case, even as we make use of some of the UML notation, we understand that we are *not* creating a design model. We are creating an architectural model that must be *converted to* real program classes and attributes, just as it must be *converted to* database tables and columns. Even before dealing with relationships, we would have to do enough conversion to at least get rid of spaces in entity class and attribute names. For example, the **Line Item** entity class would become the table **LINE_ITEMS**✤ in a database, and the class **lineItem** in a program.♠

After the conversion of names, the next element of conversion must then be to convert the entity/relationship predicates into acceptable object-oriented design rolenames.

Since an important function of the role name in UML is to identify the object class, one approach could be to concatenate the entity/relationship predicate to the name of the object class, as shown in Figure 2-10. This both keeps all the role names unique, and it also provides an indication of what entity class is hiding behind that label.

Interestingly enough, Messrs. Rumbaugh, Jacobson, and Booch endorse doing that very thing: "In principle, a rolename is required for a navigation expression. In practice, a tool may provide a default rule for creating implicit rolenames from the names of the associated classes."[35]

✤   Different companies have different conventions for naming tables. Here, the convention (adopted by the Oracle community) is that entity class names are single, because each class represents one concept. Table names are plural, because each table contains many instances. This is truly an arbitrary distinction, but it comes in handy in many cases.

♠   UML conventions call for "camel case" (or "camelCase"?). This involves first removing all spaces. Then, for classes, the first letter of each word is capitalized. For attributes and role names, all component words have capital first letters except for the first one.

[35]   James Rumbaugh, *et. al.* 1999. *Op. cit.* 415.

Thus, to the object-oriented designer, **Order** has properties *fromParty* and *toParty*. This is derived directly from the architectural model, but it meets the needs of the design model. Similarly, **Party** has the properties *aCustomerInOrder* and *aVendorInOrder*. These are also reasonable rolenames to the object-oriented designer.

Just as database designers tinker with generated default database designs created through automated conversion from entity/relationship models, so an object-oriented designer might choose to rename "aCustomerOrder" to "aSalesOrder", and "aVendorOrder" to "aPurchaseOrder" in the final design.

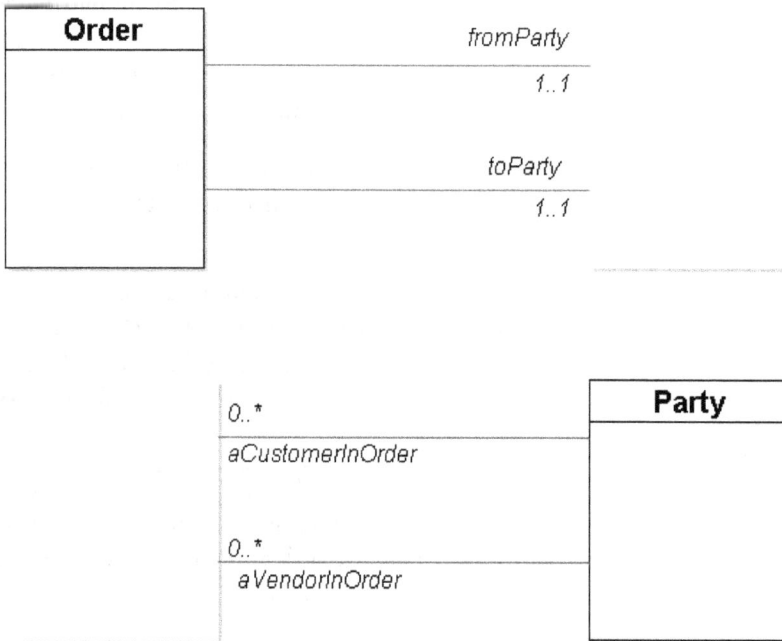

Order			
		fromParty	
		1..1	
		toParty	
		1..1	

0..*			Party
aCustomerInOrder			
0..*			
aVendorInOrder			

Figure 2-10: Object-Oriented Design Implementation

Domains, Data Types, and Enumerations

In an entity/relationship model, each attribute may be described by its data type—numeric, character, date, etc. Clusters of attributes, however, can have not only the same data type, but also a common set of constraints on their values. In entity/relationship language, this common set of characteristics for a set of attributes is called a *domain*. It can be as simple as a format, it could be a list of values, or it could be as complex as some sort of validation formula.

Domain is a concept with an evolving definition and a history of weak implementation in relational systems. Moreover, it addresses issues that are handled differently in the object-oriented vocabulary.

Mr. Barker defines a domain as follows:

"A set of business validation rules, format constraints, and other properties that apply to a group of attributes: for example:

- a list of values

- a range

- a qualified list or range

- any combination of these.

Note that attributes and columns in the same domain are subject to the same validation checks."[36]

In addition to the things just listed, a domain can also be described by:

- data type

- length

- a list of legal values

- edit rules

- a precision factor

- a mathematical expression

Some entity/relationship-oriented data modeling tools have explicit support for documenting domains behind the scenes as part of an attribute's documentation—others do not.

A *data type*, in effect, is a simple domain. If we require that a value of an attribute be an integer, we are assigning it to a data type. If we require that a value of an attribute be a positive integer between 1 and 10 (inclusive), then we are assigning it to a domain.

UML does not have what entity/relationship modelers are accustomed to calling "domains". Its concept of "data type", however, is extensible and can be used in the same way.

---

[36]   Richard Barker, 1990, *Op. Cit.*

The only caution is that in a conceptual entity/relationship model, a *value set* for a domain is a list of *meanings*. This is different from the *code set* that constrains the values a column in a database may take. A value set, for example, could be the States in the United States, which is then effectively implemented via several code sets in a database. Corresponding code sets could consist of names, two-character post office abbreviations, the older set of four-letter abbreviations, sequence numbers, and so forth. One of the code sets (like "state names") can be designated as "primary", to be used for revealing the value set, but even it is still not the same thing as the value set.[37]

UML doesn't have quite the same idea explicitly, but the components for defining domains are available, at least for data type and list of values.

First of all, UML has a basic list of what it calls "data types". This describes the nature of characters that can be used: "String (Character)", "Number", "Date", and so forth. This is analogous to the set of data types available for, say an Oracle database, even though the definition of each may be slightly different (UML "String" vs. Oracle "Varchar"). The principle is the same, however. This list can be extended to include such things as "US Telephone Number", "US Social Security Number", and so forth.

One alternative to specifying a domain which is a list of values is to represent it as a "reference" entity type. For example, **Internal Organization** might have had the attribute "Internal Organization Type" with a domain that is a list of values such as "Division", "Department", "Section", etc. This could be documented in the definition of the attribute, or it could be shown as an entity class, as in Figure 2-11. This is a solution which applies to both entity/relationship and UML modeling.

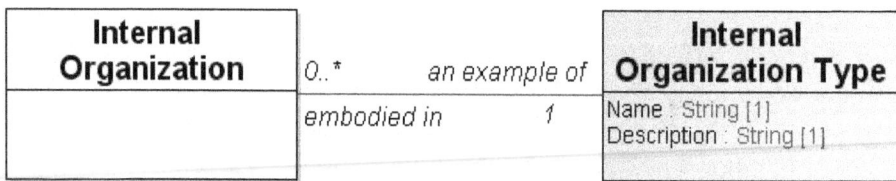

Internal Organization			Internal Organization Type
	0..*	*an example of*	Name : String [1]
	embodied in	1	Description : String [1]

Figure 2-11: Entity Classes as Domains

---

[37] For more on value sets and code sets, see David C. Hay. 2006. *Data Model Patterns: A Metadata Map*. (Boston: Morgan Kaufmann).

UML, however, has another way to represent a "list of values". An *enumeration* is "a user-definable data type. It has a name and an ordered list of enumeration literal names, each of which is a value in the range of the data type—that is, it is a predefined instance of the data type."[38] It is represented in this book by a class box with the *stereotype* <<enumeration>>, as shown in Figure 2-12. Enumerations are described in more detail in Chapter Three. Note that in Figure 2-12, **Internal Organization** has an attribute "Internal Org. Type"[♣], which has as a data type "internal". This is linked to the <<enumeration>> **Internal Organization Type**.

The advantage of this structure is that instead of displaying the assumed attributes of "Name" and "Description", the diagram shows a *list of values*.[♥] In the example of Figure 2-12, they are "Department", "Division", or "Section".

An association line may be drawn to clarify that the enumeration **Internal Organization Type** is related to the entity class **Internal Organization**, but it is not necessary.

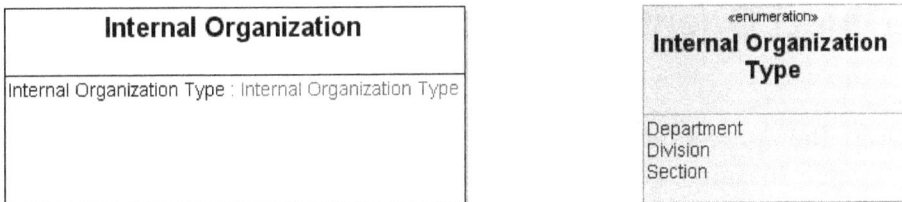

Internal Organization
Internal Organization Type : Internal Organization Type

«enumeration» **Internal Organization Type**
Department Division Section

Figure 2-12: An Enumeration

---

[38] James Rumbaugh, *et. al.* 1999. *Op. cit.*

[♣] MagicDraw, the software used to produce all the model drawings in this book, has only one shortcoming that I have discovered: a limit on attribute name length. Hence "Internal Organization Type" had to be abbreviated. The idea should be clear, however.

[♥] In a typical model of any size there can be many **…Type** entity classes. Each one has the attributes "Name" and "Description". Displaying them isn't very useful. Displaying the list of values in each case is much more useful.

Namespaces

UML is organized around the object-oriented concept of *namespace*, which refers to a collection of objects to be treated as a named group. The architecture of object-oriented programming is predicated on this concept. The problem with this, however—as described above in the section on relationships—is that it makes it extremely difficult to treat a subject/predicate/object as a logical unit, since the object class cannot be contained in the namespace that is the subject class. A "property" of the subject class is the *rolename* only, without the class that is being named. For example, in Figure 2-11, above, "*an example of*" can be a property of **Internal Organization,** but "*an example of* **Internal Organization Type**" cannot. Moreover, since in the object-oriented world, there can be no duplicate role names, there could not also be "*an example of* **Internal Organization Class**", or some such—even though the total meaning of the predicate is *not* duplicated.

Here is another place where the architectural entity/relationship modeler must part company from the object-oriented designer.

Object Oriented Design vs. Relational Database Design

Given the conversion described above, it is certainly appropriate for an architectural entity/relationship model to provide a starting point for an object-oriented UML design, just as it can provide a starting point for relational database design. Indeed, the point of architectural modeling is that it is technology independent and can therefore serve as the starting point for any kind of design. The real differences are between the different approaches to design. In one sense, these are not the concern of this book, but it is worth discussing them to provide context.

Persistent Data

At the technology level, one significant difference in point of view between the object-oriented design and database design camps is the fact that the latter are concerned with *storing* data. This means the structure of data is important, since it determines how to organize data that are relatively permanent. Object-orientation, on the other hand, originated in real-time systems, and it is thus primarily concerned only with the *manipulation* of data. Originally, the data describing the objects manipulated (chiefly fluid flows and the valves that controlled them) were not expected to survive the end of the program's processing. Object-orientation became a force in commercial data processing in about 1980, with the advent of the personal computer and its graphical user interfaces. As in process control, windows and cursors are transient. By virtue of the applications driven by these interfaces, however, the object-oriented world is now required to deal with **persistent data** – data describing objects that continue to exist after the program is complete. Thus, the issues of connecting to a database, with its different kinds of data structure, take on new importance. What kinds of transformations are required to convert to that structure? Who defines class structure, and how are object-oriented classes mapped to a database? These have become important questions, which, in each case, require a great deal of negotiation to resolve.

Inheritance

Most significantly, the way data are organized in an object-oriented program is very different from the way they are organized in the industry's most popular storage medium—the relational database. The structure of object-oriented data makes extensive use of *inheritance* (super-types and sub-types) that cannot be supported directly in relational databases. In addition to being an issue between object-orientation and data management technologies, the problem of this impedance mismatch actually occurs *within* the data world as well. An architectural data model makes extensive use of this same object-oriented concept. Invariably, such models have many super-type/sub-type combinations. From the beginning, it has always been a challenge to translate an entity/relationship model with sub-types into a relational database, with its simple two-dimensional tables and their rows and columns.

Within the data world, however, that's a translation problem that only occurs when designing a database. Database designers have always recognized two alternatives for dealing with it. Neither is perfect, but each is workable under the right circumstances.

- Make one table for the super-type, subsuming all the sub-types. This has the following effects:

  Columns specific to one of the sub-types must accept null values for the instances that are of another sub-type.

  Relationships to one of the sub-types cannot be mandatory.

- Make one table for each sub-type including the super-type columns in each. This has the following effects:

  The super-type columns are duplicated for each sub-type table.

Relationships to the super-type must be duplicated for each sub-type table—constrained by a mechanism insuring that only one of the sub-types tables is referred to at a time by the outside table.

- Make one table for the super-type with its attributes as columns, and one for each sub-type with its attributes as columns. A mandatory, one-to-one foreign key is established from each sub-type to the super-type. A constraint must then be added to ensure that each instance of the super-type is referred to by exactly one instance of a sub-type.

  This eliminates the shortcomings of both of the previous approaches, but the constraint mentioned can be very complex to implement.

If the assignment happens once and the issues are resolved for a particular database design, that is a reasonable task.

When an object-oriented designer or programmer has to map an object-oriented data structure to a relational database, the same (imperfect) translation process is required, but it must be navigated frequently, on an ongoing basis. This may require the program to be more complex, but again, once the issues have been resolved, implementing the translation should be straight-forward.

This should not be an issue, although it has generated a disproportionate amount of discussion.

Security

The object-oriented designer and programmer are accustomed to creating object classes as necessary to solve particular problems. Even if they are presented with a conceptual data model as a starting point, there is nothing in their normal work practices to keep them from at least adding system-oriented classes. Indeed, many of the classes are only defined to last for the life of the program's execution. Only "moral persuasion" discourages them from changing the architectural model's class structure.

Once stored, the persistent data are the responsibility of the database administrator, who must implement the mechanisms for enforcing security policies. Above all, the database administrator is responsible for the integrity of the database. This includes both the database structure and its contents. The object-oriented designer and programmer are, in fact, obligated to respond to the security requirements identified by the database administrator. Persistent object classes should not be created without approval from the data base administrator. Programs retrieving data and updating them in a database must be subject to security restrictions. These constraints put an added burden on the object-oriented designer and programmer. This cannot be helped.[39]

Summary

This chapter laid out the essential distinctions between data modeling and object-oriented modeling.

The issues are actually more subtle than first appears, however, since the data modeling world itself is divided between the database design and the architectural modeling perspectives. So, in this chapter, we distinguished first between architectural entity relationship modeling and object-oriented design (as represented by UML). After that, we distinguished between relational database design and UML's object oriented design.

In the first category, there are five issues between architectural models and object-oriented design models. Specifically, creating an architectural model using the UML notation will require:

- Limiting the classes addressed to the things of significance to the domain.

- Addressing behavior with models other than the class model.

- Instituting a discipline in the naming of relationship/association "roles", and modifying the assumptions of UML to allow this approach to be captured as "role names".

- Making use of data types and enumerations to address the entity/relationship concept of "domain".

- Understanding the constraints imposed by "namespaces".

In the second category, there are three differences between the two *design* approaches that have generated friction between these two groups for many years:

- Objects created in an object-oriented program do not "persevere" unless provision is made to store it. Storing it in a relational database is not straightforward.

---

[39]   Ted Neward. 2006. *Op. Cit.*

- Specifically, the concept of "inheritance" is central to the way an object-oriented program organizes objects. Relational databases have no way explicitly to recognize this.

- Programmers tend to create objects as needed. They can begin with those derived from the architecture model, but there is no inherent restriction on the creation or modification of objects. Database administrators, on the other hand are primarily concerned with security—constraining who can change the data structure and who can actually change—or even view–the data.

A well done architectural model can be the basis for both coherent object-oriented program design and coherent database design. The processes of converting to each are simply different.

Chapter 3:
How to Draw an
Essential
Data Model in UML

Given the issues between object-oriented modeling in UML and entity/relationship modeling, how do we set out to create an architectural entity/relationship model using the UML notation? This chapter provides the answer. We begin with a summary of the approach, followed by a detailed description of each step.[*]

Summary of the Approach

To create a conceptual (semantic or essential) entity/relationship model using a UML diagramming tool, follow these guidelines:

1. ***Show domain-specific entity classes only***. Consider only classes that are collections of things of significance to the enterprise or the domain being addressed. These are referred to here as ***entity classes***.

2. ***Use Symbols Selectively***.

   ➤ Use only ***appropriate*** symbols

      • Class (entity class)

      • Attribute

---

[*] Your author used the MagicDraw software sold by No Magic, Inc. to prepare his book, *Enterprise Model Patterns: Describing the World.* He found it very versatile in dealing with the non-standard UML structures in this book. It was able to handle every modification described here. Should you find that other tools make such adjustments either very difficult or impossible to do, please notify him at UML@essentialstrategies.com.

- Association (relationship)
- Cardinality for attributes and relationships
- Exclusive or (xor) Constraint

➢ Use **some UML-specific** symbols with care

- Sub-types and Relationship Sub-types
- Enumeration
- Derived Attribute
- Package

➢ *Do not use* any other UML symbols

- Abstract entities
- Association class
- Behavior
- Composition
- Navigation
- Ordered
- Visibility

➢ *Add* one symbol

- **<<ID>>** stereotype
- (Or use new property {isID})

3. Define Data Model Relationship ends as Predicates, not UML Roles

4. Define domains

5. Understand "Packages and "Namespaces"

6. Follow Display Conventions:

   ➢ *Sub-types* – Show sub-type boxes within super-type boxes.

   ➢ *Spaces in Names* – Include spaces inside multi-word entity class and attribute names.

   ➢ *Role Positions* – Position the predicate next to the object entity.

➤ **XOR** – Do not include the label in an "XOR" relationship.

➤ **Cardinality Display** – Display mandatory one cardinality as "1..1", not "1".

The rest of Chapter 3 describes each of these points in detail. Chapter 4 covers the following:

7. For **aesthetic** reasons, do the following.

➤ Place sub-type boxes inside super-type boxes.

➤ Stretch and position entity class boxes so that no relationship has an "elbow" (There are no bent lines).

➤ Turn off the ability to display operations, so the entity class box has only one horizontal line.

➤ Arrange the entity classes so that the "many" end of each relationship is at the left or top (the "starry skies" approach).

➤ Limit a subject area to no more than 15 entity classes to show on one page.

➤ Present the model in a succession of diagrams. On the first diagram, show no more than 2-5 entity classes, all highlighted. On each successive page, add no more than 2-5 entity classes and highlight them.

➤ In general, display attributes only in the diagram where their entity class first appears. Suppress them on all subsequent diagrams, unless they are needed to explain a particular concept. (Suppress them by coloring them white.)

1. Show Domain-Specific Entity Cases Only

As described in the last chapter, the only classes of interest to the architectural entity/relationship modeler are what are called here "entity classes"—that is, classes of things of significance to the business (or the domain being modeled). These may include such things as "Person", "Product", and so forth. While that does also include abstract entity classes such as "Project Assignment", or "Party", it does *not* include any technological object classes like files, personal computer screens and windows, nor anything else of that type.

Names of entity classes must be normal English (or other natural language) terms, and must not be acronyms, technical terms, or table names.

Entity class names are always in the singular, representing a prototypical instance of the class. For example, the class name is **Person**, not **People**.

2. Use Symbols Selectively

Comparing entity/relationship modeling with UML modeling is fundamentally about the symbols used. Many concepts are shared between the two approaches, so, for the most part, the symbols map cleanly from one to the other. Some symbols in one have no corresponding symbols in the other, and vice versa. Here you see the common symbols that can be selected from UML, and common symbols that can be used with a slight change of meaning. There are also UML symbols that are not used, and one entity/relationship symbol that is not available in UML and must be added.

Use Appropriate Symbols

Architectural entity/relationship modeling uses a relatively small sub-set of the symbols that comprise UML. Here is the list:

- Class (entity class)

- Attribute

- Association (relationship)

- Cardinality for attributes and relationships

- Exclusive or (XOR) Constraint

The following sections describe each of these in detail.

Class (Entity Class)

As stated above, an *entity* is the name of a "thing or object of significance to a business, whether real or imagined, about which information needs to be known or held."[40] This may be a concrete thing, such as "Charles Smith", or "Oxfordshire County", or it may be an abstraction, such as "Purchase Order 230493" or "The fact that George Saunders was made Project Manager of the Interstate 10 project on 23 October, 2005". An *entity class* is a named *set* of such things, all with the same set of attributes. Each box on the diagram represents an entity

---

[40]   Richard Barker, 1990, *Op. cit.* 4-1.

class. For example, the entities just described might be instances of **Person**, **Geographic Location**, **Purchase Order**, and **Project Role Assignment**, respectively.

This is a *subset* of the UML concept of **class**. The UML symbol for class can be used if it is understood to mean only entity/relationship model classes—that is, things of significance to the enterprise—and only if the conventions described here for naming are followed. Thus, as stated, the only classes we are interested in are *entity classes*.

This is an example of the need to identify the model, as a whole, as an architectural model, not a design model. Other examples follow. What is significant is that architectural model notation and constraints apply throughout.

By convention, the name of an entity class is in the singular, and refers to an instance of that class.[♦] Hence, as shown in Figure 3-1, **Order** and **Line Item** are acceptable. The name "Project History" is not. An entity class called **Project**, on the other hand, could contain instances over time, so it may, in effect, be a project "history". "Project History" as a name, however, is not acceptable. Database table names are not allowed, nor are abbreviations or acronyms.[♣] Classes that are computer artifacts ("window", "cursor", and the like) are not allowed.

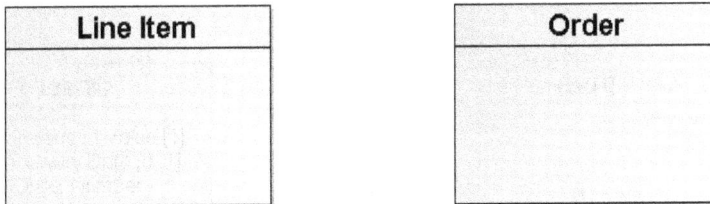

Line Item

Order

Figure 3-1: Entity Classes

♦   Also by convention in this book, UML entity classes are shown in lower case, with an initial upper case character. Where models are shown using the Barker-Ellis notation, entity class names are shown entirely in upper case. (This is a restriction of the modeling tool used for those.)

♣   *If* the acronym is widely accepted in the organization, and *if* everyone agrees on what it means, and *if* to spell it out would be too long and clumsy, then it *may* be permissible to use it in an entity class name. Maybe.

Attribute

The UML definition of *attribute* is effectively the same as that for entity/relationship modeling. That is, it is a characteristic of an entity class that "serves to qualify, identify, classify, quantify, or express the state of an entity".[41]

Note the phrase "state of an entity". Each attribute must be about the entity it is attached to. If it is describing a related entity, it should be an attribute of that entity, not this one.

As with entity class names, attribute names must be common English names for the characteristics involved. Abbreviations and acronyms should be avoided. In general, it is not necessary to include the entity class name in the attribute name, but in some companies, standards dictate that the entity class name be inserted in front of at least the common attributes—as in for example, "Person Name" and "Person ID".

In Figure 3-2, below, attributes of **Order** are "Order Number", "Order Date", and "/Total Value". Attributes of **Line Item** are "Line Number", "Quantity", "Price", "Delivery Date", "/Extended Value", and /Order Number. That is, the definition of the entity class **Line Item** is that it is any set of entities that have values for the attributes "Line Number", "Quantity", "Price", "Delivery Date", and "/Extended Value".

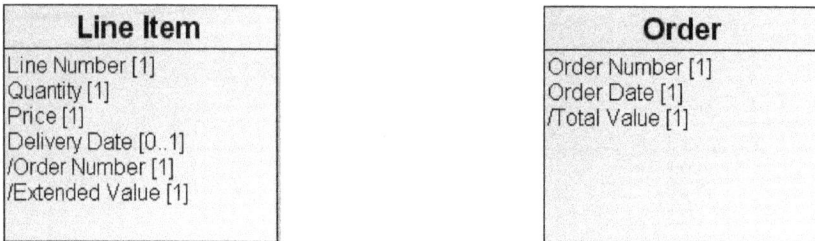

Line Item		Order	
Line Number [1]		Order Number [1]	
Quantity [1]		Order Date [1]	
Price [1]		/Total Value [1]	
Delivery Date [0..1]			
/Order Number [1]			
/Extended Value [1]			

Figure 3-2: Attributes

The "/" in front of various attributes in the Figure 3-2 is a UML symbol identifying a *derived attribute*. For example, for each instance of **Line Item**, the value of "/Extended Value" is determined by multiplying the value of that instance's "Quantity" by the value of its "Price". ("/Order Number" in **Line Item** and "/Total Value" in **Order** are described below (page 65), after a relationship is added.)

---

[41] Richard Barker. 1990. *Op. cit.* 4-6.

The derivation algorithm is not shown in an entity/relationship drawing, but must be documented behind the scenes. Even though UML has the notation for derived attributes, and the derivation can be documented behind the scenes, it can also be shown as an *annotation* on the drawing.♥

UML has the ability to display a large number of things about an attribute: in addition to its optionality, UML can show its *data type*, its *visibility*, whether it is *read-only* or not, and others. In the entity/relationship version, however, the only things to display are the *attribute name*, whether it is *optional* or not (its "minimum cardinality"), its optional *"<<ID>>" stereotype* (described further on pages 75 ff, below), and the optional "/" that designates it as a *derived attribute*, as just discussed. Data type must be documented behind the scenes, but, as it adds clutter, it is normally not shown on a diagram used for presentations. It can, however, be included on a diagram that is solely used for documentation.

Some UML characteristics of attributes are not shown at all: "Visibility" applies to an attribute's *use* in a particular context, and does not belong on an architectural entity/relationship diagram. Whether an attribute is "read-only" or not is a characteristic of its use, and is therefore not appropriate in an architectural entity/relationship model, either.♠ These inappropriate characteristics are described further in the section "Do Not Use Other Symbols", beginning on page 79, below.

Association (Relationship)

In architectural entity/relationship modeling, a *relationship* between two entity classes consists of two assertions about them (one going each way). Each assertion is a logical statement of fact about the area of interest being modeled, not simply recognition that two things are somehow associated with each other. This can be described in a UML diagram

---

♥   By convention, in other tools, your author always surrounds derived attributes with parentheses, which is useful for exposition, but it is not logically connected to the model—although in Oracle Designer, the derivation can be documented explicitly in the repository behind the tool.

♠   Indeed, the only time an attribute might be "read-only" would be if it were a duplicate of another attribute being maintained. This would be a flaw in the model.

using the symbol for an *association*, but the way it is labeled is different from the way it is labeled in the UML design context.

It is important to keep the structure and language of architectural entity/relationship modeling when using UML. A relationship going each way represents a strong assertion about the nature of the organization being modeled. The UML concept of *rolename* applies, but its use for the architectural model, is very different from the way it is used in a design model. (Chapter 2, above, had a much more extensive discussion of the differences between UML associations and data modeling relationships. See pp. 34-45.)

The notation in an architectural model can be read according to the following template:

Each

<Subject Entity Class>

Must be (or)	…if the second entity class has "1.." next to it
May be it	… if the second entity class has "0.." next to it

<role name>*

One or more (or)	…if the second entity class has "..*" next to it
exactly one it.	… if the second entity class has "..1" next to it

<Object Entity Class>

.

For example, the relationship shown in Figure 3-3 translates into the following two sentences:

- Each **Order** may be *composed of* one or more **Line Items**.

- Each **Line Item** must be *part of* one and only one **Order**.

---

* See page 69 for a description of positioning these elements on the drawing.

Line Item		Order
«ID»Line Number [1] Quantity [1] Price [1] /Order Number [1] Delivery Date [0..1] /Extended Value [1]	«ID» 0..* part of composed of 1..1	«ID»Order Number [1] Order Date [1] /Total Value [1]

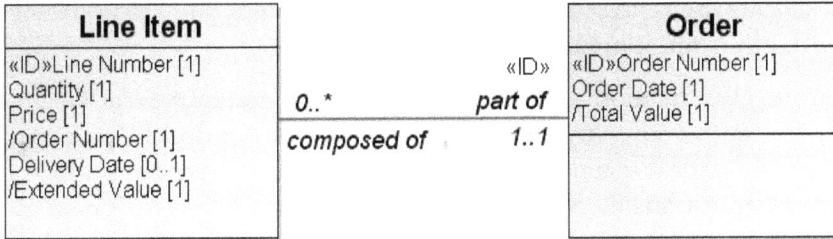

Figure 3-3: Relationships in UML

Now it is possible to describe the attributes "/Order number" in **Line Item** and "/Total Value" in **Order**. "/Order Number" in **Line Item** is inferred from the entity class **Order**, since, by definition, there is only one **Order** for each **Line Item**. Multiple instances of **Line Item's** "/Extended Value" can be summed together across all of an **Order's Line Items** to produce the value in **Order** for "/Total Value". The discussion on "Derived Attributes" below (page 72) explains the algorithms to be used for including inferences and summations in a derivation formula.

While developing the semantics of a business model, especially in initial interviews, many-to-many relationships are common. By the time the model has been turned into an architectural model, however, these should all have been resolved into one-to-many relationships. This is important because often a many-to-many intersection of the two entity classes contains important business information. Simply saying that each A is related to many Bs and each B is related to many As tells you nothing about each occurrence of an A being related to a B. Creating an *intersect entity* (defined as the fact that a particular instance of A is related to a particular instance of B) captures attributes of that association.

Note that this is preferable to the UML practice of defining an *association class,* which is simply attached to the relationship. It is true that you can then define attributes for the relationship, but you have no flexibility in defining the subtleties of the relationship. For example if an association class resolved a many-to-many relationship between **Project** and **Person**, that structure would not permit one person to be on the same project multiple times.

Cardinality

Both entity/relationship modeling and UML object-oriented modeling recognize that attributes and relationships are both *properties* of an entity class. In entity/relationship notations, maximum and minimum cardinality are represented differently for attributes and relationships. In UML, the same approach is taken for all properties.

In the Information Engineering notation, minimum cardinality in *relationships* is shown by either a circle ("o") for "optional", or a vertical line ("|") for "mandatory"—both next to the second entity class. Maximum cardinality is shown by a second vertical line ('|') next to the maximum.

The Barker-Ellis notation shows minimum cardinality by the half line closest to the first entity class. If it is solid, the relationship in this direction is mandatory. If it is dashed, the relationship is optional. Maximum cardinality is also shown with the crow's foot next to the second entity class for an unlimited maximum, but it is simply without a crow's foot and no other notation if the maximum is "1".

The cardinality constraints for *attributes* in entity/relationship models depend on the tool or the approach. In the Barker/Ellis notation, attributes are identified as follows:

*   - mandatory

\#   - part of a unique identifier

O   - optional

Different tools show these with different symbols. In most cases, the information engineering tools flag optional attributes with "<null>" and mandatory ones with "<not null>". Identifying attributes are in a separate part of the entity class box.

UML uses the same notation to describe cardinality in *both attributes and associations*. The expression is **<min>...<max>**. Here "**<min>**" is either "**0**" or "**1**", meaning, respectively, that the attribute or relationship is either optional or required. The variable "**<max>**" is typically "**1**" or "*****" meaning respectively that the attribute or relationship may be either "no more than one" or "any number more than one".

In the case of *attributes*, in the relational world an attribute is *never* permitted to have more than one value. In this case, the only legal combinations are **0..1** (for an optional attribute) or **1..1** (for a mandatory attribute). The maximum cardinality **..*** is not permitted for attributes. Figure 3-3, above, shows this. In the example, each **Line Item** must be *part of* one and only one **Order**. (Note that for attributes, **1..1** is often abbreviated **1**.) Going the other way, each **Order** may be *composed of* one or more **Line Items**.

The most common configurations are **1..1**, for "…must be … exactly one…", and **0..*** for "…may be…one or more…" As mentioned above, because it is so common, **1..1** is often abbreviated **1**. That means, when reading such a role, the reader must parse "1" into its two components.♥

Unlike in entity/relationship modeling, UML can have any combination for maximum cardinality. For example **0, 2-5, 9** means zero, between 2 and 5 (inclusive), or 9, are all legal values. In practice, complex rules like that are not appropriate for supposedly long-lived architectural models, although it is not completely out of the question. And this form, of course, is not permitted for attributes.

As we've seen, the UML cardinality (both maximum and minimum) are shown using the same symbols for both attributes and relationships. In the case of relationships, it is desirable to suppress the modeling tool's inclination to collapse **1..1** into **1**, since the two elements form separate parts of the assertion sentence. In the case of attributes, it is only the minimum cardinality character that is needed, so any abbreviation that takes place automatically does not hurt. The only choices are **0..1** and **1..1**. If the second one is described as **1**, it's not completely consistent, but it is acceptable.♣

Exclusive or (XOR) Constraint

Some entity/relationship notations have the ability to describe an "exclusive or" arrangement of relationships. For example, Figure 3-4 shows how the Barker-Ellis notation represents the assertion:

- Each Line Item must be <u>either</u> *for* exactly one Product <u>or</u> *for* exactly one Service.

The "arc" across the relationship lines denotes this.

♥ As mentioned at the beginning of this chapter, your author used the modeling tool "MagicDraw" from No Magic, Inc. and found it to be an outstanding tool for developing conceptual UML models. There was one problem, however: All **1..1** roles were displayed as "**1**". It was several months into the project before the company's Technical Support Group finally described to him the "secret handshake" for forcing it to display "**1..1**". Contact him at UML@essentialstrategies.com if you want to know more.

♣ Actually, compressing the optionality configuration to "[0]" for attributes would make it more symmetrical.

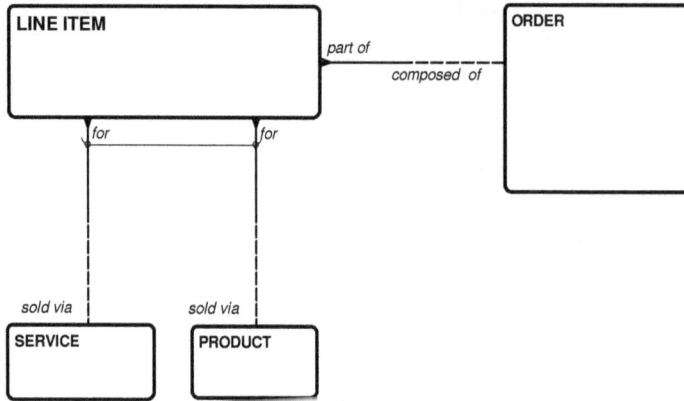

Figure 3-4: Exclusive Or in the Barker-Ellis Notation

Not all entity/relationship notations can show this, but, in fact, UML can. In UML, it is called an "XOR Constraint" and is shown in Figure 3-5.

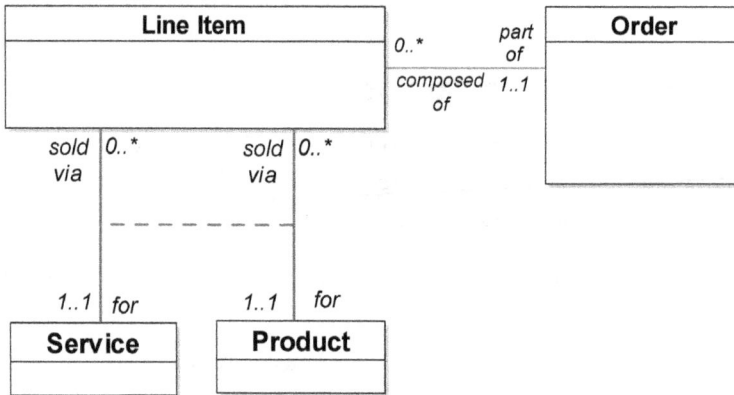

Figure 3-5: Exclusive Or in UML

UML, in fact, has a number of constraints available, so in that context, the dashed line would be labeled "XOR". Since this is the only constraint used in an entity/relationship model, however, the label can be left off.

Use Some UML-specific Symbols with Care

The last section notwithstanding, there are some elements of UML that, while not present in standard entity/relationship models, can add information, and therefore can be used to advantage. These are *enumeration, computed attributes,* and *packages.*

Entity Class Sup-types and Relationship Sub-types

While the concept of super-types and sub-types is essentially the same in UML and essential data models, they are represented differently. Chapter Four will describe the change in how (entity class) sub-types are shown in essential entity/relationship models. (See pages 91-97.) Specifically, unlike the native UML layout of showing sub-types *alongside* super-types, the sub-type boxes in an entity/relationship model are shown as being *inside* their respective super-types. In the interest of continuity with UML, the sub-type relationship symbols are maintained, however, even as they are between an interior box and its container.

There is another feature to UML that requires mention, however. While writing *Data Model Patterns: a Metadata Map,*[42] your author discovered that if you begin the narrative with a set of detailed entity classes and their relationships and then moved to more general classes, the more general *relationships* were in fact *super-types of* the more specific relationships. Nowhere in data modeling literature had he encountered that, and was quite pleased with himself for figuring it out. You'll see it for the first time in data modeling literature in the ...*Metadata Map* book.

Imagine his annoyance then, when he discovered that UML's designers had already figured that out–and included the ability as a feature in UML.

Ah well.

So, yes, you can show relationships as sub-types of other relationships, using the same symbol connecting the two as is used in connecting sub-type and super-type entity classes. Figure 3-6 shows the way UML entity classes are "nested" when they appear in an entity/relationship model. (This is described in detail, below.) That is, **Employment Contract** is a *sub-type of* **Party Relationship; Person** and **Organizations** are each *sub-types of* **Party. Internal Organization, Government, Company**, and so forth, are all *sub-types of* **Organization.**

But note the effects of the entity class sub-type structures on the relationships. First, each **Party Relationship** must be *from* one **Party**

---

[42]   David C. Hay. 2006. *Data Model Patterns: A Metadata Map.* (Boston: Morgan Kaufmann).

and *to* another **Party**. Second, the diagram shows that each **Employment Contract** must be *for* one **Person** and *with* one **Organization**.

More significantly, it also shows that:

- **Employment Contract** *for* **Person** is a <u>sub-type of</u> **Party Relationship** *from* **Party**.

- **Employment Contract** *with* **Organization** is a <u>sub-type of</u> **Party Relationship** *to* **Party**.

And of course for the inverses:

- **Person** *employed via* **Employment Contract** is a <u>sub-type of</u> **Party** *on one side of* **Party Relationship**.

- **Person** *employer in* **Employment Contract** is a <u>sub-type of</u> **Party** *on the other side of* **Party Relationship**.

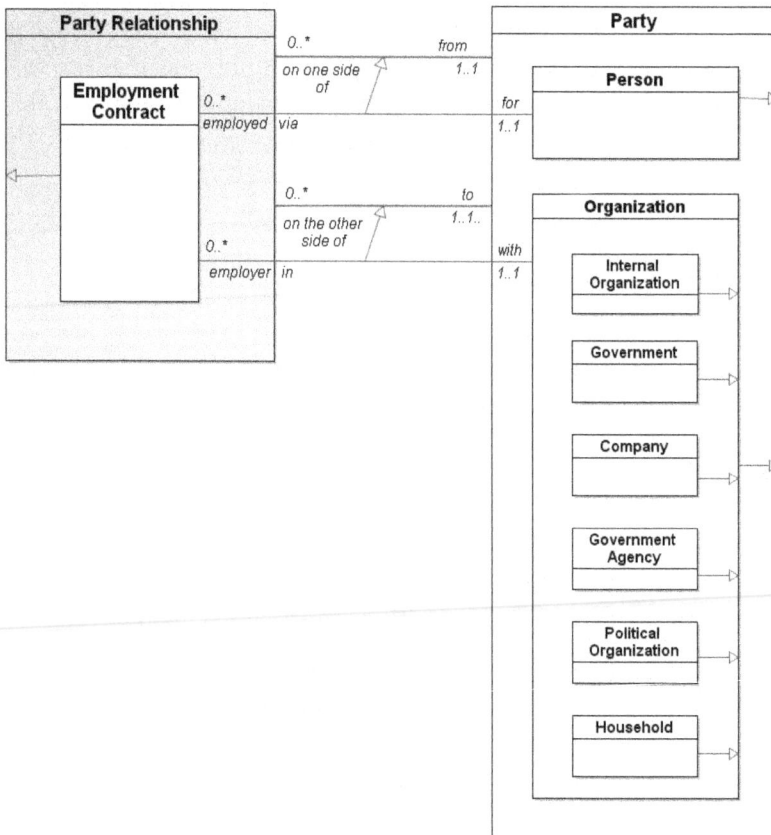

Figure 3-6: Relationship Sub-types

<<Enumeration>>

Commonly, in entity/relationship models, a ...Type♥ entity describes a list of elements used to qualify another entity class. For example, each **Status** may be *an example of* one and only *one* **Status Type**. The attributes of such an entity class are typically just "Name" (or "Code") and "Description". It is the list of instances that are actually more interesting to the reader of a model. In this case, instances might be "Pending", "In Force", and "Closed". Identifying these instances invariably has to be part of the documentation of the model.

UML has a very clever way of dealing with such "lists of values". A UML *stereotype* is defined to characterize a class specifically defined for this purpose. A box labeled **<<enumeration>>** displays not the attributes, but the list of values. An <<enumeration>> is a special kind of class used to capture and display such a list of values. In an entity/relationship model, where the number of instances is relatively short, this UML feature can be a nice enhancement. Figure 3-7 shows an example where **Status Type** is a list of possible values for the **Project Status** attribute "Status Type". Note that "Status Type" has a data type of "Internal Organization". This has an effect similar to that of a *foreign key* in a relational database, where the attribute name is equivalent to an enumeration name. It is not necessary to explicitly define the relationship between the entity class and the enumeration, but it does clarify the existence of the relationship, so it is shown in this drawing.

Enumeration was discussed in detail in Chapter 2 (page 48 ff.), and is discussed briefly below, in the discussion on Domains, below (page 82).

Beware, though, in entity/relationship models it is also possible to use the ...Type entity class to reproduce the sub-type structure of the entity class being "typed". For example, the entity class **Party** typically has many sub-types. The entity class **Party Type,** then, reproduces all of those sub-types in a list. That is, the first set of instances of **Party Type** would be "Person", "Organization", "Company", "Government Agency", etc. An additional relationship asserting that each **Party Type** may be *the super-type of* one or more (other) **Party Types** neatly accommodates the structure of **Party**.

♥   That is, **Party Type, Geographic Location Type, Activity Type,** etc.

Project Status
«ID»Sequence Number : Integer [1] Effective Date : Date [1] Until Date : Date [0..1] Status Type : Internal Organization [1]

embodied in   0..*   in   0..*

an example of

1..1   1..1   for

«enumeration» Status Type
Planned Open Delayed Complete Pending Overdue

Project

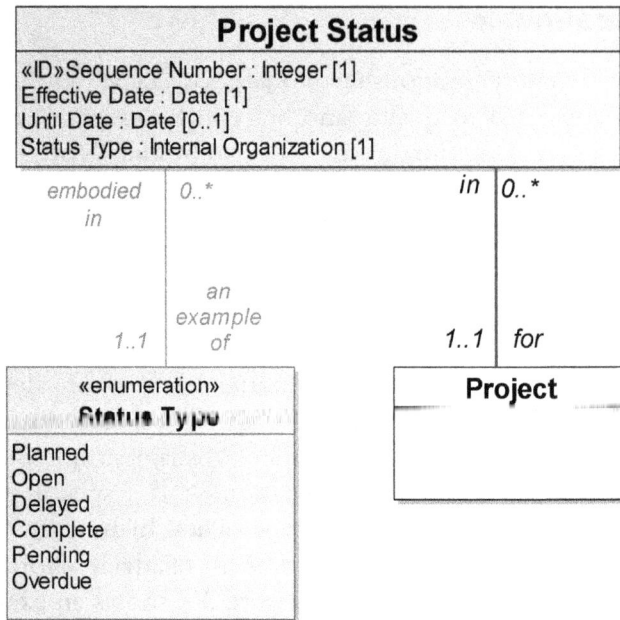

Figure 3-7 : Enumeration

As another example, instances of **Geographic Location Type** include "Geographic Area", and "Geopolitical Area", where the latter is *a sub-type of* the former.

In neither case will <<enumeration>> work.[43]

Derived Attributes

Most entity/relationship notations have no special symbol for derived attributes, and this is a shortcoming in the available tools. So, by convention, one can always surround an attribute name with parentheses if it is derived, and Oracle Corporation's Designer does provide for documenting the formulae for such an attribute.

Using derived attributes is an extremely powerful way to present many important concepts in a model, and using them, when appropriate, is highly recommended. Back in ancient times (around 1981), your author encountered a database management system (called "Mitrol Information Management System"—MIMS) that had a feature he had never before

---

[43]   Both of these examples were taken from the companion volume to this book: David C. Hay. 2011. *Enterprise Model Patterns: Describing the World*. Bradley Beach, NJ: Technics Publications.

(and has never since) encountered. You could specify a "computed field" in a file. This was not stored, but any time you did a query on the file you could refer to that field just as though it were any other kind of field. The computer was then clever enough to compute the value on the fly, based on other fields in the database. That proved to be an incredibly powerful feature that allowed development of massive manufacturing applications in a very short time.

Of course once you ran a query, the lights tended to dim. Having all the values calculated at query time proved to be, shall we say, not entirely satisfactory. Clearly it was useful to calculate many of those values when you entered the data. This becomes a design tradeoff, depending on how stable the results were and how frequently they will be requested. The criteria to be applied to that decision are different now, since computer processing is many times faster than it was in 1981. The point is still valid, however, since we can be sure the demands on the computer have increased as well.

Even so, the concept of computed fields established a profound logical structure. Even in a properly normalized structure, it is possible to imagine attributes of entity classes that are not "stored", but are derived from others. As a way to fully present and understand complex data, it is extremely valuable to include them (with formulae properly documented, of course) in the essential data model.

To be sure, it is a *design* decision (based on volume and expected usage) whether to have the calculations done when the data are coming into a database or when the data are being retrieved. But to be able to describe the calculations in a meaningful way–in context–has a profound effect on the thoroughness and readability of a model.

In MIMS, the language for expressing values was simple algebra, plus two very significant functions:

INFER-THROUGH (<relationship name>, <Entity Class Name> <attribute name>) - Treat an attribute in a parent entity class (via the specified relationship) as though it were in this entity class.

SUM-THROUGH (<relationship name>, <entity class name>, <attribute name>) - compute the sum of the values of a specified attribute in all related instances of the child entity class, via the specified relationship.

For example, in Figure 3-8:

- "/Extended Value" in **Line Item** = **Line Item** "Quantity" times **Line Item** "Price".

- "/Order Number" in **Line Item** = INFER-THROUGH (*part of*, **Order**, "Order Number")

- "/Total Value" in **Order** = SUM-THROUGH (*composed of*, **Line Item**, "/Extended Value")

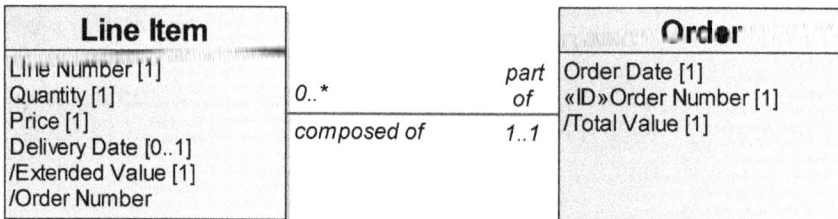

Line Item		Order
Line Number [1] Quantity [1] Price [1] Delivery Date [0..1] /Extended Value [1] /Order Number	0..* *part of* *composed of* 1..1	Order Date [1] «ID»Order Number [1] /Total Value [1]

Figure 3-8: Derived Attributes

Alas, database management systems since the days of MIMS never picked up on the idea. Well, not directly. Stored procedures can accomplish almost the same thing, but documenting them isn't nearly as tidy as simply describing an attribute.

NOTE: UML does *not* have the facility to describe the formulae in the way described above.[*] You can describe calculations in notes or in supporting documentation, but there is no automated way to implement the formulae. As in E/R models, the modeler must simply describe and document them, to be implemented as the designer sees fit.

Package

In the object-oriented world, a *package* is "a general-purpose mechanism for organizing elements into groups"[44]. Specifically, packages are "containers whose purpose is to group elements primarily for human access and understandability, and also to organize models for computer storage and manipulation during development."[45] In the entity/relationship context, a package can be defined for a subject area,

---

[*] Pity that.

[44] James Rumbaugh, *et. al.* 1999. *Op. cit.*

[45] *Ibid.*, 354.

or it can be defined simply to refer to "the model" as a whole. "Package" has no inherent semantics, after all, beyond its being a collector. Each object (entity class, attribute, or relationship) can be *owned by* one and only one *package*, although an entity class, with its associated properties, can *appear* in *any* diagram in *any* subject area. Be careful, though to tell the diagramming software which package will be the *owner* of each entity class.♣

Note that a "package" in object-oriented language is *not* the same as a "package" in some relational database management system products.

Add One Symbol

The <<id>> stereotype

In an entity/relationship model, a unique identifier distinguishes each instance of an entity class from every other instance of it.

In the object-oriented world, there is no concept of a *"natural"* or meaningful identifier. In an object-oriented program, every object in the system is uniquely identified by a generated surrogate key called an *object identifier* (known as an "OID"). Indeed, even in entity/relationship models, reference entity classes, like **Person**, often use "surrogate" identifiers (like "Person ID", in our example). In dependent entity classes, however, it is important to know whether instances are identified by all of the roles involved, just some of them, or some of them plus an attribute. The meaning of the entity class is based on that.

For example, in Figure 3-9, **Project** and **Person** are called *reference entity classes*, since they have no mandatory relationships with any other classes. They are also called *independent entity classes*. For these, unique identifiers are only attributes.

That is, for **Project**, the, the judgment was made that in this organization, all project names are unique, so the attribute "Name" can be used to identify instances of **Project**. On the other hand, **Person** is simply

---

♣   MagicDraw, for one, is perfectly capable of placing an entity class into any package that it chooses, if the correct package is not clearly identified when the entity class is defined. It is valuable to take control of this. Well organized packages (as with well-organized directories in MS-Windows) are important in the management of large models.

identified by an attribute that is a "surrogate" (automatically generated) identifier: "Person ID".

Identifying attributes are indicated on the drawing by the octothorpe (#)[*] next to the attribute name.

Dependent entity classes are those which have mandatory relationships with one or more other entity classes. That is, their unique identifiers include relationships (predicates) with other entity classes. Instances of **Constrained Project Assignment** in Figure 3-9, for example, are not identified by attributes at all. Instead, each instance of **Constrained Project Assignment** is identified by the **Person** it is *of* and the **Project** it is *to*. In this notation, each relationship involved is designated as an *identifying relationship* by a line across the relationship line (–|—) at the end next to the identified entity class.

In information engineering, a non-identifying relationship is represented by a dashed relationship line, and an identifying relationship is represented by a solid relationship line. The assumption is that identification applies only to the entity class on the "many" end of the relationship

---

[*] Blame Bell Labs in the United States for "octothorpe". The name was created by this subsidiary of American Telephone and Telegraph Company. (The current high-tech company, AT&T doesn't advertise that "telegraph" used to be part of its name.) In 1963 they came up with this name for the key showing "#" on the newly invented "Touch-tone™" telephone keypad. In the United States, this is known as the "number sign" or the "pound sign". In the United Kingdom, it is known as the "hash mark". (It is not called the "pound sign" since there is already a symbol (£) with that name.) A neutral, international word like "octothorpe" seemed like a good idea at the time. Pity it didn't take off.

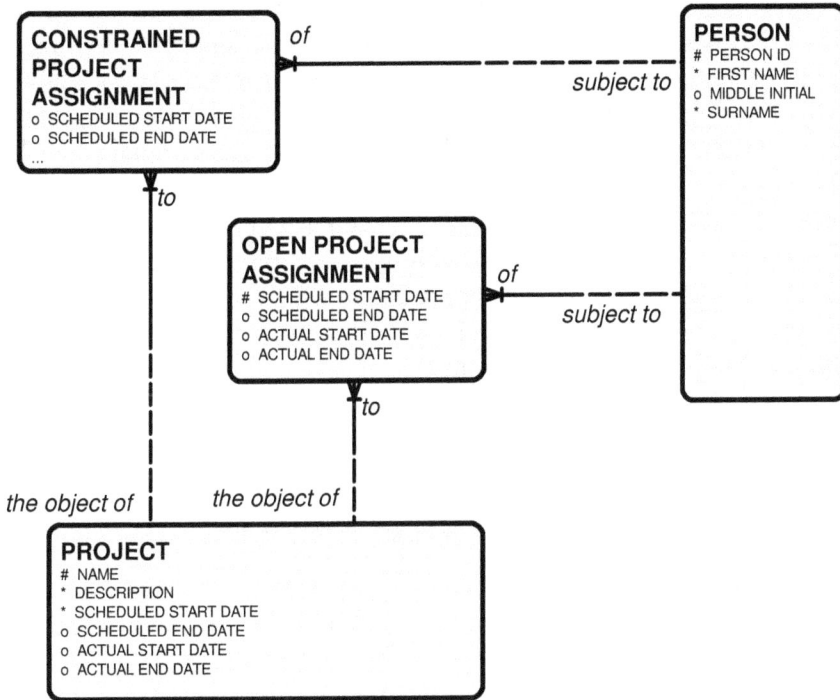

Figure 3-9: Projects

Take note of a significant characteristic of the set of identifiers of **Constrained Project Assignment**: if each assignment is uniquely identified by the **Person** and the **Project**, no **Person** can work for the same **Project** twice. There can be no more than one instance of "Charlie" working on the "I-10 upgrade project". If he leaves and wants later to return to the job, he is out of luck. This is exactly the constraint described above on UML's ***association class*** described previously. (See page 65.)

This may be exactly what the organization wants to say. Using natural identifiers allows this rule to be expressed, while surrogate object identifiers would not. If this is not the enterprise's intent, of course, the model is incorrect. As an alternative, instances of **Open Project Assignment** are identified not only by the roles they play, but also by the values of the attribute "Scheduled Start Date". Thus, if Charlie worked for one period that was scheduled to start on January 25, 2007, actually stopped working ("Actual Stop Date") on June 15, 2007, and then returned to the project November 3, 2007, this would be no problem. Different dates on the two instances would keep the instances unique.

It may be that "Scheduled Start Date" is not always known, in which case, it cannot practically be used in the unique identifier. In that case, another kind of surrogate key, such as a "Sequence Number", could be added to the entity class, and the unique id would then be the relationships plus the "Sequence Number". This opens up other possibilities. It may be that the business is mostly concerned with who works on the project, and wants to set up a sequence number series for each project. In that case, the role "to one **Project**" and the attribute "Sequence number" would be sufficient. The second assignment of Charlie to this **project** could be identified as, for example, the "fifth **Open Project Assignment**" *to* this **Project**.

Figure 3 10 shows the UML version of the same model. Note that in the absence of specific UML symbols, the stereotype "**<<ID>>**" has been added next to the attributes and the predicates involved. This serves the same purpose as identifying notations in entity/relationship notation.♥

Note that the concept of a unique identifier is carried through to relational database design as a *primary key*. This designates one or more columns to uniquely identify rows in a table. Roles are converted to relational tables by conversion of all many-to-one relationships to *foreign key* columns in the entity class that is the subject of the relationship. Each of these columns corresponds to a primary key column in the object entity class.

This means that a primary key can consist of both columns native to the table and columns that are foreign keys to other tables. This exactly implements the entity/relationship concepts of a unique identifier consisting of both attributes and roles.

♥   UML stereotypes actually have an advantage over the two most commonly used entity/relationship notations. The notation for predicates is more visible than the Barker-Ellis line, and it is less imposing than the Information Engineering solid and dashed lines.

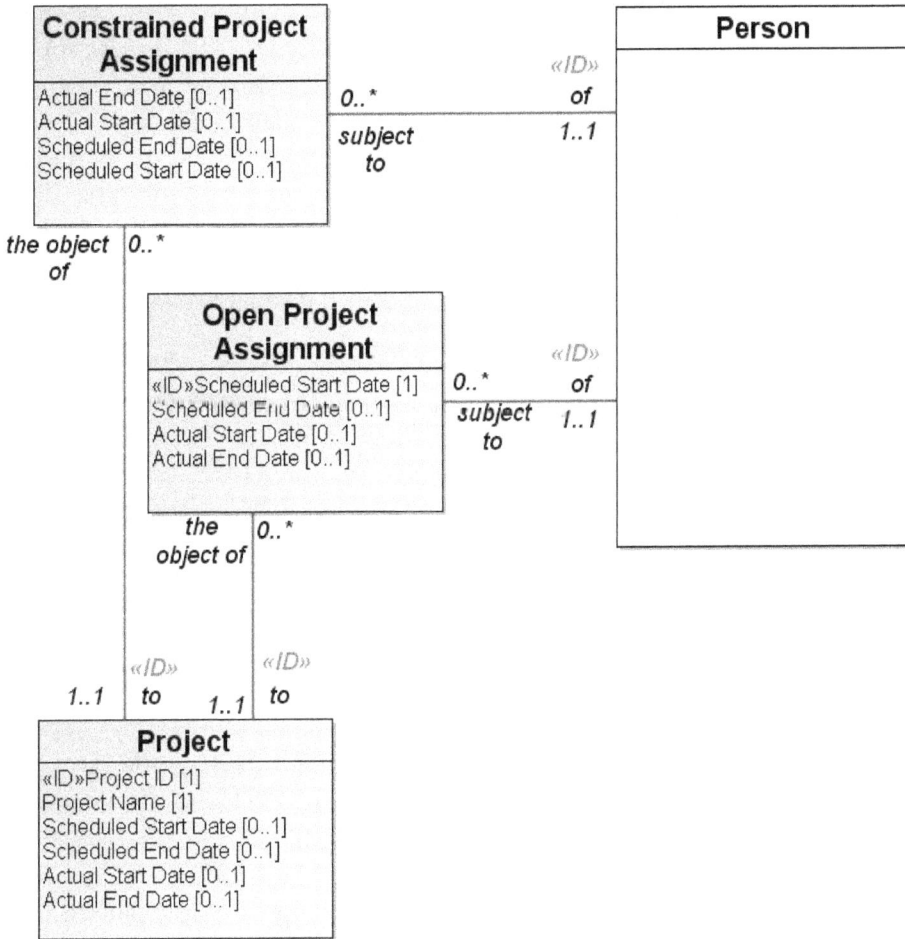

Figure 3-10: Projects in UML

Do Not Use Any Other Symbols

Ok, you now have the basic elements required for an entity/relationship model: the entity class, the relationship, and the attribute.

This is all you need from UML to create an equivalent entity/relationship model.

Nothing else is required.

UML has a number of features to describe concepts important to object-oriented designers and programmers. These are features that have no place in a conceptual entity/relationship diagram. They include:

- **Abstract Entities** – In UML, every instance of an "abstract entity" is defined to be at least one of its sub-types. That is, the super-type is an abstraction, with no physical existence apart from its sub-types. Based on the constraints described here, in an entity/relationship model every instance of a super-type must— by definition—be an instance of exactly one of its sub-types. The additional designation of calling it an "abstract entity" is unnecessary. Moreover, in some tools, it affects the way the entity is portrayed graphically, which can be a distraction.

- **Behavior** – The advertised advantage of the object-oriented approach is that it addresses behavior together with class structure. But the behavior included is often simply the name of object-oriented program modules. While it might be interesting to know how the real-world objects represented by entity class instances are created, what may be done with them, and how they disappear, this is not something that can be described in a small compartment of an entity class box. So, no, behavior is not an appropriate subject for an entity/relationship diagram, even if it is rendered in UML.

  The object-oriented movement has, of course, accentuated the point that entity/relationship modeling cannot be done in isolation from activity and event modeling. This is absolutely the case. But the notation (and even the UML Class diagram notation with its "behavior") is not an appropriate tool for doing this. Other notations, from process modeling to entity life history modeling, provide much more expressiveness for real world behavior to be presented.

- **Composition and aggregation** – Some will say that we could add a "composition symbol" (◆) on the model, or an "aggregation symbol" (◇) to denote "composed of". But in an entity/relationship model, we don't need an extra symbol, since we already have available the ancient symbols c, o, m, p, s, e, d and f at our disposal. * Yes, in this case, the older approach uses many more symbols (and for example, here reuses the "o" twice), but experience has shown that most observers of the models have had more experience with—and are therefore more comfortable with—the ancient symbols than with the UML

♣   ...rim shot...   (See Glossary, if necessary.)

symbol that is new and has no intuitive meaning. Adding a new symbol is unnecessary in this context. Most business-oriented viewers prefer the older symbols.

There is an interesting additional meaning to these UML symbols, though: They express some of the rules for *referential integrity*. This in spite of the fact that these are database concepts, not object-oriented design ones. If it is a solid diamond (called "composition"), it means that the referential integrity rule "cascade delete" applies. That is, if the parent is deleted, all the children are deleted. If it is an open diamond (called "aggregation"), the referential integrity rule "nullify" applies. That is, if the parent is deleted, the children are left as orphans, not connected to anything.

While it would be valuable to be able to designate referential integrity rules in entity/relationship diagrams, this isn't an adequate approach, since these symbols reflect only two of the three possible referential integrity rules, but not the third: there is no symbol for the "cascade restricted" rule— the rule that says that, if children exist, the parent cannot be deleted. (Perhaps: ⬦ could be added to the notation?)

Without the complete set of referential integrity rules, there is no point to placing the composition and aggregation symbols on an entity/relationship diagram.

Note that some UML modelers use these symbols *instead of labeling* the roles. In that case, they are better than nothing, but in the entity/relationship environment we are aspiring to here, the roles must be labeled anyway.

- *Navigation direction* – In an entity/relationship model, the relationship exists as a structure with two ends. You cannot talk about half a bridge. In object-oriented programs, on the other hand, there is no declarative structural component to associations. That is, typically a programmer must write program code to navigate a relationship in each direction. In UML—in deference to the object-oriented designers and programmers—it is permitted to designate that the primary path of navigation is in one direction or the other. In Figure 3-3 (above, on page 74) for example, you could add an arrowhead from **Order** to **Line Item** to indicate that it is expected for someone to want all the line items in an order, but it is expected much less frequently to ask for order information about a line item.

In an entity/relationship diagram, this is not shown. We make no such assertions. The diagram is about structure, and there is no reason to limit the direction in which it can be navigated.

- *Ordered* - UML aficionados will also suggest that we do not need "Sequence number" as an attribute, since, when we are inclined to use such an attribute, we could simply characterize the entity class as **ordered**. The sequence number would then be implicit. The problem with this approach is that it presupposes that the "ordered" approach will be implemented by a technology that can create sequence numbers and manipulate them behind the scenes. This is to say, leaving the sequence numbers implied in the model implies the use of a particular technology to generate them. More significantly, if we were to use the "ordered" approach, the sequence number would not be available for designation as part of an identifier.

- *Visibility* – in an object-oriented program, a class and/or its attributes may be accessible to other classes or not. This characteristic is called "visibility" and is very specific to object-oriented design. It is meaningless in an entity/relationship model.

3. Define Domains

In entity/relationship models, the common set of characteristics for a set of attributes is called a *domain*. It can be as simple as a format, it could be a list of values, or it could be some sort of validation formula.

Mr. Barker defines a domain as follows:

"A set of business validation rules, format constraints, and other properties that apply to a group of attributes: for example:

- a list of values

- a range

- a qualified list or range

- any combination of these.

"Note that attributes and columns in the same domain are subject to the same validation checks."[46]

In addition to the things listed above, a domain can also be described by:

- data type

- length

- a list of illegal values

- edit rules

- a mathematical expression

- precision factor

Some entity/relationship-oriented CASE tools have explicit support for documenting domains behind the scenes as part of an attribute's documentation—others do not.

UML does not have what entity/relationship modelers are accustomed to calling "domains". Its concept of *data type*, however, is extensible and can be used in the same way.

First of all, UML has a basic list of what are standard "data types". This describes the nature of characters that can be used: "String", "Number", "Date", and so forth. This list can be expanded to include the kinds of domain constraints just described.

One alternative to specifying a domain is to represent it as a "reference" entity type. For example, **Internal Organization** might have had the attribute "Internal Organization Type" with a domain that is a list of values such as "Division", "Department", "Section", etc. This could be documented in the definition of the attribute, or it could be shown as an entity class. This is a solution for both entity/relationship and UML modeling.

In addition, UML, as was described above, can display a "list of values" explicitly with an <<enumeration>>. (See page 71.) Enumerations are described in more detail in the last section. (See page 48.) Note in Figure 2-12 (page. 30), that **Internal Organization** has an attribute "Internal Org Type", which has as a data type "internal". This is linked to the <<enumeration>> **Internal Organization Type**. Instead of displaying the assumed attributes of "Name" and "Description", the diagram shows a

---

[46]   Richard Barker, 1990, *op. cit.*, G1-3.

list of values. In this case, they are "Department", "Division", or "Section".

4. Understand "Namespaces"

In UML, a *namespace* is "a part of the model in which the names may be defined and used. Within a namespace, each name has a unique meaning. All named elements are declared in a namespace, and their names have scope within it. The top-level namespaces are packages (including subsystems), containers whose purpose is to group elements primarily for human access and understandability, and also to organize models for computer storage and manipulation during development."[47]

That is, a namespace is "owner of" a set of objects, and no duplicate names are allowed within that namespace. In our UML version of an entity/relationship model, the parent package that is the entire model, plus any sub-packages we may define, plus each entity class, are all namespaces. So is each relationship. The rule against duplicate names only applies at the lowest level of namespace, so you cannot have duplicate attribute names within a class, but you can have duplicate attribute names across classes. You cannot have duplicate class names at the lowest package level, but you can duplicate class names across packages.

As just mentioned, in a UML class model, each class is defined as a namespace. One class cannot be contained in another class's namespace, which means that for a property that is a relationship, the object entity class in a predicate sentence cannot be contained in the subject class's namespace. More significantly, this is why, in the design model, role names (properties of the subject class) are used only to *label* object classes, not to describe the entire relationship. (See the discussion of "Associations and Relationships" in Chapter Two.)

This is the source of problems we entity/relationship modelers have in naming relationships, since the object-oriented community sees attributes and relationships as properties of the subject class. The solution rests in the fact that the association is also a namespace. Both classes and the predicate can be members of that namespace.

---

[47]　James Rumbaugh, *et. al.* 1999. *Op. cit.* 353-4.

5. Follow Display Conventions

Chapter Four describes in detail the aesthetic principles to follow to create a suitable diagram for presentation. That chapter is about issues of organization and presentation style. Here are some detailed recommendations for dealing with the particulars of the UML notation.

Name Formats

Since entity/relationship models are intended to be presented to non-technical people, the names of entity classes, attributes, and relationships should be as readable as possible. So include spaces between two word names: "Line Item", not "LineItem". And capitalize each word in either an attribute name or an entity class name. Don't capitalize at all in relationship names.

Role Positions

Position the predicate next to the object entity class. Since both cardinality terms are there, it makes it easier to read the relationship sentence.

For those who use both the Barker/Ellis notation and UML, the position of role names can be confusing, since relationship names are at the other end for the Barker/Ellis notation. To keep your sanity, in each notation always position the predicate so that it can be read in a clockwise direction. This means, (in UML) for a vertical relationship line, the lower one is to the right and the upper one is to the left. For a horizontal relationship line, the one to the right should be above and the one to the left should be below. In each case the cardinality terms are on the other side of the line at the same end as the role to which they refer.

For example, Figure 3-8, above, is reproduced in Figure 3-11, below. Note that each relationship sentence is constructed by reading clockwise:

- "Each **Line Item** must be (1..) *part of* one and only one (..1) **Order**."

- "Each **Order** may be (0..) *composed of* one or more (..*) **Line Items**."

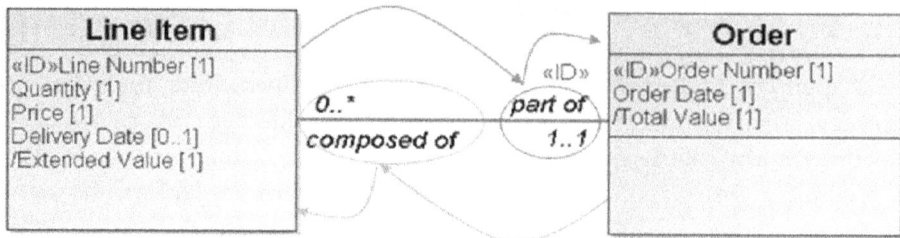

Figure 3-11: Role positions – UML/ER

"Exclusive or" Relationship Constraint

Because this is the only UML constraint used in this context, it is possible to eliminate display of "XOR".

Cardinality Display

Because it is a very common combination, the cardinality "must be one and only one", which should appear as "1..1", is collapsed into the single symbol "1" in UML modeling tools. This is unfortunate, since the two components form the two parts of the natural language sentence describing the predicate. If at all possible, adjust the tool to make all of these appear as "1..1".♣

Summary

To draw an architectural entity/relationship model, using the UML notation, follow these steps:

    1. Show domain-specific entity classes only.

    2. Use symbols selectively.

        ➢ Use only recommended symbols.

        ➢ Optionally, use selected UML symbols not available normally to entity/relationship modeling.

        ➢ Do not use UML design-oriented symbols.

♣   You should be aware that it took considerable time for your author to discover the "secret handshake" for doing this in No Magic, Inc.'s product "MagicDraw". Eventually I found a technical support person who knew how to do it, however. Interested parties should contact me (uml@essentialstrategies.com) for the secret.

➤ Add the symbol for identifiers.

4. Define Domains.

5. Understand "Namespaces".

6. Follow display conventions.

In addition, be sure to follow the aesthetic guidelines and best practices for entity/relationship modeling described further in Chapter 4, below.

Chapter 4:
Aesthetic guidelines and Best Practices

What distinguishes an entity/relationship model from a UML design model—or a database design, for that matter—is that its first purpose is to be presented to the community concerned with the domain being modeled. It may be business executives, government employees, or someone studying an intellectual domain. In short, it will be presented to human beings, most of whom have no prior experience with data models and who have little patience with things technical or technological. For this reason, aesthetics is important.

Introduction – Aesthetic Considerations

It is true, first of all, that in terms of aesthetics, UML starts at a disadvantage:

Cardinality indicates whether an instance of an entity class is associated either with one or more instances of another entity class or with no more than one instance. In a conventional entity/relationship diagram, this is represented by *graphic symbols to be viewed*—typically a "crow's foot" (<) to represent more than one, and either the absence of a crow's foot or a mark across the line (—|—) to represent just one. This may also be referred to as *maximum cardinality*.

Optionality indicates whether an instance of a relationship is required in the first place. This is represented by either a dashed relationship line next to the subject entity class or a circle {O} across the end of the line next to the object entity class. This may also be referred to as *minimum cardinality*.

In UML, these concepts are represented by *text to be read*: "**0..**" means the relationship is optional; "**1..**" means that it is required; "**..1**" means that an instance of the first entity class can be associated with no more than one instance of the second class; "..*" means that it can be associated with an unlimited number of instances of the second class.[48]

Thus, the relationship portrayed in Figure 4-1 shows cardinality and optionality in graphic terms. The optionality and multiplicity can be *seen* immediately. The equivalent relationship shown in Figure 4-2 shows these characteristics portrayed with digits and other characters. Instead of *seeing* these concepts graphically, the viewer has to *read* the symbols before *understanding* them.

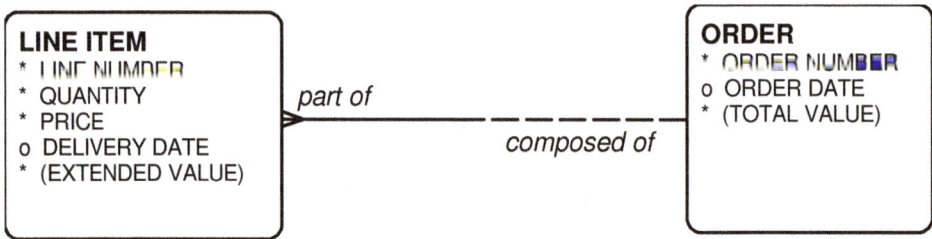

Figure 4-1: A Relationship in Barker-Ellis Notation

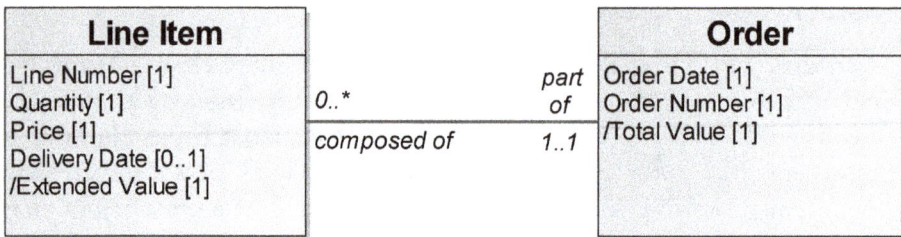

Figure 4-2: A Relationship in UML

This means that in presentations, patience will be required in explaining the cardinality and optionality notation to the viewers. It can be done, however, if the other aesthetic standards described here are followed. In that case, viewers can accustom themselves to this one quirk.

---

[48] For a comprehensive comparison of data modeling notations, including all described here, see Appendix A of [Hay, 2003] or go to http://www.essentialstrategies.com/publications/modeling/compare.htm.

This chapter presents principles and best practices for documenting and presenting an architectural entity/relationship model, regardless of the notation used. Many data modelers are, shall we say, cavalier about these practices, but they are important if you are using Information Engineering, IDEF1X, or Barker-Ellis, and—because of the inherent disadvantage described here—particularly so if you are using UML.

The basic principles are:

1. Place sub-type boxes inside super-type boxes.

2. Eliminate bent lines

3. Orient the "many" ends of relationships to the left or top of the diagram.

This is in addition to the typographical standards described in the last chapter. The following guidelines apply no matter which notation you are using.

Place Sub-types Inside Super-types

When instances of an entity class can be categorized into two or more other entity classes and each of these subordinate classes "inherit" the attributes and relationships of the original entity class, these subordinate classes are called *sub-types*. The parent class is called a *super-type*. This concept is known in the object-oriented world as *inheritance*—each sub-type "inherits" the attributes and relationships of its super-type.

Condensed Entity/Relationship Approach

In the Barker-Ellis version of an entity/relationship model, these are represented with the boxes representing sub-types being *inside* the box representing their super-type. For example, in Figure 4-3, **Person** and **Organization** are sub-types of **Party**. That is, every instance of **Party** is an instance of either a **Person** or an **Organization**. **Organization**, in turn, is a super-type of **Internal Organization**, **Government**, **Company**, **Government Agency**, **Political Organization**, and **Household**.

In this diagram, the boxes representing **Person** and **Organization** are shown *inside* the box representing their super-type, **Party**. Similarly, the boxes representing **Internal Organization**, **Government**, **Company**, **Government Agency**, **Political Organization**, and **Household** are all shown *inside* the box representing their super-type **Organization**.

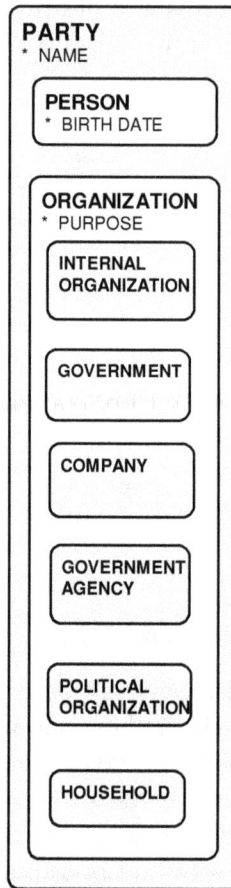

Figure 4-3: Sub-types in Barker-Ellis Notation

The UML (and that of some entity/relationship notations) Approach

Figure 4-4 shows the way UML (and Information Engineering, for that matter) represent sub-types: These are shown *outside* the super-type box, attached via specialized arrows.

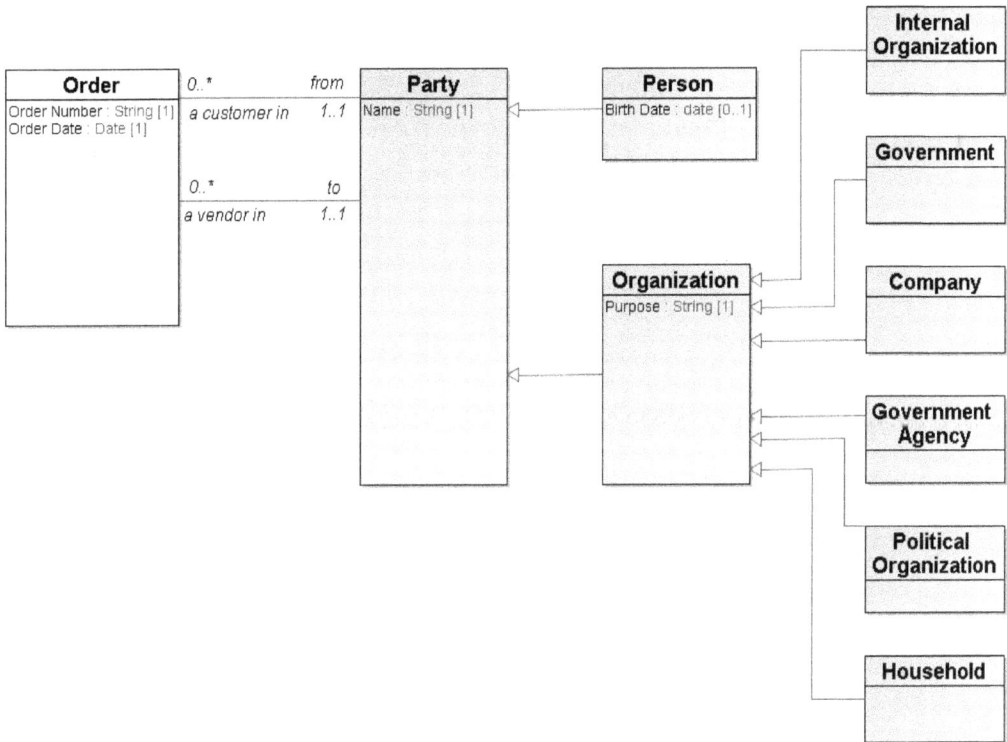

Figure 4-4: Sub-types in Conventional UML

The problem with this approach is that if you have many subtypes, your diagram quickly fills up, distracting from other, often more important, structures. Moreover, as the nesting gets deeper and deeper, it is progressively more difficult to *see* that an instance of the sub-type *is* in fact an instance of the super-type several levels up. The attributes and relationships at the upper levels are not obviously attributes and relationships of the lower level sub-types. In Figure 4-4, for example, it is not obvious that a **Government Agency** may be *a customer in* an **Order**.

Many UML tools do, in fact, allow you to display sub-type boxes inside the super-type boxes. The result for our example is shown in Figure 4-5.

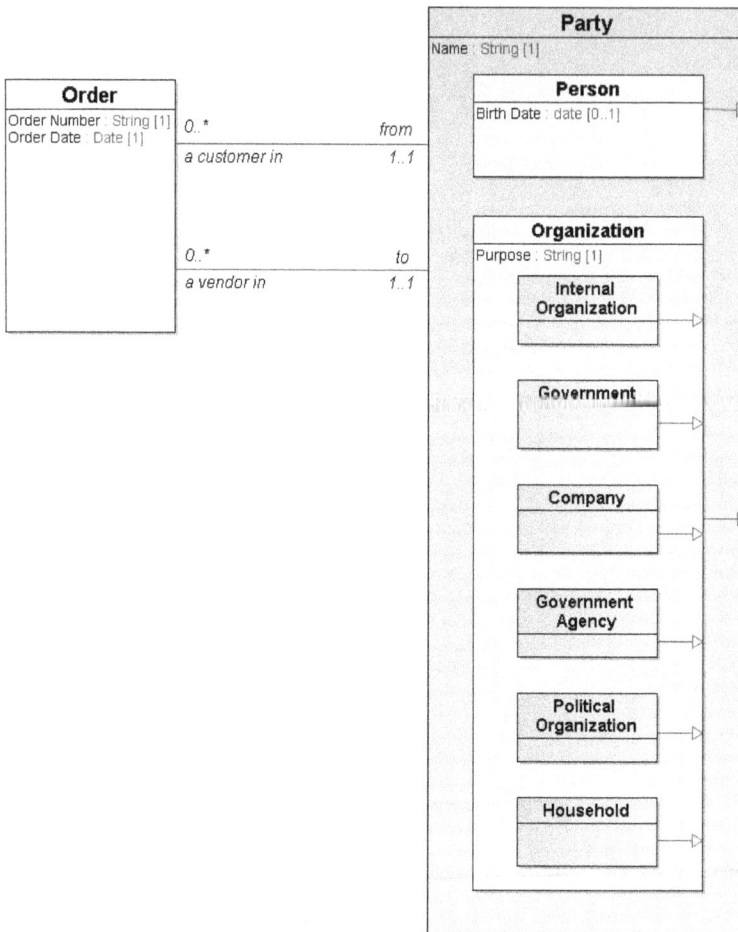

Figure 4-5: Sub-types in ER UML

The "box-in-box" approach has the following advantages:

- It is more compact. Given the constraint that a model must fit on an 8 1/2 X 11 (or A4) piece of paper, having to take up space for sub-types is a significant cost in drawing real estate.

- It is more representative of the business reality. An instance of a sub-type really *is* an instance of its super-type. (Think about Venn diagrams.) That is, an attribute or relationship for a super-type is clearly also an attribute or relationship of all the sub-types. **Company**, for example, may be *a customer in* one or more **Orders**, just as a **Political Organization** may be. Both of these have as attributes "Name" and "Purpose", inherited from **Party** and **Organization**, respectively.

One Problem

Unfortunately, to use this notation in UML, we have to recognize that it has already been taken. In UML version 2.0, a *composite structure diagram* is used to describe run-time architectures that aren't clear from a typical object or class diagram. Specifically, "UML 2 has added a composite structure diagram that shows the participating elements and their relationship in the context of a specific classifier such as a use case, object, collaboration, class, or activity."[49]

Solution

According to the UML specification, a composite structure is "a composition of interconnected elements, representing run-time instances collaborating over communications links to achieve some common objectives."[50] That is, it is analogous to a product structure, where the interior boxes are *components* of the outer box.

A composite structure diagram is represented by a larger rectangle, with its components (which may be classes, packages, or operations) contained as symbols within it. To look at the diagram shown in Figure 4-5 as a composite structure diagram is to imagine that **Person** and **Organization** are components of **Party**, not sub-types of it.

To solve this ambiguity, Figure 4-5 includes the *generalization lines* in the boxes. This keeps the aesthetic orientation we are looking for, but signals to UML aficionados that this is inheritance, not composition. This should not really be an issue because any viewer of this model should understand that it is an architectural model describing an enterprise, and not a run-time model describing a physical system.

Constraints

In the approach to entity/relationship modeling described in this book, there are three constraints on the treatment of super-/sub-types:

---

[49]   H-E. Eriksson, Magnus Penker, Brian Lyons, and David Fado, 2004, UML 2 Toolkit. (Indianapolis: Wiley Publishing), 34.

[50]   Object Management Group, "OMG Unified Modeling Language" (OMG UML), Superstructure, V2.1.2". OMG Document Number: formal/2007-11-02, 161.

- *Completeness* - Each instance of the super-type must be an instance of one of the sub-types. This is equivalent in UML to calling the super-type "abstract". That is, in UML you can impose this constraint or not. In the version of entity/relationship modeling described here, the constraint always applies, but it can be finessed by adding a sub-type **Other... (Other Organization, Other Geographic Area**, etc.).

- *Exclusivity* – No instance of the super-type may be an instance of more than one of the sub-types.

- *No multiple inheritance* – Each sub-type may have only one super type.

Note that these constraints are not followed by all modelers, even in the entity/relationship modeling community. Information Engineering, for example, makes it possible to have overlapping and incomplete sub-types. Some would permit an instance of a super-type to be an instance of more than one sub-type.

One constraint that is reinforced by the sub-type-within-super-type approach, is a prohibition of **multiple-type hierarchies** (called **generalization sets** in UML), where a super-type has more than one *set* of sub-types. This violates the basic concept that a sub-type is a *fundamental* category of the super-type. Multiple-type hierarchies are much better represented by the "categorization model", described below. (See Figure 4-6, "Categorization", on page 98, below.)

Similarly, it is common to display *only some* of the sub-types that actually exist. This is acceptable in the course of a presentation to build up the model slowly—but eventually all sub-types have to be accounted for. (OK, if necessary, as mentioned above, you can finesse this constraint by including the entity class **Other...**)

Multiple inheritance (an entity class with more than one super-type) is controversial in both the object-oriented and data modeling worlds. Your author contends that, in his experience, every time it looked as though multiple inheritance was necessary, looking at the model from a different perspective removed the need.

Again, the topography of the sub-type-within-super-type approach does not permit multiple inheritance.

These constraints are important. They ensure that the classification shown in sub-types is *fundamental*. In this example, it is not possible for someone to be both a **Government** and a **Company**♥. Moreover, it is not possible for an **Organization** to change from being a **Government** to being a **Company**, even over time.

Categories

There are more flexible ways to categorize things, of course, but these should be represented in a data model separately, without using sub-types. Figure 4-6 shows a reasonable way to do this for **Party,** by adding the entity classes **Party Category** and **Party Categorization**. A **Party Categorization** is the fact that a particular **Party** falls into a particular **Party Category** *for a period of time*. That is, each **Party Categorization** must be *of* exactly one **Party** *into* exactly one **Party Category**—at a particular time. The **Party Categorization** is effective on an "Effective Date", and ceases to be effective on an "Until Date".

This structure allows a **Party** to be categorized into multiple **Party Categories** at a time, and also allows for that **Party Categorization** to change over time.

Note that, in addition to being *of* a single **Party,** the **Party Categorization** must be *by* a single **Party**, as well. This supports the concept of data stewardship, and, moreover, recognizes that different people in an organization might well categorize **Parties** differently. **Parties** may be *subject to* different **Party Categorizations** *by* different **Parties**, each for its own purpose. For example, the **Internal Organization** "Market Research Department" might place the **Household** "Hay family" in a different **Party Category** than the **Internal Organization** "Sales" does.

Moreover, each **Party Category** must be *defined by* exactly one **Party**. The set of **Party Categories** that is of interest to Market Research may be very different from the set of **Party Categories** that is of interest to Accounting. A **Party** must be appointed as a steward for every **Party Category**.

For example, a **Party Category** that would apply to **Person** could be "Income Level". This might be *defined by* the **Internal Organization**, "Market Research Department". The **Person** "David Letterman", then, would be *subject to* **Party Categorization** *into* the **Party Category** with the "name" "Over $500,000". This might be according to the **Person** "Sam Sneed", who happens to be Mr. Letterman's Gardener.

♥   Sometimes a **Government** may be the owner of a **Company**, but that is a different kind of relationship.

This is a very different approach to categorization than sub-typing, but if you are looking for multiple inheritance or multiple type hierarchies, this is the way to go.

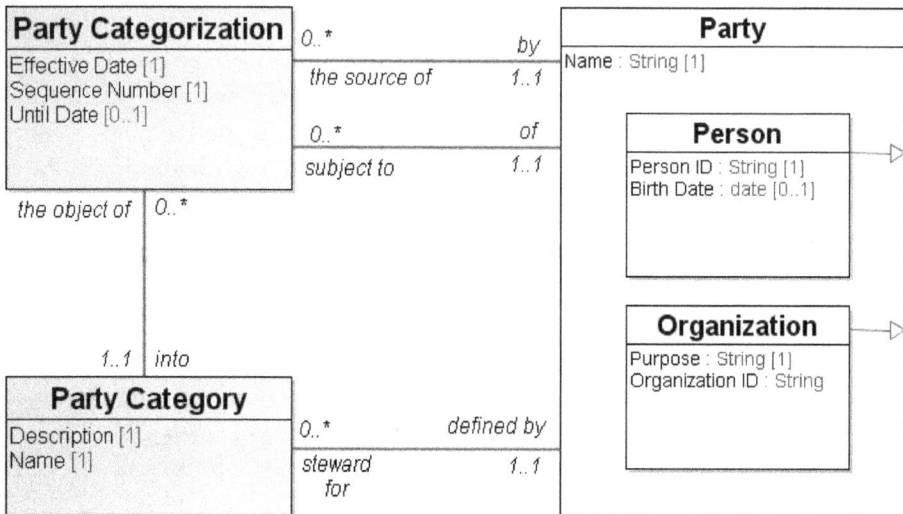

Figure 4-6: Categorization

Eliminate Bent Lines

On a drawing, any angle or intersection is a symbol that will draw the viewer's attention. For this reason, there should be no "bent" lines, since each of these will appear to be a symbol for something. There is no meaning to the bend, so it is an unnecessary distraction to the eye.

The first step, then, is to stretch boxes as necessary to ensure that all relationships are represented by a straight line from one entity class to the other. Note that if you do this, it is suddenly less critical to avoid crossed lines. While that is still desirable, if there is an occasional crossed line, the viewer typically doesn't notice it, since it cannot be two adjacent right angles. It can only be a crossing of two straight lines. The viewer's eye is focused on the line connecting two entities.

Figure 4-7 shows a drawing with a "spaghetti" approach to drawing relationship lines. You've been give this drawing with no documentation. How easy is it for you to grasp what it is about? Tests and measurements, yes. But what about them? Note the crossed lines. It is a standard rule that you should not cross lines, and this is the setting where that is particularly true. The line from **Person** to **Sample** clearly crosses both the line from **Test Type** to **Test**, and the line from **Expected Measurement** to **Test** crosses the line from **Test Type** to **Measurement**. Or do they? In fact, the line from **Measurement** to **Expected Measurement** turns 90° right at the point where the line from **Test Type** to **Test** does the same. The two lines are *adjacent*, not crossing.

Also, no rules about the positioning of the role names were followed, so even understanding individual relationships is hopeless.

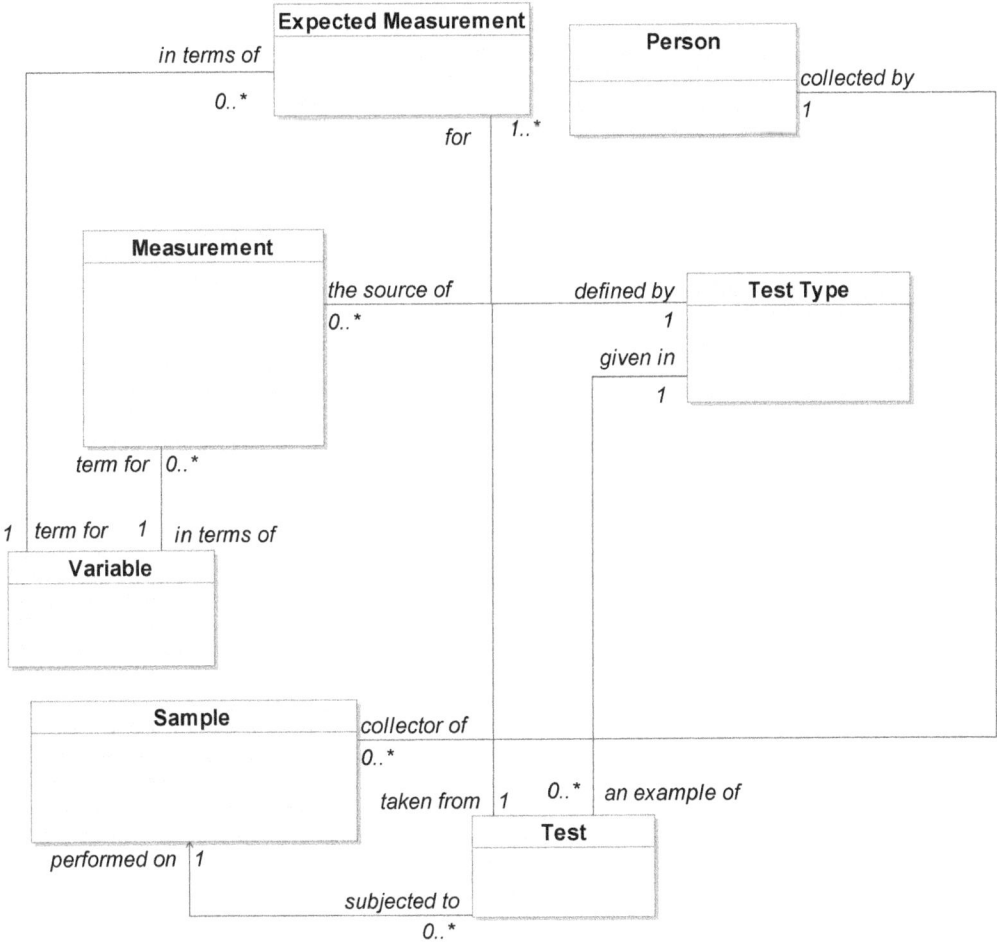

Figure 4-7: Bent Relationships

Instead of bent lines, Figure 4-8 shows the same model with straight relationship lines. This is easier. Also, all relationship sentences may now be read clockwise. Tests are performed on samples, and measurements are in terms of variables.

Note that in this case, the one example of crossed lines is not a problem. The only way to interpret it is as two relationships that happen to cross each other.

Still, the overall structure is not yet as clear as it could be.

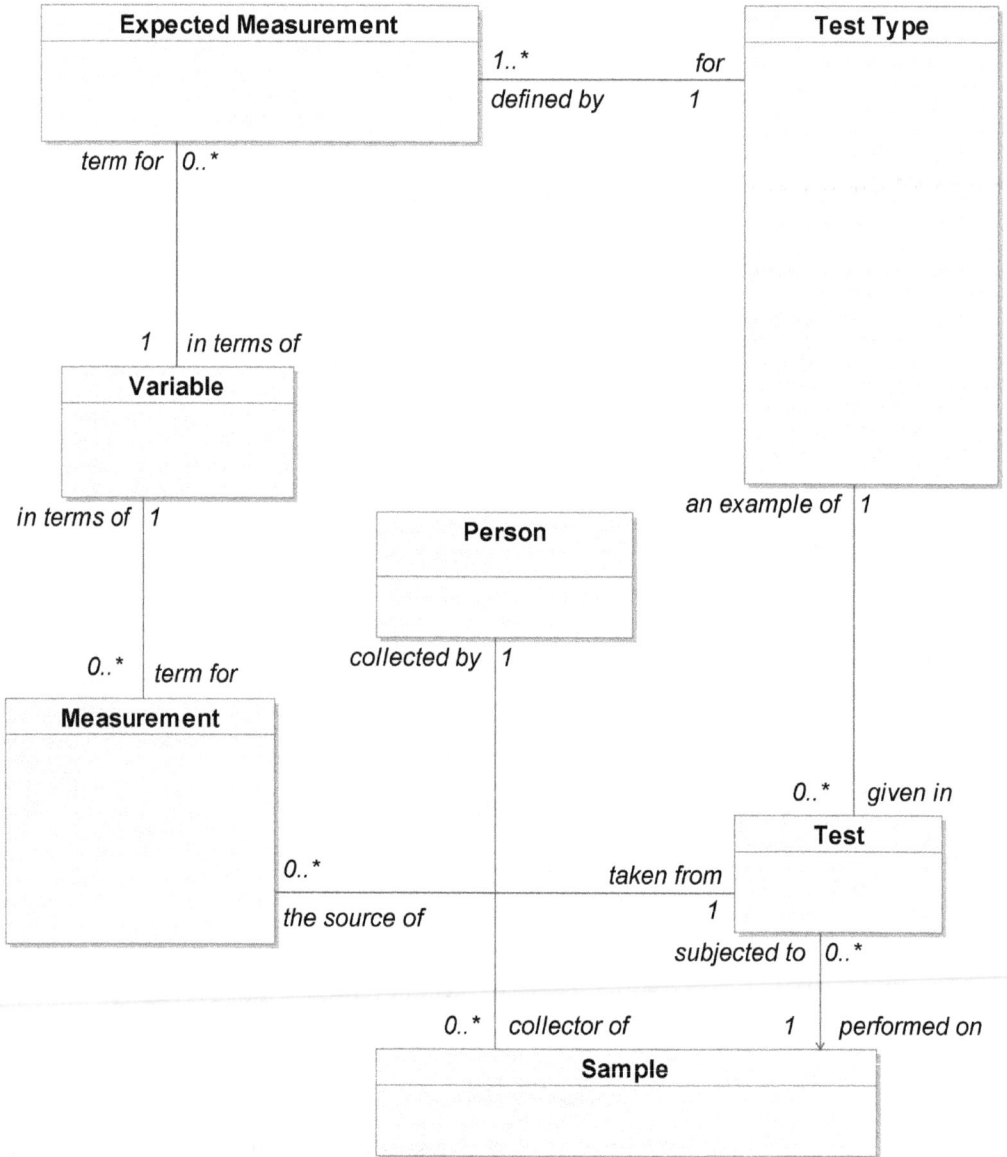

Figure 4-8: Straight Relationships

Orient "Many" End of Relationships to Top and Left

Notice that in Figure 4-8, even with the lines straight, it is not clear what the model is about. What is the "subject" of the model? Expected measurement? Sample? It's hard to tell.

Orienting the relationship lines so that the "..*" ends are at the left or toward the top of the diagram makes that clearer, as shown in Figure 4-9.

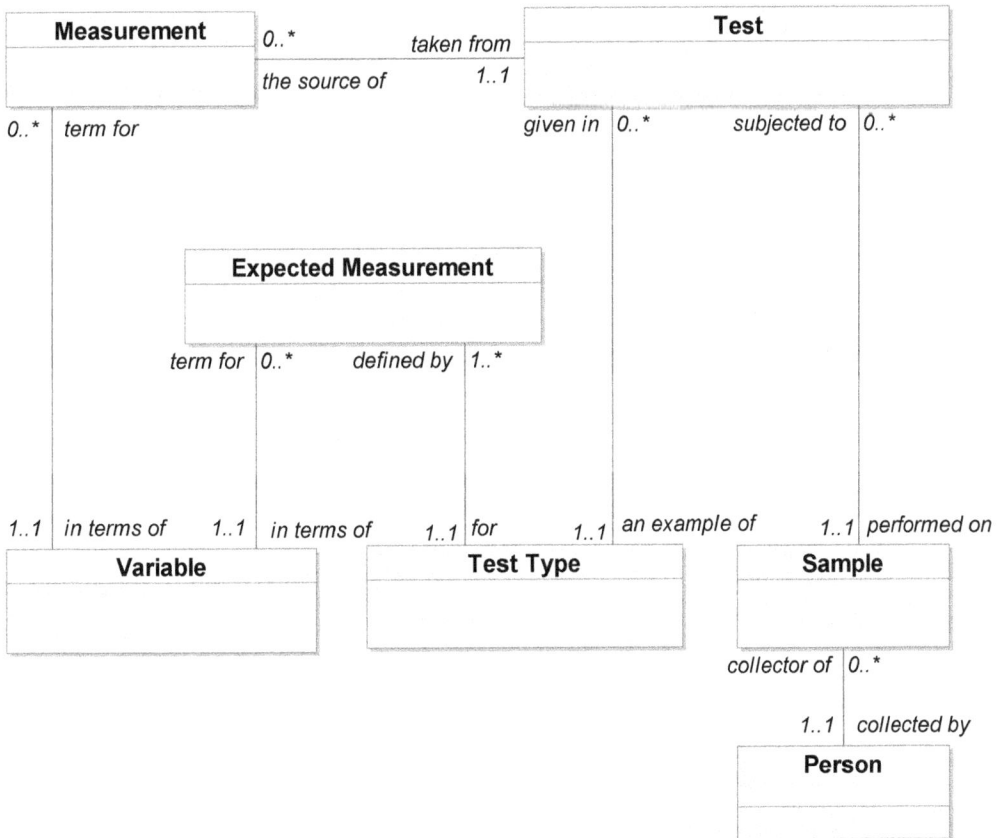

Figure 4-9: Properly Oriented Relationships

Here, the "reference" entity classes, that describe relatively tangible things (**Test Type**, **Person**, and **Sample**, for example), tend to collect in the lower right, while more transactional entity classes that are more abstract (such as **Measurement**), tend to collect in the upper left. Now you can see what the diagram is about (the reference entity classes) and what is describing those things. **Tests** are *performed on* **Samples**, and these are the *source of* **Measurements**.[51]

Among other things, the resulting drawing can be made more compact.

Presentation

Probably the worst thing to happen to data models was the invention of the plotter. This permits modelers to create wallpaper-sized models that are completely unintelligible.

Presentation Rule

If you have a plotter at your disposal, ***turn it off.*** Quietly and carefully...***walk away***. Pretend it does not exist.

If a model is to be presented to a human audience, it must be composed of individual sections, each describing a particular area of interest, typically called a "subject area". Each subject area must be small enough to fit on one sheet of 8 ½" by 11" (or A4) paper. Ideally, each subject area drawing would have no more than 9-10 boxes, but keeping the number small is hard.

The absolute maximum limit, however, if the drawing is to be at all intelligible, is 15 boxes. Show even that many on a screen without any highlighting, however, and your audience will immediately bring out Blackberries, knitting, and/or origami paper—and tune out completely.

Note two things about presenting data models to an audience:

1. You are *not* in front of this audience to present the drawing. They are only for taking notes. You are there to make the English

---

[51]   Yes, it's true that there are some heretics among you (Canadians?) who prefer to orient the relationships with the "many" end towards the right and the bottom. "How can this be?" we ask.

(Ok, it *can* be, and it actually is fine, as long as you adopt it as a convention and use it consistently.)

language *assertions* that the drawing represents. Is it true that each clinical trial must be *about* exactly one compound? (It turns out that it is not. Each clinical trial must be *to test* exactly one compound. See how relationship names are important?)

2. You are there *to be wrong*. You are not there to have the audience pat you on the head and be impressed. You will have made mistakes in your understanding of the business. It is *much* cheaper to learn about them now, and mark up the model, than it is to find out after a system based on your (incorrect) assumptions has been installed.

Present the model in small pieces, beginning with a diagram containing between one and three entity classes. Discuss the meaning of each. Discuss the attributes. Read the relationship sentences and get acceptance. Is it really only one? Might there be more?

An ideal medium is overhead transparencies,* so you can mark them up. At the very least, take notes (and be seen to be taking notes) for corrections.

The next slide will add between one and three more entity classes. On this drawing the new entity classes are highlighted. Use a contrasting color, but not one that is so dark as to make the text unreadable. (Dark yellow is good.) Again, discuss the added entity classes and relationships. Continue this build up sequence until the subject area is complete.

Had you presented the last drawing first, you would have completely lost your audience. This way, though, the last drawing has only one to three entity classes highlighted. Some viewers will pretend that's all they are seeing. Others can be pleased with themselves that they actually understand a complex drawing. No one (well, ok, almost no one) will have fallen asleep.

In 1956, G.A. Miller was decades ahead of his time when he published a landmark article that profoundly identified what is wrong with most

---

* One sad victim of the assent to power of the PowerPoint® presentation is the overhead projector. With physical slides, you can mark them up, erase the markings, and then mark them up again with a different color. In ancient times (say ten years ago), the measure of success in a feedback session was the number of scribbles on the transparencies. Nothing in the Microsoft world can compare to that.

PowerPoint presentations.[52] His research determined that human beings can hold no more than nine "things" in their heads at one time. Specifically, people are most comfortable with "seven plus or minus two" things. This is why, when area codes were meaningful, most people could remember seven-digit local telephone numbers. Now that it's really a ten digit number it's hopeless.♥

The upshot is that if a slide has less than five bullets it usually looks trivial. If it has 10 or more, it is too complicated to follow. Either way, the viewer immediately loses interest.

The same thing is true for data model presentations. If it is necessary to have up to 15 boxes, no more than three or four should be highlighted for the topic of any one slide. The collection of boxes that are not highlighted becomes just another "thing".

(By the way, when the time comes to write up the model, take the same approach: Explain it in the text a little bit at a time.)

Summary

What distinguishes an entity/relationship model from either a UML design model—or a database design, for that matter—is that its first purpose is to be presented to the business community. It will be presented to human beings, most of whom have no prior experience with data models and who have little patience with things technical or technological. For this reason, the aesthetic characteristics are critical.

This chapter laid out the basic guidelines for producing a model that can be presented to a non-technical audience. Given the textual business of UML's approach to cardinality, some patience will be required from the audience initially, but if all other guidelines are followed, the presentation should be a success.

Success, you must note, is measured in terms of the number of corrections identified. If no changes come out of the meeting, you failed. The reason the relationship names are as explicit as they are is so that the

---

[52]   G. A. Miller. 1956. "The Magical Number Seven, Plus or Minus Two: Some Limits on Our Capacity for Processing Information", *The Psychological Review*, Vol. 63, No. 2 (March, 1956). Pp. 81-97. Available at http://www.musanim.com/miller1956/.

♥   Speed dialing was invented just in time…

viewer will not be able to say simply "Sure, looks ok to me." In each case, the assertion should be clearly true or truly false. And the viewer should be compelled to speak up if it is false.

The basic principles are:

1. Place sub-type boxes inside super-type boxes.

2. Eliminate bent lines.

3. Orient the "many" ends of relationships to the left or top of the diagram.

This is in addition to the typographical standards described in the last chapter.

Chapter 5: An Example: Party

As an example of both the use of UML notation to describe an architectural model, as well as best practices for presenting any architectural model, this chapter consists of an excerpt from the companion book, *Enterprise Model Patterns: Describing the World*.

Take note of the following characteristics:

1. No more than five entity classes are highlighted in each Figure.

2. Logical business rules (extensions of the logic of the model, rather than rules that are business policy) are included.

An enterprise cannot exist without people. Whether one is an employee, a vendor agent, or the president of a company, a **Person** can clearly be assumed to be a "thing of significance" to most companies and government agencies. A few of the things to be known about a *Person*, such as **Name**, or **Birth Date** are attributes of the **Person** entity. Others (more than you might suppose) are not attributes, but relationships to other entities, as we shall see. A *Person* may enroll in one or more courses, for example, or may play a role in one or more activities, and so forth.

If an enterprise is concerned with people, it must surely also be concerned with aggregations of people. Such an aggregation (called henceforth an *organization*) may be a department, a committee, a vendor, a labor union, or any other collection of people or other organizations. It is described by such attributes as **Purpose, Federal Tax ID**, and so forth.

Figure 5-1 shows entity classes for **Person**, a human being of interest, and **Organization**, a collection of human beings.[*] We'll discuss attributes in

---

[*] Yes, it is possible to define an organization without specifying the people it contains. The presumption is that even if it is being postulated, it is expected to consist of human beings.

detail later on, but here for the sake of argument, **Person** has the attribute **Birth Date**, and **Organization** has the attribute Purpose.

Five kinds of **Organization** (sub-types) are shown:

- **Company** – a legally recognized commercial business, which, in the United States, is a corporation, a partnership, or a sole proprietorship.

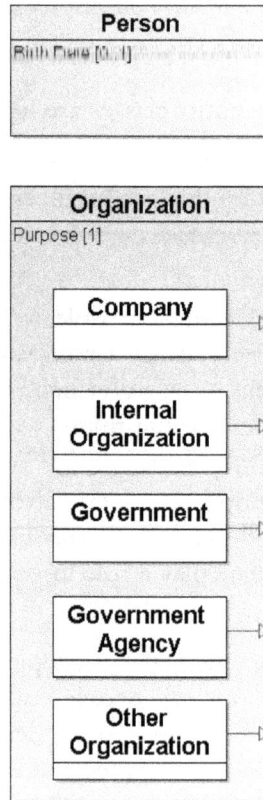

Figure 5-1: People and Organization

- **Internal Organization** – an organization within the enterprise, such as a department.
- **Government** – the body which is responsible for administration of a geopolitical area, such as a country or a state.

- **Government Agency** – a component of a **Government** usually concerned with regulating a particular area of concern, such as pharmaceuticals, air travel, criminal activities, and so forth.
- **Other Organization** – the sub-types shown here are pretty standard, but every enterprise has its own way of segmenting **Organizations**. **Other Organization** is for any **Organization** not covered by the other categories.[*] Examples might include labor unions and professional societies, political parties, and the like.

Note that **Person** is described by the attribute **Birth Date**, while **Organization** is described solely by the attribute **Purpose**. So far they have no identifying attributes, but these will come next.

Parties

People and organizations share many attributes and relationships to other entities. A corporation is, after all, a legal **Person**. Both people and organizations can be described by "Names" and "Addresses", and both may be party to contracts. For this reason, while **Person** and **Organization** are useful entities, so too is the super-set of the two, which we will here call **Party**. This is shown in Figure 5-1.

In this example, **Party** has the common attributes **Global Party Identifier** and **Name**. In Figure 5-1 we saw that **Person** has the attribute **Birth Date**, and **Organization** has the attribute **Purpose**. Now we can see that both **Person** and **Organization** also have *Global Party Identifier* and *Name*.

Of course, **Person** actually has *two* names (plus a middle initial, if you want to get thorough). This could be handled by moving **Name** to **Organization** and giving **Person** **First Name** and **Last Name**. An alternative is shown here, with the principle **Name** being equivalent to a

---

[*] Note that according to the data modeling approach being followed in this book, sub-types do not overlap. The same **Organization** may not be both an **Internal Organization** and a **Company**. Note also that the constraint that every instance of a super-type must be an instance of one sub-type. This constraint is finessed by including **Other Organization** for the ones we haven't thought of yet.

Person's surname, and only the given name is specific to **Person**. Names will be treated in a much more comprehensive way, below.[*]

Notice that **Global Party Identifier** is specified as a unique identifier for both **Person** and **Organization**. This is a fairly strong assertion: no **Person** can have the same identifier as any **Organization**. The modeler may, instead, choose to have a separate set of identifiers for **Person** (say, **Person ID**) and for **Organization** (say, **Organization ID**).

The answer to the question of which approach to take is, as they say, beyond the scope of this book. This is, after all, only a "pattern". It is for the reader to apply it appropriately.

Note that in Figure 5-2, each **Party** must be *an example of* exactly one **Party Type**. This is a structure that we'll see again often. In this case, **Party Type** is defined as the definition of a kind of **Party**. That each **Party** must be *an example of* <u>exactly one</u> **Party Type** suggests some overlap with the sub-type structure, where each **Party** must be either a **Person**, a **Company**, a **Government Agency**, and so forth. Indeed, **Party Type** does exactly reproduce the sub-type structure. That is, instances of **Party Type** include "Person", "Organization", "Company", and so forth. Note the relationship that permits us also to say that, for example, "Company" may be *a sub-type of* "Organization".

The generalization structure of **Party** is further represented by the assertion that "each **Party Type** may be *a super-type of* one or more other **Party Types**". (Alternatively, "each **Party Type** may be *a sub-type of* one and only one other **Party Type**".)

This redundancy is a bit of a gimmick, but it allows us both to see graphically the principal categories of **Party**, and to make use of them in the formulation of business rules. We will see examples of this later.

Business Rule

- Instances of **Party Type** must at least include one for each sub-type of **Party** shown. Other, more detailed instances are permitted.

---

[*]   Henceforth, unless there is reason to display them (as there was here, to make a point), attributes will only be shown in the first figure where the entity class appears. For the sake of clarity, they will not be shown after that.

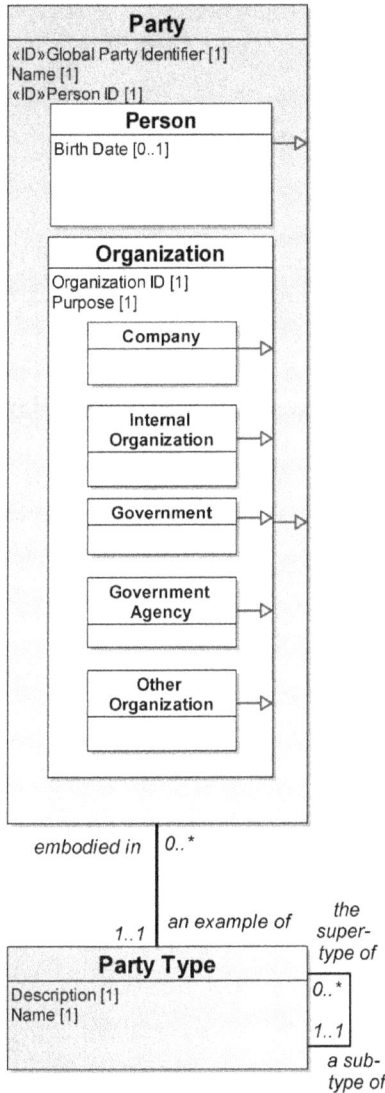

Figure 5-2: Parties

Party Relationships

People are related to each other; people belong to unions and clubs; departments are contained in divisions; companies band together into industrial associations, buying groups, and so forth.

To address this diversity of possible associations among **Parties**, the entity class **Party Relationship** is introduced in Figure 5-3. This allows us to represent *any* relationship between two parties. That is, each **Party Relationship** is defined to be *from* one **Party** and *to* another **Party**.

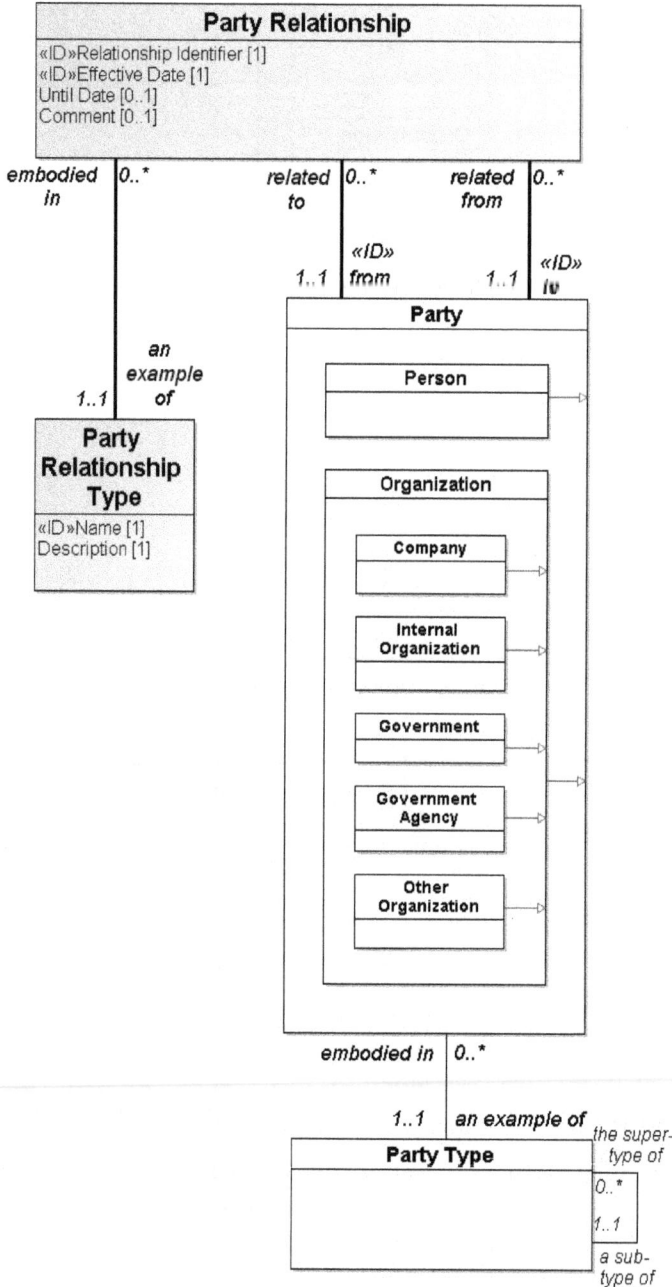

Figure 5-3: Party Relationships

Thus, a **Party Relationship** *from* **Person** "George Gobel" *to* **Organization** "The Screen Actors' Guild" between the relationship's **Effective Date** of "June 18, 1952" and its **Until Date** of "February 24, 1984"—would be *an example of* the **Party Relationship Type**, "Member".

The important attributes of this are the **Effective Date** of the **Party Relationship** and its **Until Date**. Note that each **Party Relationship** must be *an example of* exactly one **Party Relationship Type**, such as "organizational structure", "club membership", "family relationship", and so forth.

Thus, George Gobel may go down in history as having been in a relationship (of type "membership"), with "The Screen Actors' Guild", "Effective" June 18, 1952, "Until" February 24, 1991.

Party Identifiers and Names

Back in Figure 5-2, **Party** is shown with the attribute **Global Party Identifier**, marked with <<ID>> to show that it is a component of the unique identifier for the entity class. This symbol is an extension to UML to show that each instance of an entity class is uniquely identified—at least in part—by the annotated attribute. In this case, it shows that each instance of **Party** has a unique value for **Global Party Identifier**. It is also only a dream today. Many are working on schemes for eliminating duplicate records and neatly being able to identify everyone. It hasn't happened yet. Many systems have a surrogate key that forces uniqueness for all instances of **Party** within the system, but there is no guarantee that in the world there aren't multiple instances of the same **Person** or **Organization**.

Figure 5-4 shows an alternative approach. This acknowledges that there are lots of identifiers for people (Social Security Number, passport number, employee number, and so forth.) and for organizations as well (Employer Identification Number, department number, and so forth.) This structure allows us to capture all the possible identifiers in the entity class **Party Identifier,** and then to give each a **Value** as it is evaluated in **Party Identifier Value**. Each of these must be *for* one **Party Identifier** and *assigned to* one **Party**.

The identification of instances of **Party Identifier Value** is via a combination of the attribute **Identifier Value**, and the two relationships:

- Each **Identifier Value** must be *assigned to* one **Party**.

• Each Identifier Value must be *for* one Party Identifier.

Note the "<<ID>>" symbol next to both the attribute and the role names. This means that George Smith can have two different values of Employee ID. There could be a business rule preventing that, but if the situation exists, it should be captured—and then revealed.

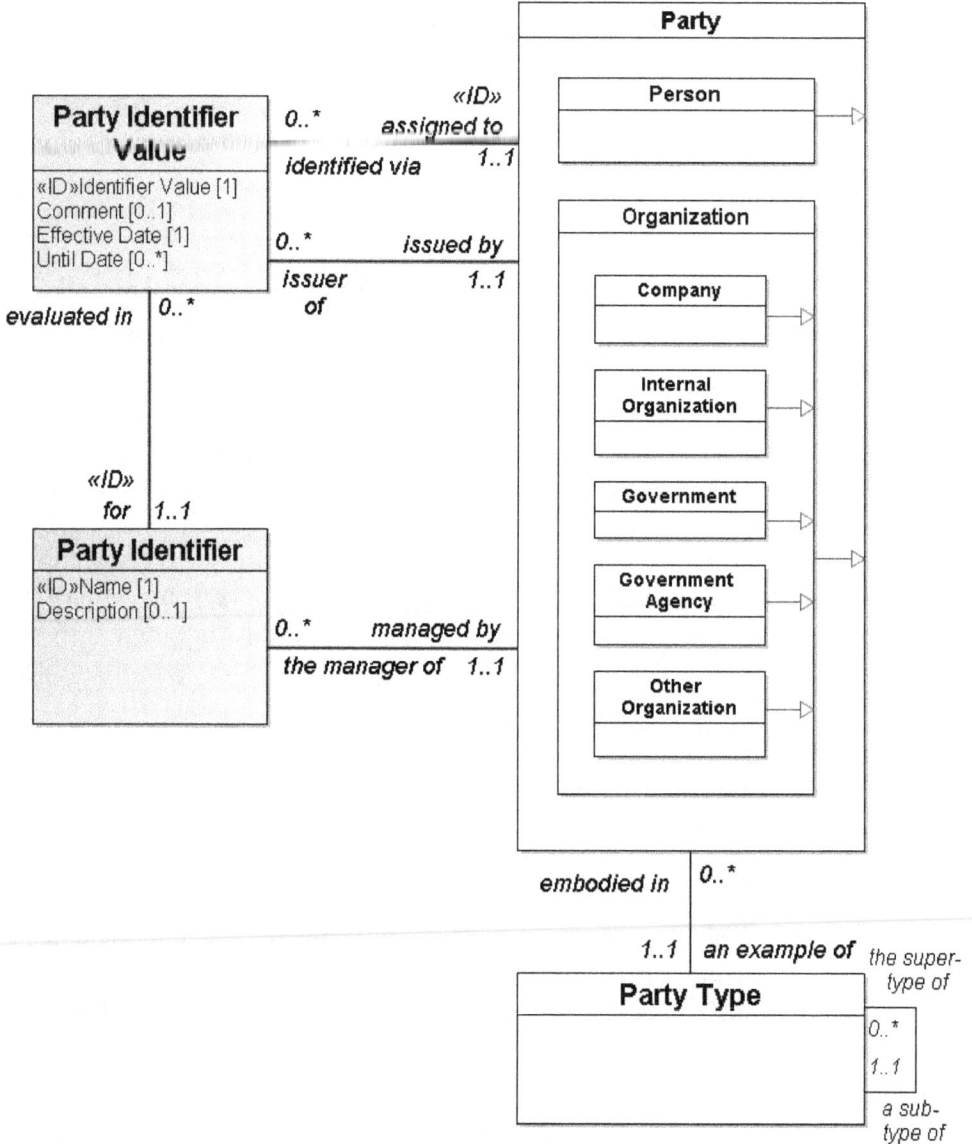

Figure 5-4: Party Identifiers

Tables 5-1 and 5-2 show examples of tables derived from these entity classes. The names of identifying columns are highlighted. In Table 5-2, the reference to **for Party Identifier** matches the value of **Party Identifiers Name** shown in Table 5-1. Note that including the Identifier Value to the unique identifier allows for George Smith to have two values for "Employee Number" at two different times. Without that, George Smith could not be employed more than once.

Table 5-1: Party Identifiers

Name <<ID>>	Description	Managed by
Social Security Number	Number used to identify individual people who are present or future pensioners.	U.S. Social Security Administration
Employer Identification Number	Number used to identify corporations.	U.S. Social Security Administration
Emp No	Number used to identify individual employees	a specified **Company**
...		

Table 5-2: Party Identifier Values

<<ID>> assigned to Party	<<ID>> for Party Identifier	<<ID>> Identifier Value	issued by Party	Effective Date	Until Date
Marlon Brando	Social Security Number	234-99-3122	Social Security Administration	February 4, 1940	July 1, 2004
The Company Company	Employee Identification Number	99-1234567	Social Security Administration	August 4, 1989	--
George Smith	Employee Number	241533	Lockheed Martin	December 15, 2004	December 16, 2004
George Smith	Employee Number	242687	Lockheed Martin	January 24, 2006	August 15, 2009

The Figure also shows that each **Party Identifier** must be *managed by* a **Party**. For example, the concept of the Social Security Number is managed by the U.S. Social Security Administration. The Employee ID is managed by the company's Human Resources Department. Along the same lines, the actual assignment of an **Identifier** to a **Party** is *issued by* a **Party**, such as an **Internal Organization**, or even the **Party** itself.

Moving from identifying people to the task of identifying data (instances of **Party Identifier Value**, in this case), each instance of **Party Identifier Value** is identified by the combination of the two relationships just described, plus the attribute Identifier Value. That is, there is only one instance of Essential Strategies having an "Employee Identification Number" of "99-1234-123". With this configuration, it is possible for Essential Strategies, Inc. to have another Employer Identification Number.

To constrain it so that, for example, Essential Strategies, Inc. may never have more than one Employer Identification Number, simply remove the designation of Identifier Value as part of the unique identifier. Then, there could be no more than one instance of the combination of **Party** and **Party Identifier**.

Note that each **Party Identifier** must be *managed by* a **Party**. For example, the concept of the "Social Security Number" is managed by the U.S. Social Security Administration. The "Employee ID" is managed by the company's Human Resources Department. Along the same lines, the actual assignment of a **Party Identifier Value** to a **Party** is itself *issued by* one **Party**, such as an **Internal Organization**, a **Government Agency**, or the **Party** itself.

An obvious attribute for **Party**, as we have seen, is Name. Well, not exactly. You can have a name for an organization, but what about people's names? In addition to simple first and last name, what about middle? Or Jr.? What about the title? No, it's more complex than even that. For that matter, companies have official names, nicknames, and stock tickers. And on top of everything else, names change. No, a simple name attribute just won't do.

Figure 5-5 shows that, as with **Party Identifier**, **Party Name** has been pulled out from the **Party** entity class, so that each **Party** may be *labeled by* one or more **Party Names**. That is, each **Party Name** must be *of* one **Party** and (significantly) it must be *of* one **Party Name Type**. This allows a woman, for example to have one **Party Name** that is of **Party Name Type** "married name", and another of **Party Name Type** maiden name.

Note that each **Party Name** is uniquely identified by both the **Name Text** and the **Party** being named. The name "David Charles Hay" can only exist once for the fellow who is the author of this book.

The **Company** IBM may be *labeled by* the **Name Text** attribute of **Party Name**, "International Business Machines Corp". That **Party Name** is *an example of* **Party Name Type Name** of "official name". IBM is also *labeled by* the **Party Name Name Text**, "IBM", where that **Party Name** is *an example of* **Party Name Type Name** of "official abbreviation".

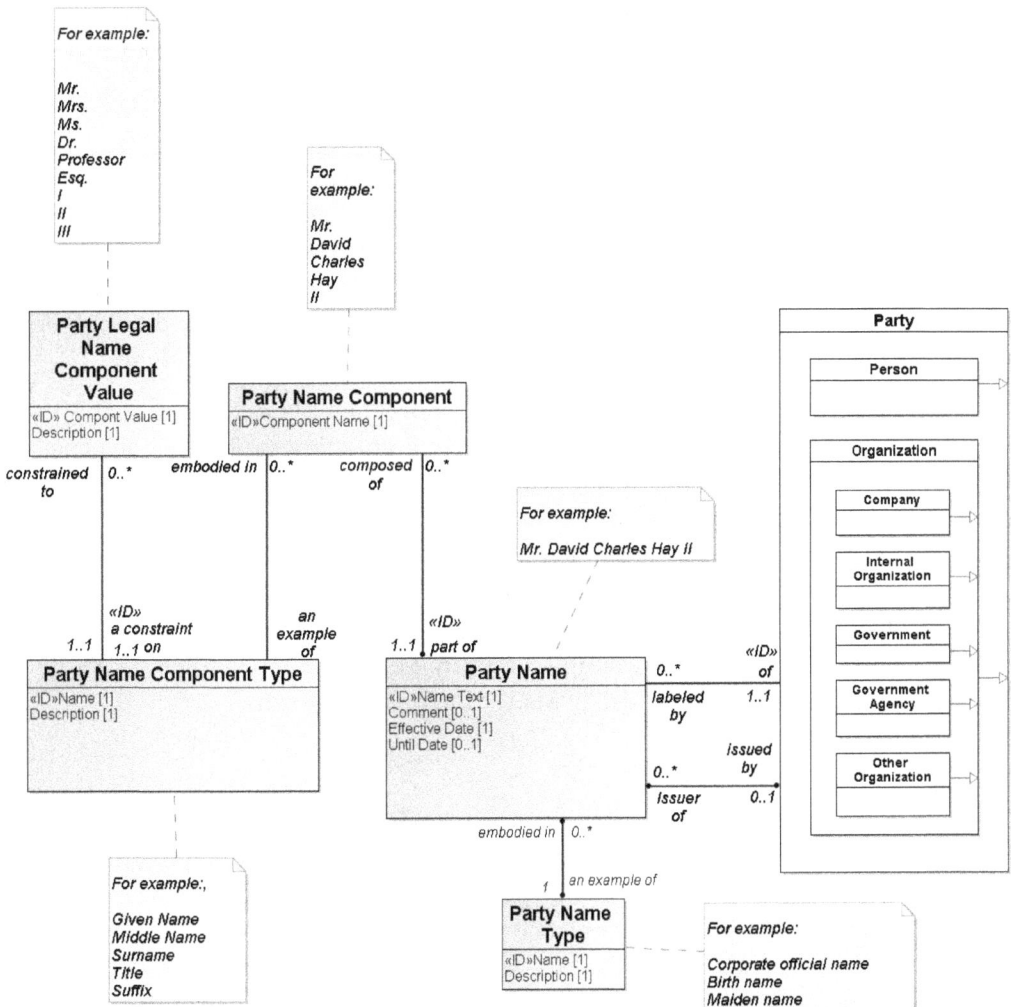

Figure 5-5: Party Names

The entity class **Party Name** has attributes **Effective Date** and **Until Date**, which allows capture of the history of names. For example, Table 5-3 shows a history of names for the company known since 2000 officially (if redundantly) as FedEx Express.

Table 5-3 The Names of Federal Express

Party	Effective Date	Party Name Text	Party Name Type Name
Federal Express	6/1/96	Fed Ex	Nickname
Federal Express	1/1/98 (became subsidiary of FDX Corp)	Federal Express	Official name
FDX Corp	1/1/2000	Fedex Corp	Official name
Federal Express	1/1/2000	FedEx Express	Official name

Note that while each **Party Name** must be *of* one **Party**, it may also be *issued* by a **Party**. Presumably, in the case of a **Person**, that **Person** is responsible at least for reporting h'♥ own name (rare is the organization that requires parents to sign off on someone's name), but in the case of **Organizations**, it could be important who specified the **Party Name**.

The naming problem for people is more complicated than that. As pointed out above, people's names have a complex structure. Each may be *composed of* one or more **Party Name Components**, where each **Party Name Component** must be *an example of* exactly one **Party Name Component Type**, such as "first name", "last name", "suffix", "title", and so forth. Some **Party Name Component Types** are constrained to certain values, though. That is, the Component Name in a **Party Name Component**, if it is an example of **Party Legal Name Component Value** "Title", must then be "Mr.", "Ms.", "Dr.", and so forth.

♥   As a modern man, your author is properly reticent to use "he" to mean "he or she". As a grammarian, however, he also objects to using "their" when only one person is involved. (Although he does acknowledge that this practice goes back at least to the 17th century). He also finds "he or she" to be incredibly clumsy. So, in the interest of conciseness and logical consistency, he hereby proposes the following conventions: **'e** means "he or she"; **h'** means either "him or her" or "his or her".

Remember, you saw it here first.

Figure 5-5 showed annotations with examples of the primary entity types. Table 5-4 shows the example in tabular form.

Table 5-4: An Example of a Name

Party Name	Party Name Type	Party Name Component Type	Legal Party Name Component Type Value	Party Name Component
Mr. David Charles Hay II	Birth name	Title	Mr.	Mr.
			Mrs.	
			Ms.	
			Dr.	
			Professor	
		Given name	(no list of values)	David
		Middle name	(no list of values)	Charles
		Surname	(no list of values)	Hay
		Suffix	II	II
			III	
			IV	
			Esq.	

Business Rule

If a **Party Name Role Type** is constrained to one or more **Legal Name Component Value**s, then any instance of **Party Name Component** that is an example of that **Party Name Component Type** must have as its Component Name the "value" of one of those **Legal Name Component Value**s.

Translation: If a Party Name Component Type is *constrained to* one or more Party Legal Name Component Value, any Party Name Component must be *an example of* one of those values.

Constraints

The structure for identifiers and names has the advantage of being supremely flexible. Any name value can be given to any **Person** or **Organization**. Any identifier value can be given to any **Person** or **Organization**. But only certain kinds of **Party Identifier**s are appropriate for certain kinds of **Parties**, just as only certain **Party Name Types** are appropriate for certain kinds of **Parties**. For example, the **Party Identifier** "Social Security Number" is only appropriate for **Person**. The **Party Name Type** "corporate abbreviation" is only appropriate for **Company**.

Here is where splitting out **Party Type** becomes useful. Figure 5-6 shows that we can specify that each **Party Identifier** is only appropriate for particular **Party Types**.

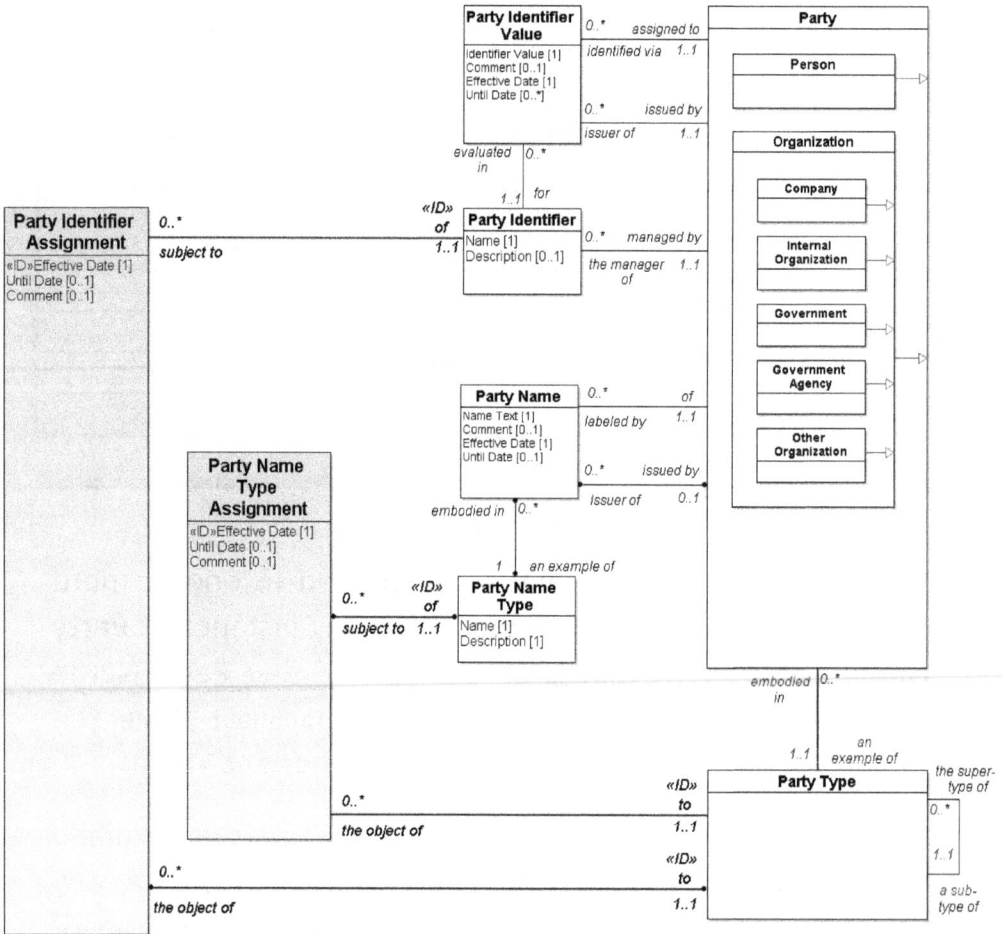

Figure 5-6: Party Name and Identifier Assignments

This is done through specifying a **Party Identifier Assignment** that is *of* a **Party Identifier** and *to* a **Party Type**. That is, for example, one can assert that the **Party Identifier "Employer** Identification Number" may only be assigned to a **Party** that is an *example of* the **Party Type** "Company".

The same constraint is described by **Party Name Assignment. Party Names** such as "married name" and "personal name" can only be *embodied in* **Party Names** *of* **Parties** that are *examples of* the **Party Type** "Person". (Indeed, the **Party Types** "male person" and "female person" could be added as **Party Types** that are each a sub-type of **Person**, even though they don't appear as sub-types. In that case, the **Party Name Type** "maiden name" could be constrained to "female person").

Table 5-5 shows some examples of **Party Name Types** being assigned to **Party Types**.

Table 5-5: Some Party Constraints

<<*ID*>> of Party Name Type	<<ID>> to Party Type
Given Name	Person
Corporate Official Name	Company
Location Name	Government

Note that in a data model, only *the existence of* constraints such as these assignments can be shown. Since they will ultimately be implemented via program code, rather than database structures, the constraints themselves must be specified separately. The constraints are:

Business Rules

- A **Party Name** Name Text *of* a **Party** may only be *an example of* a **Party Name Type** if a **Party Name Assignment** exists that is *of* that **Party Name Type** and is *to* the **Party Type** that the named **Party** is *an example of*.

- That is, a **Party** may not be *labeled by* a **Party Name**, unless the **Party Name Type** it is *an example of* is *subject to* a **Party Name Assignment** *to* the **Party Type** *embodied in* the **Party** involved.

  Translation: Only certain kinds of **Party Names** can be used for each kind of **Party**.

- A **Party Identifier Value** Identifier Value *assigned to* a **Party** may only be *an example of* a **Party Identifier** if a **Party Identifier Assignment** exists that is *of* that **Party Identifier** and is *to* the **Party Type** that the named **Party** is *an example of*.

- That is, a **Party** may not be *identified via* a **Party Identifier Value** unless the **Party Identifier** it is *for* is subject to a **Party Identifier Assignment** *to* the **Party Type** *embodied in* the **Party** in question.

Translation: Only certain kinds of **Party Identifiers** can be used for each kind of **Party**.

Summary

Yes, architecture modelers, you can create an entity/relationship model in UML and have it meet all your requirements—if you're willing to adjust your way of looking at the problem (and your sense of aesthetics) just a little. And yes, UML modelers, you can create a genuine entity/relationship model and present it to business people—if you're willing to adjust your way of looking at the problem (and your sense of aesthetics), just a little.

A model developed according to the principles described in this book is an *architectural entity/relationship model*. It remains to be converted to an *object-oriented design model* and/or a *database design model*.

But lest we get too wrapped up in the perfection of our notation or our approach, we should remember:

"Essentially, all models are wrong, but some are useful."[53]

---

[53]   Box, George E. P.; Norman R. Draper (1987). *Empirical Model-Building and Response Surfaces*. Wiley. pp. p. 424.

Appendix A: A Brief Summary of The Approach

1. ***Show domain-specific entity cases only***. Consider only classes that are collections of things of significance to the enterprise or the domain being addressed. These are referred to here as ***entity classes***.

2. ***Use UML symbols selectively***:

   ➢ Use the following common symbols from UML:

      ➢ Class (entity class)

      ➢ Attribute

      ➢ Association (relationship)

      ➢ Cardinality for attributes and relationships

      ➢ Exclusive or (xor) constraint

   ➢ Use some ***UML-specific*** symbols (with care)

      ➢ Enumeration

      ➢ Derived attributes

      ➢ Package

   ➢ ***Do not use*** any other UML symbols

      ➢ Abstract Entities

      ➢ Behavior

      ➢ Composition

      ➢ Navigation

      ➢ Ordered

      ➢ Visibility

➢ *Add* one stereotype:

    ➢ <<ID>>

    ➢ (Or use new property {isId})

3. Define data model *relationship ends* as *predicates*, not UML Roles

4. Define *domains*

6. Follow *display conventions*:

➢ *Spaces in Names* – Include spaces inside multi-word entity class and attribute names.

➢ *Role Positions* – Position the predicate next to the object entity.

➢ *XOR* – Do not include the label in an "XOR" relationship.

➢ *Cardinality Display* – Display mandatory one cardinality as "1..1", not "1".

7. For *aesthetic* reasons, do the following.

➢ Stretch and position entity class boxes so that no relationship has an "elbow". (There are no bent lines).

➢ Turn off the ability to display operations, so the entity class box has only one horizontal line.

➢ Arrange the entity classes so that the "many" end of each relationship is at the left or top end (the "starry skies" approach).

➢ Limit a subject area to no more than 15 entity classes to show on one page.

➢ Present the model in a succession of diagrams. On the fist diagram, show no more than 2-5 entity classes, all highlighted. On each successive page, add no more than 2-5 entity classes and highlight them.

➢ In general, display attributes only in the diagram where their entity class first appears. Suppress them on all subsequent diagrams, unless they are needed to explain a particular concept. (Suppress them by coloring them white.)

Appendix B: A History of Modeling Objects and Data

The history of the information technology industry is a combination of successively more compact, fast, and sophisticated hardware, plus successively more sophisticated ways of organizing the software used to operate that hardware. At each stage whereby computers could process more bits, a proportion of that processing power was devoted to making the interaction between people and computers more natural and comfortable for the people.

There is a difference, however, between these two elements: whenever someone invents a new computing technology, it is often only a matter of accumulating enough financial and physical capital to mass-produce the hardware involved, in order to distribute it world-wide. On the other hand, whenever someone comes up with a good idea about *how to make use* of this technology, distribution of that idea is *very, very slow*. For the most part, it is one person sharing it with another, one at a time. Even if it is presented in a class or conference, or better yet, published in a book, it often takes years for a critical mass of people to understand and embrace it.

Of course, once it is finally accepted as the new, wonderful way to solve the industry's problems, it is then misapplied, causes great hardship, and now has to fight a bad reputation. Eventually, though, it begins to get applied more reasonably, and finally (often years after the original idea was expressed) takes its place among the tools available for intelligent design.

Looking at the current state of affairs, there seem to have been two main flows of such ideas over the past 40-some years:

- The movement from early programming languages to object-oriented methods.

- The movement from early database management systems to data architecture and data administration. Along with this has been the movement from informal systems with "casual" data quality requirements, to critical systems where data quality is an important part of the enterprise's business.

These flows are shown graphically in Figure B-1. The upper flow shows approximately the history of technology and object-oriented development, while the lower flow addresses the history of data architecture, data management, and data modeling techniques.

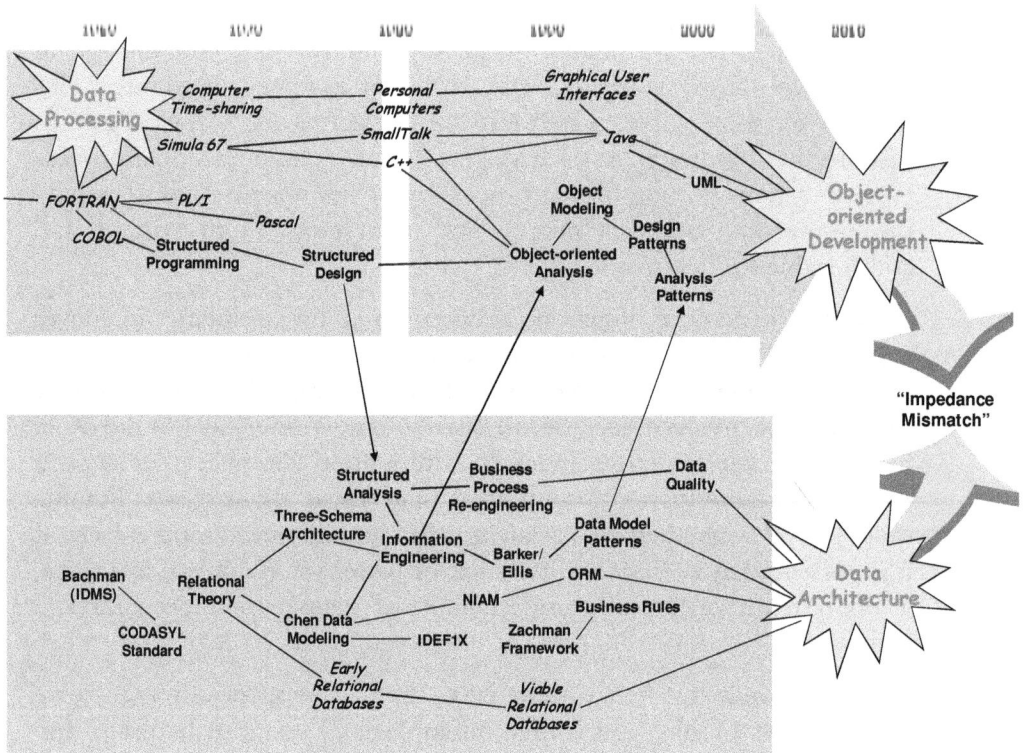

Figure B-1: Some History

Data Processing

The first widely-accepted term for this industry was "data processing", with an emphasis on "processing". The first widely accepted languages were *algorithmic languages* focused on the work done by computers, with data being a kind of "raw material" for the processes.

Early Programming Languages

In the 1950s, first Assembly Language and then Fortran allowed programmers to deal with concepts more comfortable than simple zeroes and ones. Assembly language defined mnemonic codes for machine instructions, which made them easier to deal with than zeros and ones, but programming was still very intricate work in that decade.

"Fortran (derived from IBM Mathematical Formula Translating System) is a general-purpose, procedural, imperative programming language that is especially suited to numeric computation and scientific computing. Originally developed by IBM at their campus in south San Jose, California in the 1950s for scientific and engineering applications, Fortran came to dominate this area of programming early on and has been in continual use for over half a century in computationally intensive areas such as numerical weather prediction, finite element analysis, computational fluid dynamics, computational physics and computational chemistry."[54] ♥

First specified in 1959, COBOL's "name is an acronym for COmmon Business-Oriented Language, defining its primary domain in business, finance, and administrative systems for companies and governments."[55] COBOL was originally developed by the "Conference on Data Systems Languages" (CODASYL), and has lasted several decades as the standard for business applications—as witness the efforts required to convert millions of lines of COBOL code to accommodate the four digits of 21st Century years. Successive programming languages derived from these early languages included PL/I, Pascal, and Basic.

The first computer programs were entered via switch settings, and subsequently via paper tape. During the 1950s, the medium of choice for communicating with computers was punched cards. The programmer would hand a card deck to an operator, who submitted "jobs" in

---

[54]   Wikipedia. 2009. "Fortran". Retrieved October 9, 2010 from http://en.wikipedia.org/wiki/Fortran.

♥   Through FORTRAN 77, the language name was spelled in all capitals. Since Fortran 90, it's been shown in upper and lower case. [Wikipedia. Retrieved July 17, 2011 from http://en.wikipedia.org/wiki/Fortran#cite_note-0.

[55]   Wikipedia. 2009. "COBOL". Retrieved October 9, 2010 from http://en.wikipedia.org/wiki/Cobol.

sequence. At a later time, the programmer received output—usually containing errors and requiring the process to be repeated. During the 1960's the hardware technology became faster and disk space became relatively cheaper, such that by the end of the decade *computer time-sharing* was a viable way to give people a direct link to a computer in an interactive mode. The programmer would make use of a teletype machine and interact more directly with the computer. Indeed, it was now possible to create application programs that allowed an end-user to interact directly as well.

The first "user interfaces" made use of 10-character per second teletype machines.

Object-oriented Programming Languages

These advances in programming structure, both in language design and methodology, managed the executable program code, but did not address data well. The relative levels of abstraction addressed by a structured program design did not translate into equivalent levels of abstraction for the data the programs manipulated. As programs got larger, the code could be modularized, but there was nothing in the syntax that supported a systematic way to manage the data. Parameters could be passed between modules, but there was no consistency in approach. Global data, contained in COBOL DATA DIVISIONS and Fortran COMMON statements, could keep all data in one place, but again, there was no systematic way to control which modules had access to what data and how they updated it.

In the early 1960's Ole-Johan Dahl and Kristen Nygaard, of the Norwegian Computing Center in Oslo, took a different approach by developing Simula-67, the first *object-oriented programming language*. This was organized not around formulas or processes (what Grady Booch called the "algorithmic view"[56]), but around data defining the "objects" being manipulated. Unlike its predecessors, Simula-67 was organized around the concepts of objects, classes, and sub-classes.[57] It is the definition and the *behavior* of these objects and classes that

---

[56]   Grady Booch. 1994. *Object-oriented Analysis and Design with Applications.* Redwood City, California: The Benjamin/Cummings Publishing Company, Inc. Pp. 16-17.

[57]   Wikipedia. 2010, "Simula", Retrieved September 15, 2010 from http://en.wikipedia.org/wiki/Simula-67.

constitutes an object-oriented program. This approach made it possible to simulate physical processes, which made it suitable for process control applications. This approach, as it progressed to SmallTalk and C++, remained in the background until the 1990s. Then, as on-line applications began to dominate the industry, they lent themselves far more to the object-oriented approach than they did to COBOL.

As Grady Booch puts it "the algorithmic view highlights the ordering of events, and the object-oriented view emphasizes the agents that either cause action or are the subjects upon which these operations act."[58]

Structured Techniques

Computer programming languages proved to be wonderful intellectual tools for solving problems. They each provided a language in which almost anything could be specified—unfortunately. Very quickly programs became unmanageably complex, to the point where it was often impossible to prove whether a program actually did what it was supposed to do. Initially, here was no guidance as to how programs in any language should be organized.

Structured Programming

In 1976, Edward Dijkstra published *A Discipline of Programming*—the culmination of many years' work of developing structured programming.[59] This approach to programming required all system logic to be expressed in terms of "IF/THEN/ELSE statements. Doing so creates programs that are provably correct. Among other things, this approach eliminated the "GOTO" statements that were a significant contributor to program complexity. Having these laced throughout a program made it extremely difficult to understand its logic. As one anonymous wag once said, though, "It's not the 'GOTO' statements that are the problem. It's the fact that there is no 'COMEFROM' statement." Under structured design, blocks of code are treated together and either executed or not, according to easy to read conditions.

---

[58]   Grady Booch, 1994 *Using the Booch Method: A Rational Approach* (Benjamin-Cummings Pub Co).

[59]   Edward W. Dijkstra, 1976, (New York: Prentice-Hall Series in Automatic Computation).

Structured Design

Based on these insights, Ed Yourdon and Larry Constantine subsequently introduced the world to **structured design.**[60] This provided guidance for organizing programs into coherent modules. The approach addressed the problem of how to divide a large program design into digestible modules. There were three major components to the approach:

- Begin any programming effort by designing—via a drawing—the successive levels of program structure. The drawings consist of a box for each program module and a line connecting two boxes for each subroutine call. Design the "top" module first. This consists of the calls to component modules. All next level modules are simply stubs that can be called, receive parameter values, and return dummy parameter values. Once all the problems associated with setting up these sub-routine calls have been dispensed with, flesh out the first module at the next level, and similarly call the next level of sub-routines—also initially just stubs. Write programs in the same order, fixing the structure of subroutine calls at the first level, before moving to successive levels.

  The point of this is that errors in interfaces are much more difficult to identify and correct than are errors in the code carrying out the program's functions. Address the design of those interfaces first.

- In breaking the program into pieces, minimize **coupling**—the amount of information that must be passed from one module to another. As Messrs. Yourdon and Constantine put it, this is "the degree of interdependence between modules".[61]

- At the same time, maximize **cohesion**, "how tightly bound or related its internal elements are to one another."[62]

---

[60] Edward Yourdon and Larry L. Constantine, 1979, *Structured Design: Fundamentals of a Discipline of Computer Program and Systems Design.* (Englewood Cliffs, NJ: Prentice Hall). (Widely circulated as an unpublished manuscript in 1976.)

[61] *Ibid.* 85.

[62] *Ibid.* 106.

The principles of minimizing coupling and maximizing cohesion resulted in programs whose structure more closely resembled that of the underlying problem—which again, made it easier to identify the location and cause of programming errors.

This approach also led to the concept of "reusable code" at the bottom of the structure hierarchy—which proved to be invaluable for the object-oriented designers.

Data Architecture*

Even as the world of programming and systems analysis progressed through the 1970s, there were important things happening in the world of data management.

Early Data Modeling

The first database management systems began to be developed in the late 1960s, but it soon became clear both that it was hard to organize data in a reasonable way, *and* that it was important to do so.

CODASYL

During the mid 1960's, while he was working for General Electric, Charles Bachman developed the Integrated Data Store (IDS), one of the first *database management systems.* Subsequently, IBM adopted it as their product, "Integrated Data Management Store" (IDMS). This used a network structure, which made use of programmed, hard-coded, links between elements. This meant that database structures were invariably very complex and difficult to manage, which further meant, among other things, that they were difficult to change.

It also meant that traversing the network was economical enough, but if you wanted to search based on the values of "leaf" nodes, it could get very expensive.[63]

---

* The descriptions of various data modeling techniques are taken from David C. Hay. 2003. *Op cit.* Pp. 34B-387. See Appendix A of that book for the complete comparison of the data modeling notations.

[63] Your author learned this the hard way in 1971 when using RAMIS, a database system based on a hierarchical architecture. Its query language, to be used interactively in a time-sharing environment, was

"In October 1969 the "Database Task Group" of the "Conference on Data Systems Languages" (CODASYL) published its first language specifications for the network database model which became generally known as the *Codasyl Data Model*. This specification in fact defined several separate languages: a data definition language (DDL) to define the schema of the database, another DDL to create one or more sub-schemas defining application views of the database; and a data manipulation language (DML) defining verbs for embedding in the COBOL programming language to request and update data in the database. Although the work was focused on COBOL, the idea of a host-language independent database was starting to emerge, prompted by IBM's advocacy of PL/I as a COBOL replacement."[64]

Dr. Edward Codd (1970)

As an alternative to the hard-coded hierarchical approach, in 1970, Dr. Edward Codd presented his *relational theory* to the world.[65] Based on set theory in mathematics, it provided a systematic way to organize data so that they reflected their meaning. This further had the effect of reducing redundancy. While there were no hidden links between elements, the only redundancy required was to explicitly describe such links. It took a few years for the industry to recognize the implications of his discovery, but by the end of the decade, commercial relational databases were on the market.

Dr. Codd's insight was that data could most effectively be managed in terms of two-dimensional *relations*. The term "relation" was derived from the mathematics upon which his approach was based. (The public

---

very powerful. Any query could be described in a kind of structured English. If the hierarchical database had not been organized along the lines of the query, however, it could be very time-consuming. I had organized market research data in terms of the sources, geographical dimensions, and finally by product. To ask for information about the a set of products required the computer to search every branch of the hierarchy before it could determine if the data were what was being sought.

[64]   Wikipedia. 2011. "CODASYL". Seen 7/17/2011 at
     http://en.wikipedia.org/wiki/CODASYL

[65]   Edward F. Codd, 1970, "A Relational Model of Data for Large
     Shared Data Banks". Communications of the ACM 13, No. 6 (June).

came to call these as "tables".) In each table, *tuples* (rows) were independent of each other, as were *attributes* (columns). Both tuples and attributes could be in any order. Dr. Codd asserted that the values of one or more specified attributes could be used to uniquely identify instances of tuples. These attributes constituted the *primary key* of the table. Each table would describe instances of a logical "thing".

Relationships between tuples were described by adding one or more attributes to one or more *child relations* corresponding to the attributes that constituted the primary key of the *parent relation*. The set of attributes in the child relation constitutes a *foreign key*. If the values of the foreign key attributes in a row of the child tuple match the primary key attributes in a tuple of the parent relation, the two rows are logically connected.

Dr. Codd came up with a series of constraints to apply to relations, to guarantee minimum redundancy. These *normalization* constraints are applied in a sequence, initially leading a relation to be in *first, second,* or *third normal form*. Several additional normal forms also exist, but are less widely observed.[*]

Early Relational Databases

The Oracle Database Management System began its existence as a secret project for the CIA and was subsequently introduced as a commercial product in 1978. Ingres was first created as a research project at the University of California, Berkeley, starting at about the same time as Oracle. "Ingres generally was the better-featured product, moving a little earlier than Oracle into application development tools, distributed databases, etc., whereas Oracle seems to be ahead on the most important attributes, such as SQL compatibility — Oracle always used IBM's suggested standard of SQL, while Ingres at first used the arguably superior Quel from the INGRES research project. Oracle eventually pulled ahead on superior/more aggressive sales and marketing."[66]

---

[*]   Some wags have suggested that the terminology could have been based on Richard Nixon's "normalizing relations" with China. But as it happens, his ground-breaking visit didn't take place until 1972. No, the terms here are all derived from mathematics.

[66]   Curt Monash, 2005, "Is Ingres a Serious Player? First Some History…" Computerworld. June 2, 2005.

Three Schema Architecture (1972)

In 1972, the American National Standards Institute's Standards Planning and Requirements Committee (SPARC) established a Study Group on Database Architectures. In February of 1975, they published an interim report which explained in detail the gross architecture they had developed for information systems.[67]

At the heart of the report was the "three-schema approach" to database management. The three were:

- *Conceptual Schema* – This "embodies the 'real world' view of the enterprise being modeled in the data base. It represents the current 'best model' or 'way of doing business' for the enterprise."

- *External Schema* – "The various users of the database management system operate on sub-sets of the total enterprise model which are relevant to their particular needs." These subsets are represented as "external schemas".

- *Internal Schema* – "The 'machine view' of the data is described by the internal schema. This schema describes the stored representation of the enterprise's information."

The ANSI committee viewed the problem from the point of view of a database management system. Over time, however, it became clear that the three schemas could be viewed from the point of view of data management itself[68].

For example, while the ANSI committee saw the **external schema** as the domain of application programs, it is true that they also represent the different views of various *people* in the organization, with various ways of looking at the same body of data. Among other things, the **semantics** used to describe each person's world may be different.

Moreover, the description of the **internal schema** sort of passed over lightly that there were actually two things going on: First is the organizational approach used by any particular data management

---

[67] American National Standards Institute (ANSI), 1975, "ANSI/X3/SPARC Study Group on Data Base Management Systems; Interim Report" FDT(Bulletin of ACM SIGMOD) 7:2.

[68] David C. Hay, 2003, Requirements Analysis: From Business Views to Architectures (Englewood Cliffs, NJ: Prentice Hall PTR).

technology (e.g. relational, hierarchy, network, flat files, etc.). This is called by some the "logical schema" (or *logical model*). In addition, the internal schema contains the description of 'how' the data are stored, i.e., record implementation techniques, field implementation techniques, syntax of data values, etc. This may be called the "physical schema", or the *physical model*.

It is the *conceptual schema* that brings all of these views together in a single representation that embodies the concepts of the company as a whole. Each of the concepts of an external schema must be represented in some way in a *conceptual model*, but in a way that does not conflict with other views of the same data. That is, both the elements of the *external schema* and the *logical schema* should be sub-types of elements in the *conceptual schema*.

Figure B-2 shows the schemas laid out in a bit more modern form.[69]

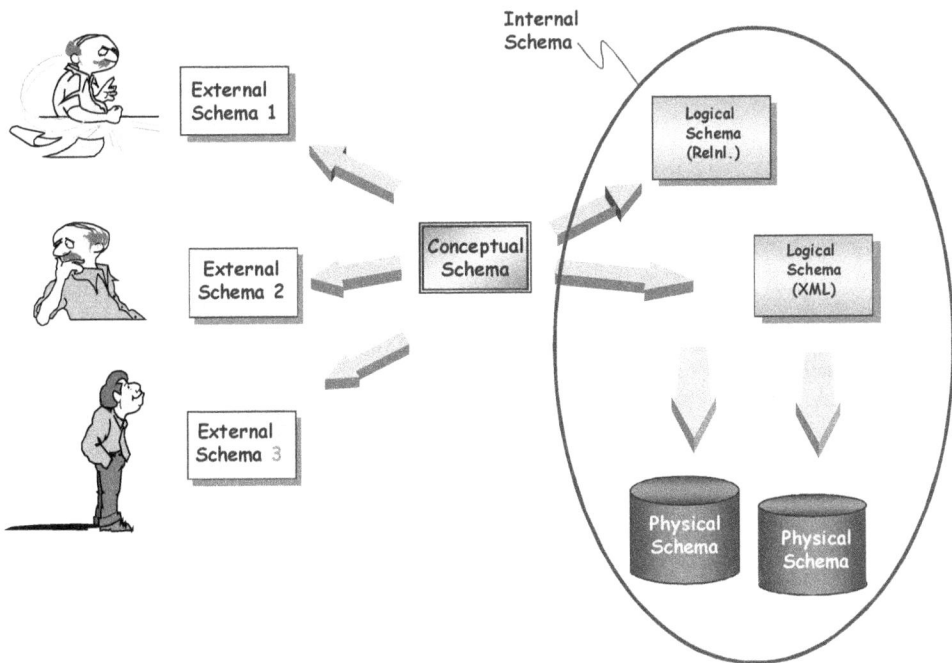

Figure B-2: The Three (Well Four, actually) Schema Architecture

---

[69]   David C. Hay, 2003, Requirements Analysis: From Business Views to Architecture (Englewood Cliffs, NJ: Prentice Hall PTR).

Note that these different views are intended to be relatively independent of each other. New database technologies can be introduced without affecting the conceptual model. The conceptual model can be changed without affecting the external views of the world.

Dr. Peter Chen (1976)

Peter Chen invented entity/relationship modeling in the mid-1970s [Chen, 1977], and his approach remains widely used today. It is unique in its representation of relationships and attributes. Relationships are shown with a separate diamond-shaped symbol on the relationship line, and attributes are shown in separate circles, instead of as annotations on each entity type. A sample model is shown in Figure B-3.

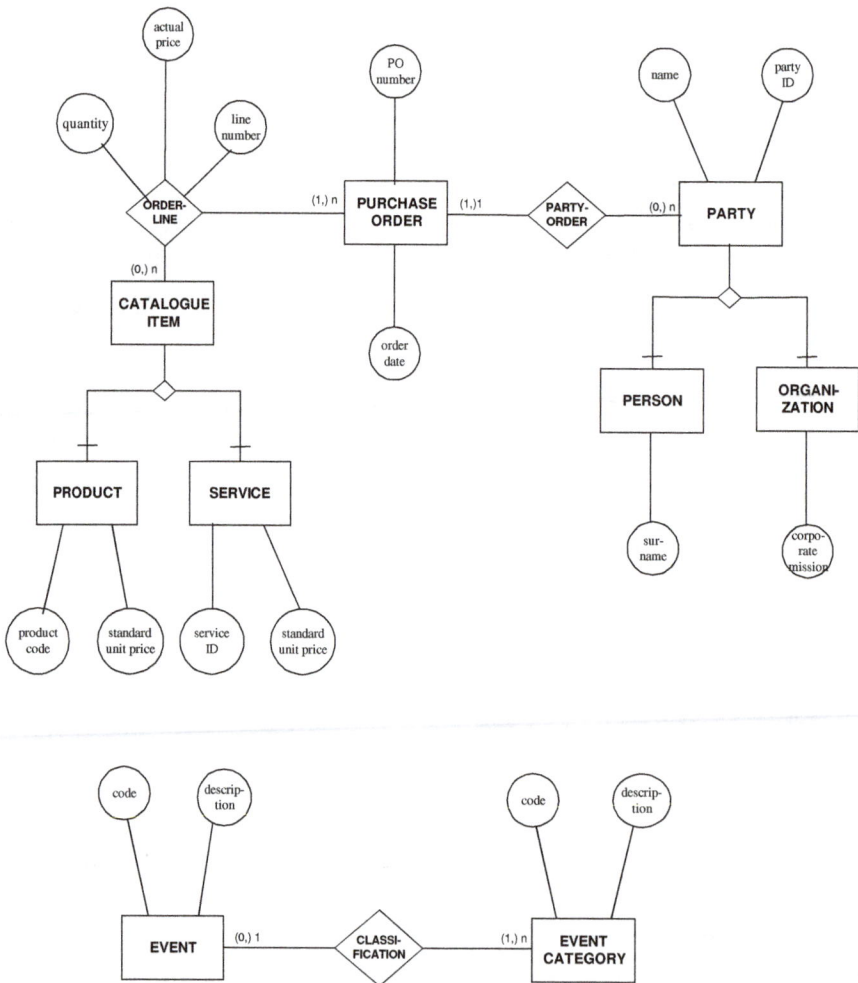

Figure B-3: A Chen Model

This same example will be used to demonstrate all the techniques that follow. The model shows entity types, attributes, and relationships. It also has examples of both a super-type/sub-type combination and a constraint between relationships.

In the diagram, each PURCHASE ORDER is related to a single PARTY and to one or more examples of either one PRODUCT or one SERVICE.

The diagram also includes two entity types (EVENT and EVENT CATEGORY) in an unusual relationship. In most "one-to-many" relationships, the "one" side is mandatory (" . . . must be exactly one"), while the "many" side is optional (" . . . may be one or more"). In this example, the reverse is true: Each EVENT may be *in* one and only one EVENT CATEGORY (zero or one), and each EVENT CATEGORY must be *a classification for* one or more EVENTS (one or more). That is, an EVENT may exist without being classified, or it may be in one and only one EVENT CATEGORY. An EVENT CATEGORY can come into existence, however, only if there is at least one event to put into it.

Table B-1 shows the standard elements that go into any data model, and the particular way each is addressed in Dr. Chen's notation.

Table B-1: Chen Model Elements

Model Element	Chen Approach
Entity Type	• Represented by square-cornered boxes.
Attribute	• Shown separately from the entity type boxes, each in a circle labeled with the attribute's name. • There are no diacritical marks to show optionality.
Relationship	• A two-dimensional symbol—a rhombus—on the line between two or more entity types. • Relationships do not have to be binary. • A "many-to-many" relationship does not require converting it into an associative or intersect entity type. • May have attributes. • (Note how "quantity", "actual price", and "line number" are attributes of the relationship Order-line in Figure B-3.)
Relationship Name	• A single noun. • The ends of relationship lines are not labeled.
Relationship Cardinality (Minimum and Maximum)	• Second number is maximum (1 => "no more than one"; n => "one or more"). • In later versions, first number was minimum (0 => "may be"; 1 => "must be").
Identifiers	• While Mr. Chen recognizes the importance of attributes as entity-type unique identifiers,[70] his notation makes no provision for showing this. • If the unique identifier includes a relationship to a second entity type, the relationship is named "E", the line into the dependent entity type becomes an arrow, and a second box is drawn around this dependent entity type. • (Figure B-4 shows a relationship part of the unique identifier of PURCHASE ORDER.) • No attributes that are part of the identifier are marked.
Sub-types	• Though not in Mr. Chen's original work, the technique was extended to include this by Mat Flavin[71] and Robert Brown.[72] • Represented by separate boxes, collectively connected to the super-type by a small rhombus, and each relationship to a sub-type has a bar drawn across it. In Figure B-1, for example, PARTY is a super-type, with PERSON and ORGANIZATION as its sub-types. Similarly, a CATALOGUE ITEM must be either a PRODUCT or a SERVICE.
Inter-relationship Constraints	(Not done)

[70] Peter Chen. 1977. *Op cit.*
[71] Matthew Flavin, 1981, Fundamental Concepts of Information Modeling (New York: Yourdon Press).
[72] R. G. Brown, 1993, "Data Modeling Methodologies – Contrasts in Style", Handbook of Data Management. (Boston: Auerbach).

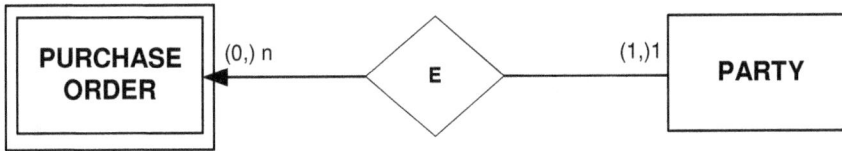

Figure B-4: Existence-Dependent Relationship.

Business Analysis

Structured Analysis

If Dr. Dijkstra's structured programming described the best practices for arranging program code, and Messrs. Yourdon's and Constantine's structured design described the best practices for organizing program modules, then it was *structured analysis* developed by Tom DeMarco,[73] as well as Chris Gane and Trish Sarson,[74] that addressed the question of what programs should be written in the first place. In two different books, they reveal *data flow diagrams*—graphic representations of the way a business processes data. The two books used different symbols, but presented fundamentally the same concepts. The diagrams were in terms of:

- *Processes,* where a process is the fact that one or more input kinds of data are transformed into one or more output kinds of data,

- *External entities,* which are the organizational units that are the ultimate sources and destinations of all data,

- *Data stores,* which are the fact that data are stored between processes, as in "pending purchase orders", for example, and

- *Data flows*, the links between all of these elements.

All data originate from one or more external entities, and then pass, via data flows, to processes, and from there either to other processes, data stores, or external entities.

---

[73]   Tom DeMarco, 1978, Structured Analysis and System Specification (Englewood Cliffs, NJ: Prentice-Hall).

[74]   Chris Gane and Trish Sarson, 1979, Structured Systems Analysis: Tools and Techniques (Englewood Cliffs, NJ: Prentice Hall).

Each process could then be "exploded" to reveal more detailed processes comprising it.

Mr. DeMarco distinguished between *physical data flow diagrams* that described processes in terms of mechanisms ("fill out order form") and *logical data flow diagrams* ("take order information"). The idea was that one would begin with a physical data flow diagram derived from interviews with the people involved, convert that to a logical data flow diagram, and from there derive a new physical data flow diagram, reflecting a new system design.

The only problem was that he was a little fuzzy about how to do the transition from "current physical" to "logical" diagram. So his colleagues Steve McMenamin and John Palmer wrote *Essential Systems Analysis*[75] to describe how that might take place. In this, the authors recommended the following steps:

- Translate all physical references into descriptions that had no reference to *how* the process takes place.

- Successively explode processes to their "atomic" level. (Where the process cannot be interrupted before it is complete.)

- Identify the *external events* that constitute the working environment of the organization.

- For each external event, identify all the atomic processes that are invoked whenever such an event takes place. Bundle them up into a next higher level process. This is called an *essential process*.

Business Process Reengineering

Business process reengineering (BPR) is the analysis and redesign of workflow within and between enterprises. BPR reached its heyday in the early 1990's when Michael Hammer and James Champy published their best-selling book, "Reengineering the Corporation".[76] The authors promoted the idea that sometimes radical redesign and reorganization of

---

[75]   Stephen McMenamin and John Palmer, 1984, Essential Systems Analysis. (Englewood Cliffs, NJ: Yourdon Press).

[76]   Michael Hammer and James Champy, 1993, Reengineering the Corporation: A Manifesto for Business Revolution (New York: Harper Business).

an enterprise (wiping the slate clean) was necessary to lower costs and increase quality of service and that information technology was the key enabler for that radical change. Hammer and Champy felt that the design of workflow in most large corporations was based on assumptions about technology, people, and organizational goals that were no longer valid. They suggested seven principles of reengineering to streamline the work process and thereby achieve significant levels of improvement in quality, time management, and cost:

1. Organize around outcomes, not tasks.

2. Identify all the processes in an organization and prioritize them in order of redesign urgency.

3. Integrate information processing work into the real work that produces the information.

4. Treat geographically dispersed resources as though they were centralized.

5. Link parallel activities in the workflow instead of just integrating their results.

6. Put the decision point where the work is performed, and build control into the process.

7. Capture information once and at the source.

By the mid-1990's, BPR gained the reputation of being a nice way of saying "downsizing." According to Hammer, lack of sustained management commitment and leadership, unrealistic scope and expectations, and resistance to change prompted management to abandon the concept of BPR and embrace the next new methodology, enterprise resource planning (ERP)."[77]

Note that this did not come out of the technology world, so the similarity of the Business Process Re-engineering approach to data flow diagrams is coincidental. Its orientation towards results rather than processes, and its lack of discipline in the notation itself, is a result of the different origins of the two approaches.

---

[77] This section is taken from: SearchCIO.com. 2001, "Business Process Engineering". Available at:
http://searchcio.techtarget.com/definition/business-process-reengineering

Later Data Modeling

Finkelstein/Martin (Information Engineering) (1981).

"Information engineering" was originally developed by Dr. Clive Finkelstein in Australia in the late 1970's. He collaborated with Mr. James Martin to publicize it in the United States and Europe,[78] and then Mr. Martin went on from there to become predominantly associated with it.[79] Mr. Finkelstein published his own version in 1989.[80]

The method included a variation on Dr. Chen's modeling notation as part of an overall revolution in the way systems were developed. This was the origin of the *Systems Development Life Cycle*, which required beginning a systems project with strategic planning and conduct of a thorough analysis of the business requirements. Only then do technicians get introduced to apply technologies to these requirements.

The Information Engineering data model technique was a way of capturing the requirements and transmitting them to designers. Figure B-5 shows the phases of a system development project:

- *Strategic Planning* – Determine the mission, vision, goals, and objectives, first of the company as a whole, and then of this particular effort as a whole. This is actually composed of "Corporate Strategic Planning" and "Business Unit Strategic Planning".

- *Requirements Analysis* – For a particular part of the company, analyze its essential nature and determine its information processing shortcomings. From this, create a vision of what future systems should accomplish.

- *Physical Design* – based on the requirements identified in the previous phase, design the database structure, the applications

[78]   James Martin and Clive Finkelstein, Nov. 1981, "Information Engineering", Technical Report, two volumes, (Lancs, UK : Savant Institute, Carnforth).

[79]   James Martin and Carma McClure 1985, Diagramming Techniques for Analysts and Programmers (Englewood Cliffs, NJ: Prentice Hall).

[80]   Clive Finkelstein, 1989, An Introduction to Information Engineering : From Strategic Planning to Information Systems. (Sydney: Addison-Wesley).

program structure, and the organizational structure that will support the world to be created.

- *Construction* – based on the design, build the desired system, including creation of physical database(s), program code, and the procedures required to operate. (This is the term from the Oracle Corporation "CASE*Development Method. Dr. Finklelstein calls this "Generation".)

Transition – of all the phases, this can be the most expensive. More than that, along with strategy, it is a phase that is not under the control of the information processing professionals. It is the task of enterprise management to understand the implications of the new technology and to manage its implementation. This includes educating the enterprise as a whole as to the implications of the new system, training the people who will use it, and populating the initial stage of the database, either through data entry or through conversion of legacy data. This phase was added by Oracle Corporation in its Case*Method.[81]

- *Production* – this is the ongoing process of monitoring the new system, fixing errors, and anticipating future improvements.

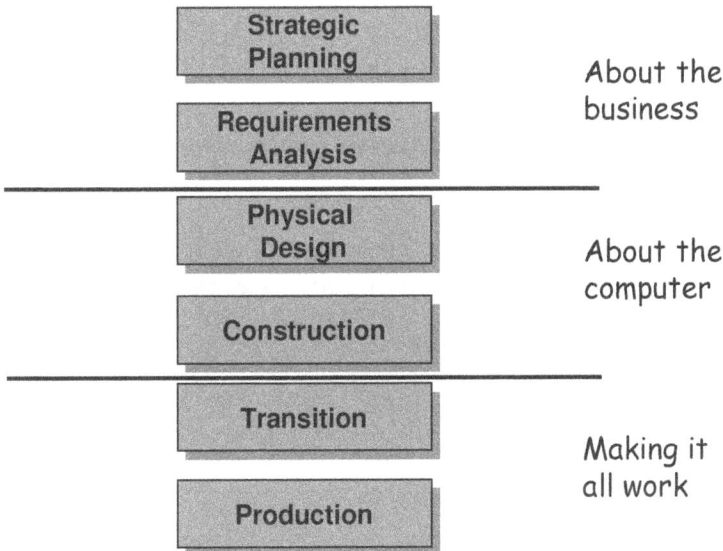

Figure B-5: System Development Life Cycle

---

[81]   Oracle Corporation, 1986, "Strategic Planning Course", SQL*Development Method (Belmont, CA: Oracle Corporation).

Because of the dual origin of the techniques, there are minor variations between Mr. Finkelstein's and Mr. Martin's notations. The Information Engineering version of our test case (with some of the notations from each version) is shown in Figure B-6.

In the example, each PARTY *is vendor in* zero, one, or more PURCHASE ORDERS, each of which initially *has* zero, one or more LINE ITEMS, but eventually it must have at least one LINE ITEM.* Each LINE ITEM, in turn, *is for* <u>either</u> exactly one PRODUCT <u>or</u> exactly one SERVICE. Also, each EVENT *classifies* zero or one EVENT TYPE, while each EVENT TYPE must be (related to) one or more EVENTS.

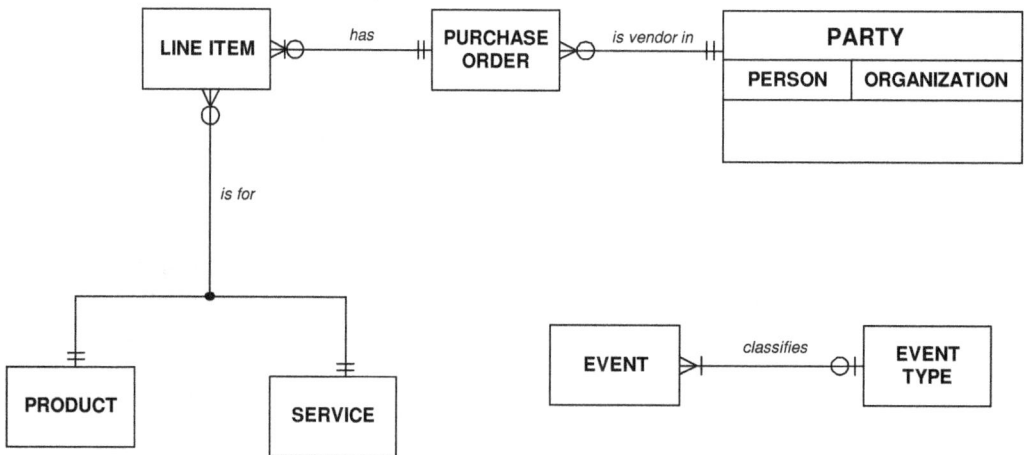

Figure B-6: An Information-Engineering Model.

Table B-5: shows the elements common to all data models and the particular way Information Engineering addresses each.

---

* Note the symbol that combines the optional circle and the mandatory bar (|O). This means "initially optional, but eventually mandatory". Dr. Finkelstein's is the only one in any modeling notation that can express this. It is actually quite profound. Conceptually, the relationship is mandatory, but in practice, it may be some time before values are captured.

Table B-5: Information Engineering Model Elements

Element	Information Engineering Approach
Entity Type	• Mr. Finkelstein defines entity type in the designer's sense of representing "data to be stored for later reference".[82] Mr. Martin, however, adopts the analyst's definition that "an entity type is something (real or abstract) about which we store data."[83] • Entity types are shown in square-cornered rectangles. An entity type's name is inside its rectangle.
Attribute	• In their original works, neither Messers. Finkelstein nor Martin included attributes in their Information Engineering data models. • Most vendors, however display them (in varying levels of detail) inside the entity type boxes.
Relationship	• A line between a pair of entity types. • Always binary.
Relationship Name	• Martin: Verbs, often in one direction only. • Finkelstein: Not named.
Relationship Cardinality (Minimum and Maximum)	• Minimum: Open circle ("may be") or line across relationship ("must be") next to object entity class. • Maximum: "Crow's Foot" ("one or more") or line across relationship ("one and only one") next to object entity class. • (For example, in Figure B-6 a PARTY is vendor in zero, one, or more PURCHASE ORDERS. A PURCHASE ORDER, on the other hand, (is to) one and only one PARTY.) • Mr. Finkelstein: additional line between circle and crow's foot. ("Initially may be but eventually must be")
Identifiers	• Originally Not represented. • Most vendors add a bit of text (usually "<pk>" next to identifying attributes. • Most vendors use the IDEF1X convention (see p. 150, below) of showing the relationship line as either dashed (for a "non-identifying" relationship) or solid (for an "identifying" relationship) on the "...1" end. • They also adopted the IDEF1x practice of showing an entity type that is at least partially identified by a relationship in a round-cornered box.
Sub-types	• Mr. Martin: nested boxes inside the super-type box. (This is shown in the figure.) • Mr. Finkelstein: separate boxes, linked with "isa" relationship lines.
Inter-relationship Constraints	• The relationship halves of the three (or more) entity types involved meet at a small circle. • If the circle is solid, the relationship between the relationships is "exclusive or", meaning that each occurrence of the base entity type must (or may) be related to occurrences of one other entity type, but not more than one. • (This is shown in the figure, where each LINE ITEM must be for either one PRODUCT or is for one SERVICE, but not both.) • If the circle is open, it is an "inclusive or" relationship, meaning that an occurrence of the base entity type or may be related to occurrences of one, some, or all of the other entity types.

---

[82] Clive Finkelstein, 1992, *Op. Cit.* 24.
[83] James Martin, and Carma McClure, 1985, *Op. Cit.* 245.

Richard Barker and Harry Ellis (1980)

The next notation was originally developed during the 1980s by Harry Ellis and Richard Barker, of the British consulting company CACI. Among other things, it is part of the European methodology, Structured Systems Analysis and Design Method (SSADM). After a decade of use by the consulting company, CACI, and Oracle Corporation, it was published by Mr. Barker,[84] and adopted by the Oracle Corporation for its "CASE*Method" (subsequently renamed the "Custom Development Method"[85]). Figure B-7 shows our example as represented in this notation.

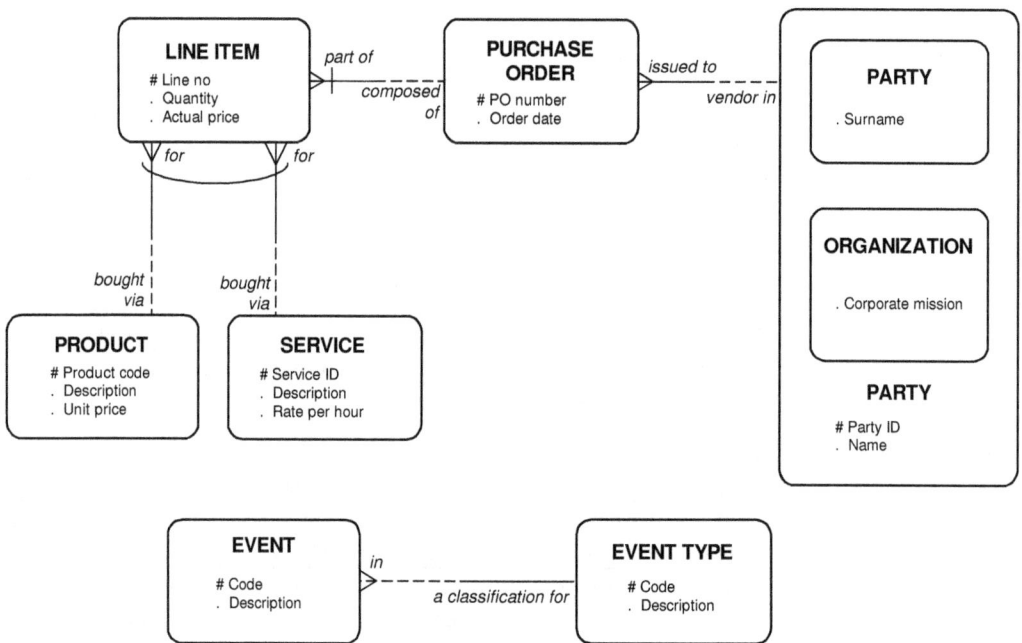

Figure B-7: A Barker-Ellis Data Model

In the diagram, each PURCHASE ORDER must be *issued to* one and only one PARTY and may be *composed of* one or more LINE ITEMS, each of which in turn must be *for* either one PRODUCT or one SERVICE. Also, each EVENT

---

[84]   Richard Barker. 1990. *Op. Cit.*

[85]   Oracle Corporation.1996. Custom Development Method (Redwood Shores, CA: Oracle Corporation).

may be *in* one and only one EVENT TYPE, while each EVENT TYPE must be *a classification for* one or more EVENTS.

Table B-7 shows the standard model elements for any data modeling notation, along with the particular way they are addressed in the Barker-Ellis notation.

Table B-6: Barker-Ellis Model Elements

Element	Barker-Ellis Approach
Entity Class	• Round-cornered rectangles.
Attribute	• Optionally displayed inside the entity boxes. • Annotations represent: * - required; O – optional; # - part of primary unique identifier.
Relationship	• Line between two entity classes. • Binary only.
Relationship Name	• Name on each end (each "role"). • Preposition as a predicate. • Structure: Each \<subject entity class\> must be||may be \<relationship name\> one and only one||one or more \<object entity class\>.
Relationship Cardinality (Minimum and Maximum)	• Minimum: "may be" = > dashed line next to subject entity class; "must be" => solid line next to subject entity class. • Maximum: "one and only one" => (no symbol); "one or more" => "Crow's foot".
Identifiers	• Attributes identified by octothorpe (#). • Roles identified by line across role attached to identified entity class.
Sub-types	• Represented as boxes inside super-type boxes.
Inter-relationship Constraints	• "Exclusive or" represented by arc across two or more relationships from one entity class.

Note that this was the first modeling approach to adopt a specific discipline for naming relationships. The "verb phrase" is divided into a form of "to be" ("must be" or "may be") to denote minimum cardinality, a prepositional phrase (to contain the meaning of the relationship) and a phrase to present the maximum cardinality ("one and only one" and "one or more"). The result is that each relationship in each direction represents a strong assertion about the nature of the organization or domain being modeled.

For example, among other things, the model in Figure B-7 asserts that "each PURCHASE ORDER <u>may be</u> *composed of* <u>one or more</u> LINE ITEMS", and that "each LINE ITEM <u>must be</u> *part of* <u>one and only one</u> PURCHASE ORDER".

IDEF1X

IDEF1X is a data-modeling technique that is used by many branches of the United States Federal Government[86]. It was developed to support the design of relational databases. It represents tables, with the relational primary keys to represent unique identifiers and foreign keys to represent relationships. It is therefore not suitable as a notation for conceptual entity relationship models.

Object-Role Modeling (ORM)

NIAM was originally an acronym for "Nijssen's Information Analysis Methodology", but more recently, since Dr. G. M. Nijssen was only one of many people involved in the development of the method, it was generalized to "Natural language Information Analysis Method". Indeed, practitioners now also use a still more general name, "Object-Role Modeling", or ORM.[87].

ORM takes a different approach from the other methods described here. Rather than representing entity types as analogues of relational tables, it shows *relationships* (that contain one or more "roles", in ORM parlance) to be such analogs. Like Mr. Barker's notation, it makes extensive use of language in making the models accessible to the public, but unlike any of the other modeling techniques, it has much greater capacity to describe business rules and constraints.

With ORM, it is difficult to describe entity types independently from relationships. The philosophy behind the language is that it describes "facts", where a fact is a combination of entity types, domains, and relationships.

ORM produces much more detailed models than other kinds of data modeling techniques, both because attributes are displayed in their own symbols—in the Chen style—and because the relationships can be much more precisely specified to reflect a wider range of business constraints. It has a much more substantial mathematical grounding than any of the other techniques presented in this section.

---

[86]   Thomas Bruce, 1992, *Designing Quality Databases with IDEF1X Information Models.* (New York: Dorset House).

[87]   Terry Halpin, 2008, *Information Modeling and Relational Databases, Second Edition* (Boston: Morgan Kaufman Publishers).

About Discipline in Data Modeling

The progression from Chen to Barker-Ellis to Object Role Modeling is one from an initial conceptualization of relational principles to the establishment of semantic structures for a business. Information Engineering introduced an approach to developing systems that was more focused on the business environment where they were to be implemented. The symbols for cardinality and optionality were also more developed. Richard Barker and Harry Ellis simplified the notation and made the relationship names more rigorous. ORM made modeling more mathematically rigorous. This turns the model into a set of descriptions of very specific assertions about the nature of the business. It is this set of assertions that can then be presented to the business community for validation.

Data Model Patterns

To go into a company and to try to infer a model based on interview notes and general knowledge of an industry is difficult. It requires numerous tries, as one attempts to identify patterns and any underlying simplicity in the problem. In the mid-1990s, several people came up with catalogues of standard data model "patterns" that make this process much easier. Instead of having to invent a model from scratch, the problem is one of recognizing standard structures and applying them to particular situations.

David Hay (1995)

In 1995, your author published *Data Model Patterns: Conventions of Thought*,[88] a book presenting a set of standard data models (in the Barker-Ellis notation) to describe standard business situations. It began by describing people and organizations, along with their addresses and geographic locations. It further had models describing physical assets, contracts, and activities. More detailed models described process industries and material requirements planning.

The models were at a level of abstraction that made them robust and generally applicable, but they also were in a language anyone could follow. They were conceptual models, in that they were without regard for what database technology might be used to implement them.

---

[88]   David C. Hay, 1995, *Data Model Patterns: Conventions of Thought* (New York: Dorset House).

In 2011, he published a successor volume, *Enterprise Model Patterns: Describing the World*. This one is more comprehensive, and it specifically addresses the issue of level of abstraction: It produces connected patterns at four levels of abstraction. Its use of UML as the notation was the motivation for producing this book as a companion.

Len Silverston, Kent Graziano, Bill Inmon (1997)

As a successor to David Hay's work, Len Silverston, Kent Graziano, and Bill Inmon published a their own set of standardized models (that they called "Universal Data Models") These were in more detail and covered different areas, and In 2001, Mr. Silverston published a two volume second edition, further described general use patterns and specialized patterns for different industries. [89] [90] In 2009, published a third volume with Paul Agnew which was about low-level patterns.[91]

Architecture Frameworks

John Zachman (1979)

In 1979, John Zachman published the first version of his "Framework for Information Systems Architecture".[92] The *Zachman Framework* brought together both data and processing perspectives, along with concerns for how data and processing take place over multiple locations. In 1992, Mr. Zachman and John Sowa added the dimensions of people and organizations, events, and motivation.[93]

It was noteworthy because it was the first formal recognition of the different perspectives taken by the players in the system development process:

---

[89] L. Silverston, 2001, *The Data Model Resource Book, Volume 1: A library of Universal Data Models for All Enterprises* (New York: John Wiley & Sons).

[90] L. Silverston, 2001, *The Data Model Resource Book, Volume 2: A library of Universal Data Models by Industry Types* (New York: John Wiley & Sons).

[91] L. Silverston and Paul Agnew, 2009, *The Data Model Resource Book, Volume 3* (Indianapolis, IN: Wiley Publishing, Inc).

[92] John Zachman, 1987, *Op. Cit.*

[93] John. F. Sowa, and John A. Zachman, 1992, *Op. Cit.*

- *Scope Description* – The "ballpark" view.

- *Model of the Business* – The owner's view.

- *Model of the Information System* – The Designer's view.

- *Technology Model* – The Builder's view.

- *Detailed Description* – Out-of-context view.

- *Actual System*

David Hay (2003, 2006)

Your author, in his books on requirements analysis[94] and metadata,[95] made extensive use of the Zachman Framework. However, as described in each of his books, he took issue with the names and definitions of some of the perspectives. Because this was largely based on Mr. Zachman's work, but not exactly the same, he called it the *Architecture Framework*. Specifically, he refined the terminology used to describe the different roles:

Planners – The planner may be the CEO, a Divisional Vice President, or simply an entrepreneur. This is the person who ultimately defines the character of the organization and sets its direction.

Business Owners – These are the people who run the enterprise. They are the shop foremen, regional managers, plant managers, and the like, who are, among other things, the source of the *language* of the organization. Their views often conflict and they often describe the same things in different ways. But these are the heart of what the organization is.

Architects – These are the "synthesists"* who integrate the collection of business owners' views to find the single, underlying nature of the enterprise. This is in terms of structures that are invariably much simpler

---

94 David C. Hay, 2003, *Requirements Analysis: From Business Rules to Architecture.* (Englewood Cliffs, NJ: Prentice Hall PTR).

95 David C. Hay, 2006, *Data Model Patterns: A Metadata Map.* (Boston: Morgan Kaufmann).

* This is, of course, what the person commonly referred to as "analysts" should be called. But that is probably a lost cause. After all, who can say "systems synthesist"?

than the collection of particular points of view would suggest. (Mr. Zachman called this the "System Designer's View".)

Designers – These are the people who understand technology. They use the architect's view as the basis for applying technology to solve the enterprise's problems. They know about relational databases, service-oriented architecture, the world-wide web, and so forth. They use this knowledge, combined with the architect's models, to design the new world. (Mr. Zachman called this the "Builder's View".)

Builders – These people know the details of the technology to be used, and then create the systems specified by the designers. (Mr. Zachman called this the "Sub-contractor's view".)

The operational system – The result of all these efforts is a system that has been implemented in one or more locations. This is the view of the people using the system.

These perspectives are significant in the book you are reading, because UML was originally developed to support object-oriented *designers* (whose domain is the fourth row of the framework.). It was not intended to support *architects,* who develop conceptual models to address the underlying structure of the organization (or other domain) being modeled. The objective of this book is to use the UML notation to support the objectives of the Architects in Row Three, not the designers in Row Four.

In 2008, Mr. Zachman and Stan Locke updated the framework to account for many of Mr. Hay's concepts. Indeed, the third row is now the "architect's" view, and the fourth row is the "engineer's" view. The fifth row is the domain of "technicians" and the bottom row the view of the enterprise's "workers".[96]

Business Rules

Among the other results of Messrs. Zachman's and Sowa's work was the development of the **business rules** movement that took on the issues raised by the business, and the natural constraints of operating on an enterprise. In Architecture Framework terms, business rules are motivation ("why?") issues that, as with the other dimensions, look

---

[96] John Zachman and Stan Locke, 2008, "The Zachman Enterprise Framework". More information available at http://zachmanframeworkassociates.com.

different from the point of view of the CEO, business owners, architects, designers, programmers, and maintainers.

Ron Ross (1987)

In 1987, Ron Ross recognized that business rule constraints were mostly outside the realm of data models. Many constraints simply could not be expressed using the data modeling structures. So, in 1994, he published *The Business Rule Book* [Ross, 1994], which both catalogued business rules and devised a notation to add to the data modeling notation to describe rules.

This was the beginning of an overall movement in the industry to analyze the nature of a company's rules in the context of analyzing other dimensions of its requirements.

Business Rule Group (1995)

A sub-committee of the IBM user group, GUIDE, was formed in the early 1990s to articulate exactly what constituted business rules, and how to describe them. In 1995, it published the white-paper "Business Rules: What Are They Really?"[97] This laid out four categories of rules:

- *Terms* – The words that describe the things that constitute the business. These are usually captured as entity classes and attributes in a data model.

- *Facts* – The linking of terms together to assert something about the business. These are usually captured as relationships in a data model.

- *Definitions* – These are terms that are derived from other terms. Computed attributes can be displayed in a data model, but the definition logic has to be captured as documentation for the model.

- *Action Assertions* – Statements about the business that cannot be described in the data model, although they may well be in terms of entity classes, attributes and relationships shown on the model.

---

[97]   The Business Rules Group, 2000, "Defining Business Rules ~ What Are They Really?" 4th ed., formerly known as the "GUIDE Business Rules Project Report," (1995). Available at http://www.BusinessRulesGroup.org

Object Management Group (2008)

A successor organization to the Business Rules Group teamed up with the Object Management Group to create a specification, the "Semantics of Business Vocabulary and Business Rules (SBVR)".[98] This is a comprehensive guide to semantics, linguistics, and how to use both effectively in describing business rules. It begins with a survey of basic principles of linguistics, including a vocabulary for meaning and representation (of propositions), and a vocabulary for formulating semantics and logic. From this, it provides semantic and logical foundations for business vocabulary and rules. Finally, it describes the structure of a business vocabulary and business rules

Sections of the specification include:

- What is a Vocabulary?

- Forms of Meaning and Representation

- Logical Formulation of Semantics

- Foundations for Business Vocabulary and Rules

- Business Vocabulary

- Business Rules

Data Management

The motivation for all the efforts to rationalize data storage, of course, was the requirement to improve the quality of data that are used by the business—both to carry out its operations and to plan for the future. Before companies were so interconnected and so dependent on computer technology, data were as accurate as they had to be to carry out specific tasks. Beginning with the advent of manufacturing planning systems in the early 1970s—that depended on accurate order and inventory data to work—the demand for *data quality* grew faster than technologies have been able to keep up. If the wrong product is shipped or raw materials are not available for manufacturing, this can be very expensive for the organization.

Achieving data quality has 4 parts:

---

[98]   Object Management Group, 2008, "The Semantics of Business Vocabulary and Business Rules" (SBVR), OMG Available Specification formal/2008-01-02.

1. Recognition that data constitute a corporate resource and must be managed accordingly.

2. From this comes organizational sponsorship of comprehensive governance policies and procedures.

3. Well-designed data handling processes

4. A well-designed and understood model of the company's data structure.

Collectively, these come under a relatively new corporate function, **data management.** The existence of this function means that the company cares about the quality of data—not only instances, but the overall architecture. Developing a coherent, well understood model of the data that run the business is important.

Object-oriented Development

A second major section of information technological history has been the phenomenal growth in the application of object-oriented design and programming. By the mid 1980s, the object-oriented community began to take an interest in modeling data to support design and programming.

Early Object Modeling

Sally Shlaer and Stephen Mellor wrote their first book on what they called "object" modeling in 1988. In this case, however, instead of modeling entity types, entities, and relationships, they took on a language closer to the world of object-oriented programming: classes, objects, and associations. In the early works, the results were similar to those of the entity modeling authors, but over time, they focused on modeling data as used in object-oriented design, more than on data as used in a business.

Shlaer & Mellor (1988)

The first book, with the title *Object-Oriented Systems Analysis,* by Sally Schlaer and Stephen J. Mellor, was published in 1988. Its sub-title was *Modeling the World in Data.*[99] This book translated the notions from what they saw as "Information Modeling" into a language more amenable to

---

[99] Sally Shlaer and Stephen J. Mellor, 1988, *Object-oriented Systems Analysis: Modeling the World in Data* (Englewood Heights, NJ: Yourdon Press).

object-oriented designers. It was based on both Dr. Codd's relational principles and the works on modeling by Dr. Chen[100] and James Martin.[101]

First, a nomenclature issue: They use the term "object" to mean "class". In their examples, an object might be a *kind of* tangible object, such as a pipe or a delivery vehicle, a kind of role, such as being a student or an instructor, and so forth. *Instances* of an object are discussed in the book under the subject of "instance data".[102]

In Figure B-8, "objects" are represented by boxes connected by associations.♦ Each is labeled with a name.

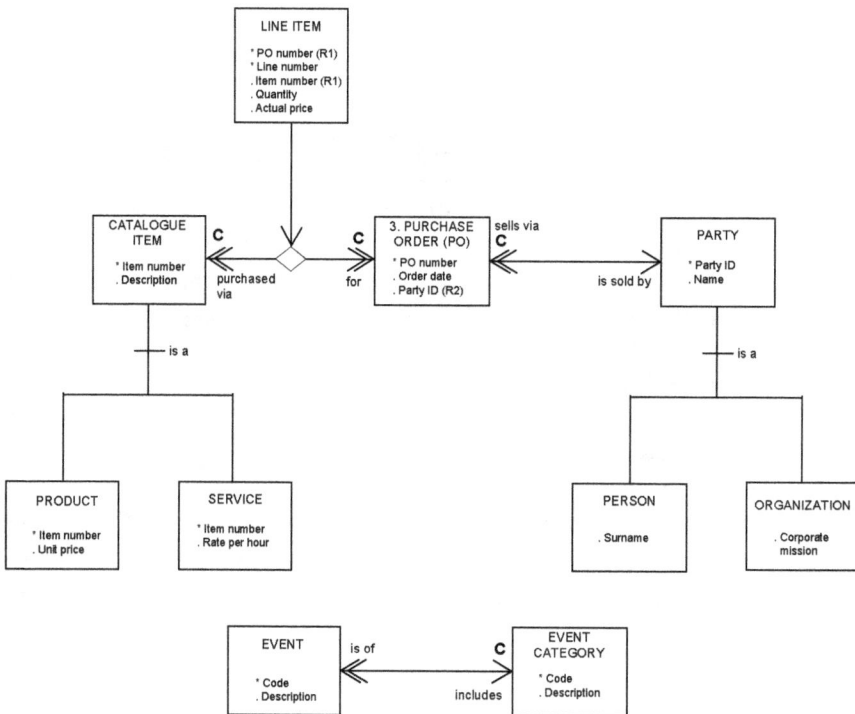

Figure B-8: Shlaer / Mellor Example

---

[100]   P. Chen, 1977, *Op. cit.*

[101]   James Martin, 1977, Computer Data-Base Organization (Englewood Cliffs, NJ: Prentice Hall).

[102]   Sally Shlaer and Stephen J. Mellor, 1988, *Op. Cit.*

♦   Note that in the object-oriented world, a "relationship" is called an "association".

As with relationships in entity/relationship modeling notations, an association is represented by a line. Unlike other notations, *maximum cardinality* (how many instances of an object are associated with an instance of another object) is shown by single arrowheads (for a single occurrence of the related object), and double arrowheads (for multiple occurrences). *Minimum cardinality* is shown by the letter "C" next to optional related entity classes. For example, "Each **Party** may *sell via* one or more **Purchase Orders.** Absence of a "C" means the relationship is mandatory.

Table B-7 shows the model elements for all notations, plus the way each of these are addressed in the Shlaer/Mellor notation.

Table B-7: Shlaer/Mellor Model Elements

Model Element	*Shlaer/Mellor Approach*
Object (Class)	• Square-cornered rectangles. • Called "objects", not "classes".
Attribute	• Displayed inside object boxes.
Relationship	• Lines between objects.
Relationship Name	• is + preposition.
Relationship Cardinality (Minimum and Maximum)	• Maximum: one => single arrowhead; more than one => double arrowhead. • Minimum: "C", for "conditional".
Identifiers	• Attributes annotated with asterisk (*).
Sub-types	• Shown as boxes outside super-type box.
Inter-relationship Constraints	• (None).

Coad and Yourdon (1990)

By 1990, the world of programming had made serious moves from COBOL and Fortran into the world of Simula-67's successors—first C++ and then Java. This brought to center stage some new concepts in the world:

• Designing programs around the structure of objects, rather than processes.

• Addressing processes as characteristics of those objects.

• Dealing explicitly with "messages" passed between objects.

- Focusing on the structures of classification and composition as the ones most important.

Messrs. Coad and Yourdon took the position in 1990 that these object-oriented concepts could contribute to the analysis of a business (The *problem space*, as they described it).[103] [Coad & Yourdon, 1990] They combined a variation on information engineering notation with a variation on data flow diagrams to show how events impinging on objects caused them to send *messages* to other objects. A message, in turn triggers a *service*.

The notation they used was basically Mr. Finkelstein's version of information engineering (no attributes and sub-types shown outside super-types), with some interesting variations. (See Figure B-9.)

This was the first case of dividing a class box into three regions for class name, attributes, and behavior. In Figure B-9, the attributes and behaviors are not shown, but the former would go into the middle section and the latter into the lower section.

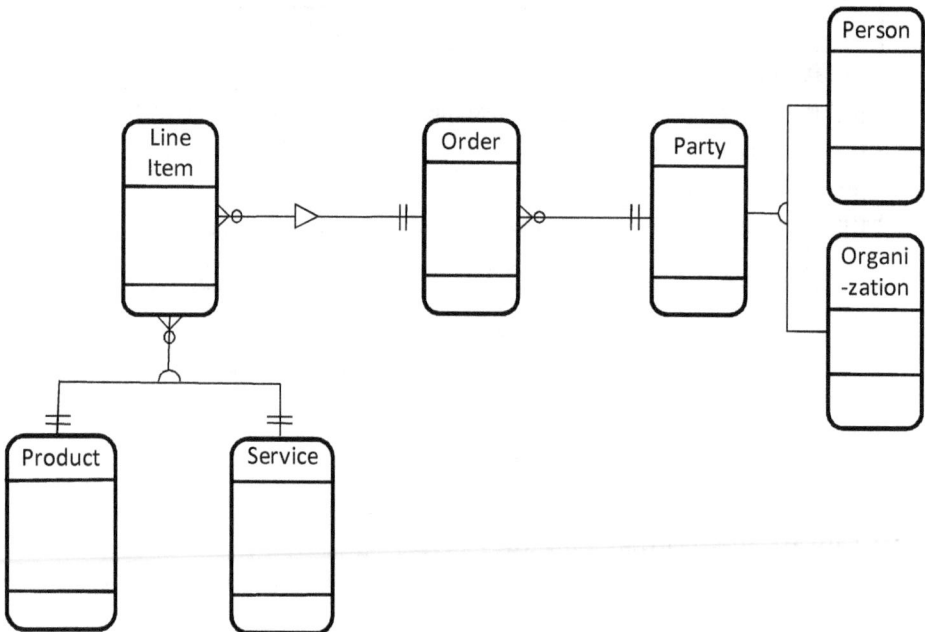

Figure B-9: Yourdon/Coad Approach

---

[103]   Peter Coad and Edward Yourdon. 1990. *Object-oriented Analysis.* Englewood Cliffs, NJ: Yourdon Press/Prentice Hall.

Interestingly, the structures of primary concern to them were two particular hierarchies: *classification structures* (sub-types and super-types), and *assembly structures* (assemblies and components). The notation for the first was Dr. Finkelstein's approach, with sub-types attached to super-types externally. The second was the first example of object-oriented modeling using a special symbol for **composition**. Note that the triangle between **Order** and **Line Item** represent the fact that the **Order** is *composed of* one or more **Line Items**.

Table B-8 shows the model elements.

Table B-8: Yourdon/Coad Model Elements

Model Element	Yourdon/Coad Approach
Class	• Round cornered box, divided into sections for: name, attributes, behaviors.
Attribute	• Optionally, shown inside the class box.
Relationship	• Line between two class boxes (binary only).
Relationship Name	• (none) • Special symbol for "composition": open triangle pointing from component to assembly.
Relationship Cardinality (Minimum and Maximum)	• (Same as Information Engineering.)
Identifiers	• (Not shown)
Sub-types	• Separate boxes external to super-type boxes, with lines connecting.
Inter-relationship Constraints	• (Not shown)

Rumbaugh, et. al. (1991)

James Rumbaugh, Michael Blaha, William Premerlani, Frederick Eddy, and William Lorensen wrote the book which set the stage for "object modeling" as it would later be practiced. *Object-Oriented Modeling and Design* was published in 1991.[104] [Rumbaugh, *et. al.*, 1991]. Mr. Rumbaugh went on to be one of the primary authors of UML, but much of what appeared

---

[104] Jim Rumbaugh, Michael Blaha, William Premerlani, Frederick Eddy, and William Lorensen, 1991, Object-Oriented Modeling and Design (Boca Raton, Florida: CRC Press).

in that language had its precursors in the Object Modeling Technique (OMT) described in this book.

Figure B-10 shows an example of an "object model" in the Object Modeling Technique. The boxes represent *classes*—sets of similarly defined objects. In this case, each class box is in three sections:

- The name of the class.

- A list of attributes.

- A list of behaviors.

Encapsulating the behavior of the class is the major difference between the approach taken by object modelers and that taken by data (entity) modelers. It is the premise behind object-orientation that the structure of objects and their behavior are addressed at the same time. An entity/relationship data model, on the other hand, is only concerned with structure.

This notation has the disadvantage that cardinality and optionality notations are not orthogonal. In the main example, the most common configuration is a solid circle to mean "zero, one, or more", paired with a simple line meaning "exactly one". As shown in the Event/Event Category example, however, "at least one or more" is represented by "1+" and "zero or one" is represented by an open circle.

The Object Modeling Technique defines a policy for naming roles that is carried forward into UML. First, relationships themselves each have a single name (a verb phrase). The modeler, however, is constrained to naming the relationship in one direction only. There are no rules for clarifying which direction to read, so your author has taken the liberty of positioning those shown in Figure B-10 to be read clockwise.

Mr. Rumbaugh and his colleagues view a binary association *role* as a traversal from one object to a set of associated objects. This is different from a data modeler's view of an association as being a predicate structure relating two classes. "Each role on a binary association identifies an object or set of objects associated with an object at the other end. From the point of view of the object, *traversing the association* is an operation that yields related objects. The role name is a derived attribute whose value is a set of related objects." (emphasis added) [Rumbaugh, 1991, p. 34].

This means that role names here are nouns. Thus, Figure B-10 asserts that **Order** plays the role of being a "whole" and **Line Item** plays the role of being a "part". More significantly, in many cases a class plays no role other than being itself. For example, relative to a Party, a Purchase Order simply plays the role of being an "order".

This issue is discussed extensively in Chapters 2 and 3 of the main body of this book.

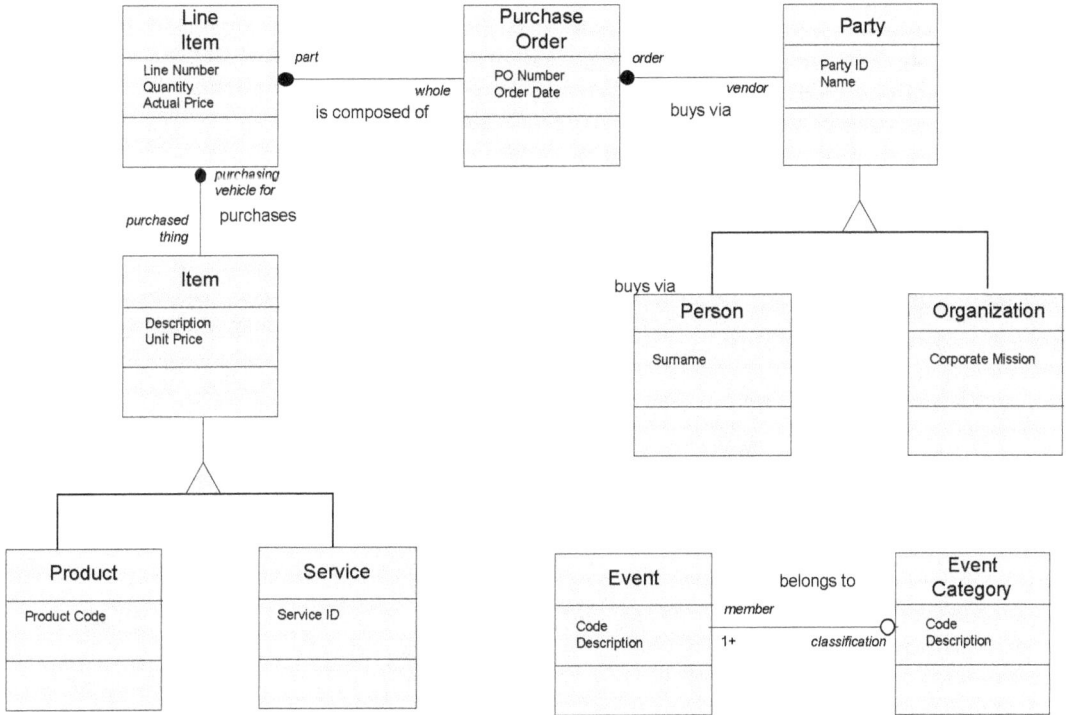

Figure B-10: Rumbaugh Example

Table B-9 shows the elements present in most notations, along with how they are treated in the Rumbaugh notation.

Table B-9: Rumbaugh Model Elements

Model Element	Rumbaugh Approach
Class	• Square cornered box. • Three sections: Name; attributes; behavior.
Attribute	• Shown inside entity class box.
Relationship	• Line between boxes. (Usually binary, but can be n-ary)
Relationship Name	• Single verb phrase for relationship. • For each end (role): noun.
Relationship Cardinality (Minimum and Maximum)	• Optional many: closed empty circle. • Mandatory many: "1+". • Optional one: open circle. • Mandatory one: (no marks).
Identifiers	• (None shown)
Sub-types	• Boxes outside super-type boxes.
Inter-relationship Constraints	• (None shown)

Embley/Kurtz/Woodfield (1992)

Many of the notation elements that later became part of UML were first published by David Embley, Barry Kurtz, and Scott Woodfield in 1992, in their book, *Object-oriented Systems Analysis*. This introduced a more elegant notation for cardinality than was used in ORT, although relationships were only named in one direction. This book, among other things was an assertion that the modeling used to support object-oriented design could be used to support business systems analysis. The book made no mention, however, of the entity/relationship work that had preceded it. Figure B-11 shows our example using their notation.

"The basic underlying concepts that make object-oriented languages and object-oriented design successful may also be used to enhance systems analysis. These concepts include developing highly cohesive but independent object classes, viewing an object not only as having static information but also as being able to act and to be acted upon, and exploiting powerful abstraction concepts such as aggregation, classification, and generalization for describing many important, but often overlooked relationships among system components."[105]

---

[105] David W. Embly, Barry D. Kurtz, and Scott N. Woodfield, 1992, Object-oriented Systems Analysis: A Model-driven Approach (Englewood Cliffs, New Jersey: Prentice-Hall). xv.

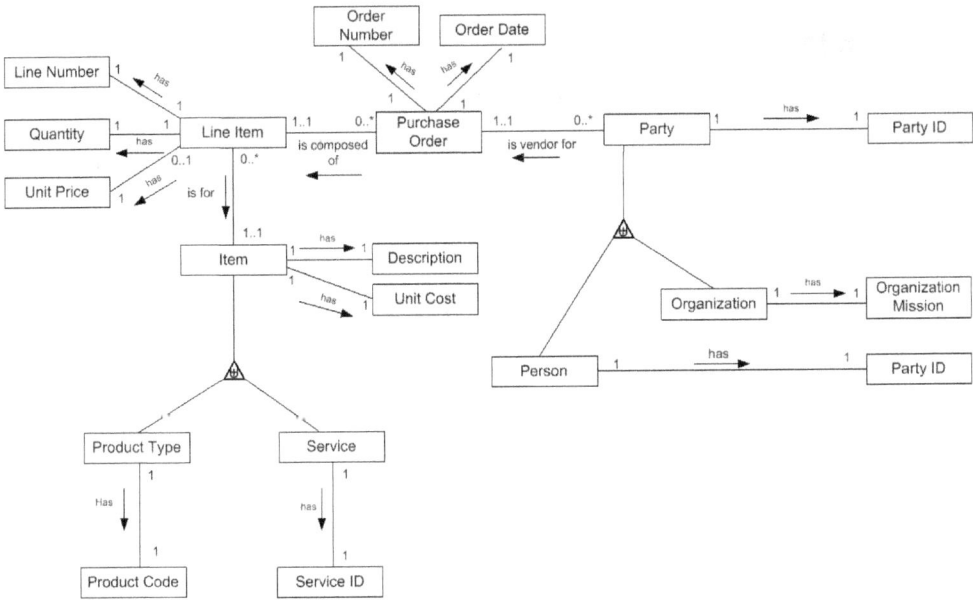

Figure B-11: Embley, et al.

Table B-10: Embley, et al. Model Elements

Model Element	Embley Approach
Class	• Rectangular box.
Attribute	• Separate rectangular box, connected to the Class box.
Relationship	• Line connecting classes (Need not be binary.) • Arrow next to it designates direction to read relationship name.
Relationship Name	• Single verb, going one way only.
Relationship Cardinality (Minimum and Maximum)	• Minimum: First character ("0" – optional, or "1" - mandatory). (Not shown if total is "0..*" or "1..1"). • Maximum: Second character ("1", "*" – unlimited, or other values, such as "< 3" or "4-8"). • If relationship to attribute, only the minimum ("0" – optional; "1" – mandatory) is shown.
Identifiers	• (Not shown)
Sub-types	• External boxes, linked to the super-type, with symbol showing the sub-types to be overlapping or exclusive.
Inter-relationship Constraints	• (Not shown)

Booch (1994)

In 1994, Grady Booch published *Object-oriented Analysis and Design: With Applications.*[106] The example with his notation is shown in Figure B-12. The way each element is treated is in Table B-10,

"Ultimately I am a developer, not just a methodologist. The first question you should ask any methodologist is if he or she uses their own methods to develop software". [Booch, 1994. Page vi.]

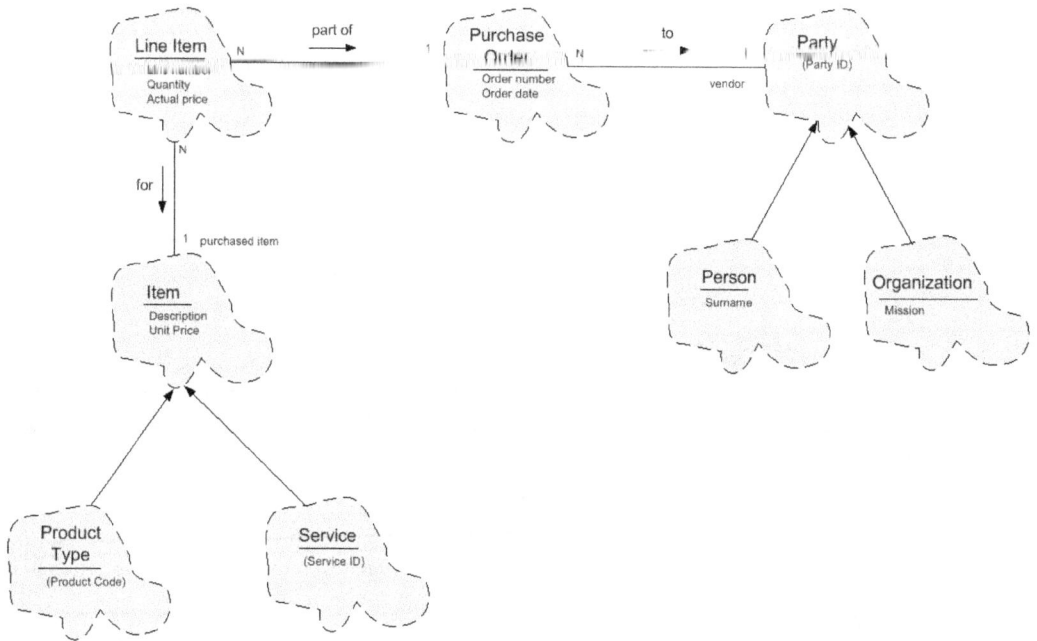

Figure B-12: Booch Example

---

[106] Booch, Grady. 1994. *Object-oriented Analysis and Design: With Applications.* (Redwood City, California: The Benjamin / Cummings Publishing Company. 16-17.

Table B-10: Booch Model Elements

Model Element	Booch Approach
Class	• A cloud. With an underlined name and attributes.
Attribute	• Shown inside Class cloud.
Relationship	• Line between Class clouds. (Binary only). • Arrow showing direction to read relationship name.
Relationship Name	• One verb.
Relationship Cardinality (Minimum and Maximum)	• Minimum: (not shown). • Maximum: "1" or "N".
Identifiers	• (Not shown)
Sub-types	• Separate clouds, with arrow pointing from the sub-type to the super-type.
Inter-relationship Constraints	• (Not shown)

Object Patterns

At the same time that data modeling patterns were being developed, the object community developed some patterns of its own.

Design Patterns

In 1995, the year that David Hay published *Data Model Patterns: Conventions of Thought*, to describe patterns of business data modeling, Eric Gamma and three colleagues published *Design Patterns: Elements of Reusable Object-Oriented Software*.[107] These pieces of C++ and SmallTalk code are designed to be widely applicable.

Martin Fowler – Analysis Patterns

Just after the publishing of David Hay's book, Martin Fowler published *Analysis Patterns: Reusable Object Models*.[108] This book also contained

---

[107] Eric Gamma, Richard Helm, Ralph Johnson and John Vlissides, 1995, *Design Patterns: Elements of Reusable Object-Oriented Software* (Reading, MA: Addison-Wesley Publishing Company).

[108] Martin. Fowler, 1997, *Analysis Patterns*. (Reading, MA: Addison-Wesley).

entity/relationship models describing business situations, but with a more object-oriented flavor. The intention was specifically that these models could be implemented via object-oriented code, and there are numerous examples of such.

UML

In 1994, Rational Software Corporation hired James Rumbaugh to join Grady Booch and the two promoted their two approaches to "object-oriented modeling". Mr. Rumbaugh's Object Modeling Technique was marketed to support "object-oriented analysis" and Mr. Booch's "Booch Method" was promoted for "object oriented design". At this point, however, they also began work to develop an approach that would unify their two approaches. In 1995, they were joined by Ivar Jacobson, who had developed the "Object-oriented Software Engineering" method.

In 1996, the "Three Amigos" began work on the truly "Unified Modeling Language" that became UML. An international consortium, called the UML Partners, was organized at this time to complete the *Unified Modeling Language (UML)* specification, and propose it as a response to a "Request for Proposal" that had been published that year by the Object Management Group (OMG).

"The Unified Modeling Language" (originally known as "The UML", but subsequently shortened to simply "UML") brought together many different techniques, including the object modeling techniques described above (called the "Class Model"). The class model represented a single technique for modeling classes and associations. The cardinality notation developed by Messrs. Embly, Kurtz, and Woodfield was combined with the segmented rectangles from Mr. Rumbaugh's Object Modeling Technique. This part of the UML suite of notations was called the "Class Model".

In addition to the "Class Model", the UML umbrella incorporated a number of techniques for modeling other aspects of the system development process:

- Use cases describing user interaction with a system
- Process flows
- Events and responses
- Software components

In recent years, an Object Constraint Language has been added, as well. Note that, prior references to "object-oriented analysis" notwithstanding, the overwhelming thrust of UML is towards object-oriented design.

UML 1.1 was submitted to the OMG in August, 1997, and adopted by the OMG in November, 1997.[109] UML version 2.0 was then adopted in two parts in 2005: The *UML 2.0 Infrastructure* defines the foundational language constructs.[110] *UML 2.0 Superstructure* defines the user level constructs.[111] The two complementary specifications constitute a complete specification for the UML 2.0 modeling language.

The Internet and the Semantic Web

Figure B-13 reproduces Figure B-1, with one addition. This is a sequence of technology development that is not directly related to the issue between object orientation and data modeling, but it may prove to be more significant than either. Everyone is involved in this technology, and as it progresses, it may overshadow all of the other discussions in this book. It is important, therefore, to include it at least in our history of modeling.

Note in the diagram the line taking off from the Data Processing events *Computer Time Sharing* and *ARPANET*. It goes to *The Internet* on the 1980 boundary between the data processing history and the object-oriented history. *The World Wide Web* lies firmly outside either, although the creation of the object-oriented language, Java, had a great deal to do with the proliferation and dynamism of the Web. The line terminates firmly in the Data Architecture stream with *The Semantic Web*. This entire thread is fundamentally about using computers on networks as an extension of our intellects.

---

[109]   Object Management Group (OMG), 1997, *Op. cit.*

[110]   2005a. "UML 2.0:Infrastructure" (OMG document 05-07-05). Published as http://www.omg.org/docs/formal/05-07-05.pdf.

[111]   Object Management Group. 2005. "UML 2.0:Superstructure" (OMG document 05-07-04). Published as http://www.omg.org/docs/formal/05-07-04.pdf.

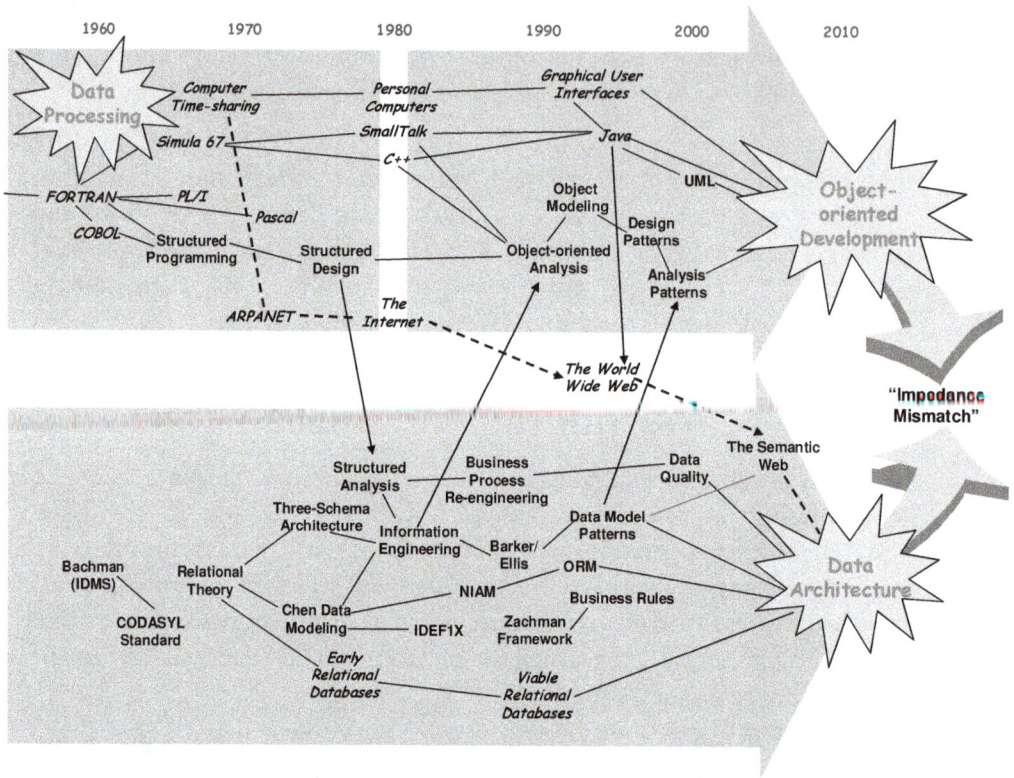

Figure B-13: History, Once More

Computer Time-sharing

Computer time-sharing, created in 1961, made it possible for a person to sit at a typewriter-like device, send messages directly to a computer that, thanks to the telephone network, could be far away. The computer would then send responses directly back to that person, across the same network. More significantly, multiple people could be working on the same computer at the same time, with each imagining that 'e was using it exclusively. Programs could be written, tested, and results examined, all while sitting at the remote device. More significantly, the resulting programs could then be turned over to end-users who could then sit in front of similar devices and have the same interactive experience of entering data and then examining the results of processing them.

It would take a decade or so before the concept of "user interface" entered the language of the industry, but its origins were here.

Computer time-sharing also meant that different people working on different aspects of a single project could communicate with each other. This was the origin of the technology later called "electronic mail" ("e-mail").[112] [113]

It quickly also became apparent that beyond having multiple people working on one computer, the computers themselves could be conected together. This was the origin of ***ARPANET***.

ARPANET

"The first recorded description of the social interactions that could be enabled through networking was a series of memos written by J.C.R. Licklider of MIT in August 1962 discussing his 'Galactic Network' concept. He envisioned a globally interconnected set of computers through which everyone could quickly access data and programs from any site. In spirit, the concept was very much like the Internet of today."[114]

The only physical network available at the time for connecting computers was the telephone system. This was a ***Circuit Network***, which required a physical connection from each device to every other device in order for them to communicate–no matter how far away. This meant that the network was extremely vulnerable to weather and natural forces that could disrupt it. More significantly, during the Cold War, it was also vulnerable to enemy attacks. For this reason, the Department of Defense ***Advanced Research Projects Agency*** (DARPA, also called at various times, simply ARPA) sought a way to build a network that would not be vulnerable in this way.

---

[112] Errol Morris. 2011. "Did My Brother Invent E-Mail With Tom Van Vleck?". *The New York Times*. Five articles, June 19-23, 2011.

[113] Tom Van Vleck. "The History of Electronic Mail". Undated manuscript reproduced at http://www.multicians.org/thvv/mail-history.html.

[114] Barry M. Leiner, V. G. Cerf, D. D. Clark, R. E. Kahn, L. Kleinrock, D. C. Lynch,
Jon Postel, L. G. Roberts, S. Wolff. "Histories of the Internet". *Internet Society*. Retrieved 7/24/2011 from
http://www.isoc.org/internet/history/brief.shtml.

The technology for computer time-sharing required a controller that would slice up the tasks received from various sources, reassemble and execute each, so the results would then be re-sliced to be sent back. Something similar would be required for secure communication across multiple computers. The communications lines themselves would have to be "time-shared" with a similar "slicing" behavior as well.

In 1961, a graduate student at MIT, Len Kleinrock, "was made aware of a problem that the military was having in what we now call data networking—sending messages around in a reliable way, in a hostile environment, efficiently. So [he] started doing some research in data networks [and he] uncovered the underlying principles of *packet switching*, of message switching, of burst communications, of data networking."[115]

Packet switching "entails packaging data in specially formatted units (called *packets*) that are typically routed from source to destination using network switches and routers. Each packet contains address information that identifies the sending computer and intended recipient. Using these addresses, network switches and routers determine how best to transfer the packet between hops on the path to its destination."[116]

The point is that there is no single route that is pre-defined from beginning to end. Each packet goes to a node, and is then passed along to what seems the most reasonable next node to get it where it is going. It is not necessarily even the shortest route. Each node independently decides the next node, according to the rules defined in a **protocol**. A protocol is "the rules for exchanging those messages in or between computing systems and in telecommunications… the rules for exchanging those messages in or between computing systems and in telecommunications."[117] (More about protocols, below.)

---

[115]   Stephen Segaller. *Nerds 2.0.1: A Brief History of the Internet.* (New York: TV Books). 33.

[116]   Bradley Mitchell. 2011. "What Is Packet Switching on Computer Networks?" *About.com Wireless/Networking.* Retrieved 7/27/2011 from http://compnetworking.about.com/od/networkprotocols/f/packet-switch.htm.

[117]   Wikipedia. 2011. "Communications Protocol". Retrieved 8/4/2011 from http://en.wikipedia.org/wiki/Communications_protocol.

Thus, each packet finds its own way to its destination and is reunited with its fellows only when all the packets that constitute a message get there.

Recognizing "the theoretical feasibility of communications using packets rather than circuits, was a major step along the path towards computer networking...In late 1966 Lawrence G. Roberts went to DARPA to develop the computer network concept and quickly put together his plan for the ***ARPANET***, publishing it in 1967."[118]

One other problem that had to be dealt with was the fact that the computers involved in all of this communication were made by different manufacturers and had different languages for communicating with the outside world.

An ***Interface Message Processor*** (***IMP***) is a small computer that translates from the communication language to that required for communication with one local machine.

In September 1969, the company, Bolt Beranek and Newman (BBN), installed the first IMP at UCLA and the first host computer was connected to a network. Stanford Research Institute (SRI) provided a second node. By the end of 1969, four computers were attached. They had a network.

Elaborating on the definition above, a ***protocol*** (or, more formally, a ***communications protocol***) is "a formal description of digital message formats and the rules for exchanging those messages in or between computing systems and in telecommunications.

"Protocols may include signaling, authentication and error detection and correction capabilities.

"The specified behavior is typically independent of how it is to be implemented. A protocol can therefore be implemented as hardware or software or both."[119]

"In December 1970 the Network Working Group (NWG) working under S. Crocker finished the initial ARPANET Host-to-Host protocol, called the ***Network Control Protocol*** (***NCP***). As the ARPANET sites

---

[118]   Barry M. Leiner *et. al. Op. cit.*

[119]   Wikipedia. 2011. "Communications Protocol". *Op. cit.*

completed implementing NCP during the period 1971-1972, the network users finally could begin to develop applications"[120]

"*NLS*, or the 'oN-Line System', was a revolutionary computer collaboration system designed by Douglas Engelbart and implemented by researchers at the Augmentation Research Center (ARC) at the Stanford Research Institute (SRI) during the 1960s. The NLS system[sic] was the first to employ the practical use of hypertext links, the mouse (co-invented by Engelbart and colleague Bill English), raster-scan video monitors, information organized by relevance, screen windowing, presentation programs, and other modern computing concepts. It was funded by the Defense Advanced Research Projects Agency, NASA, and the U.S. Air Force."[121] In December of 1968, Engelbart demonstrated a hypertext interface to the public for the first time ".♥

While tinkerers had invented e-mail-like features as far back as the 1960s, "Ray Tomlinson is credited with inventing *email* in 1972. Like many of the Internet inventors, Tomlinson worked for Bolt Beranek and Newman (BBN) as an ARPANET contractor. He picked the "@" symbol from the computer keyboard to denote sending messages from one computer to another. So then, for anyone using Internet standards, it was simply a matter of nominating name-of-the-user@name-of-the-computer. Internet pioneer Jon Postel…was one of the first users of the new system, and is credited with describing it as a 'nice hack'. It certainly was, and it has lasted to this day."[122]

The Internet

The original **ARPANET** grew from a network for government agencies and universities into the more universally available Internet we know today. "The Internet was based on the idea that there would be multiple independent networks of rather arbitrary design. This began with the

---

[120]   Barry M. Leiner *et. al. Op. cit.*

[121]   *Ibid.*

♥   This can be seen at http://sloan.stanford.edu/MouseSite/1968Demo.html. It is definitely worth an hour of your time.

[122]   Ian Peter. 2011. "The History of Email". *Net History*. Retrieved 7/27/2011 from http://www.nethistory.info/History of the Internet/email.html.

ARPANET as the pioneering packet switching network, but soon came to include packet satellite networks, ground-based packet radio networks and other networks."[123]

The Network Control Protocol (NCP), initially used, eventually proved inadequate to the job, however, since packets could be lost.

In the early 1970s Bob Kahn of BBN "decided to develop a new version of the protocol which could meet the needs of an open-architecture network environment. While NCP tended to act like a device driver from the perspective of each computer, the new protocol would be more like a communications protocol.

"Four ground rules were critical to Kahn's early thinking:

- Each distinct network would have to stand on its own and no internal changes could be required to any such network to connect it to the Internet.

- Communications would be on a best effort basis. If a packet didn't make it to the final destination, it would shortly be retransmitted from the source.

- Black boxes would be used to connect the networks; these would later be called gateways and routers. There would be no information retained by the gateways about the individual flows of packets passing through them, thereby keeping them simple and avoiding complicated adaptation and recovery from various failure modes.

- There would be no global control at the operations level."[124]

"In May 1974, the Institute of Electrical and Electronic Engineers (IEEE) published a paper entitled 'A Protocol for Packet Network Interconnection' "[125] The paper's authors, Vint Cerf and Bob Kahn, described an internetworking protocol for sharing resources using packet-switching among the nodes.

---

[123] Barry M. Leiner *et. al. op. cit.*

[124] Barry M. Leiner *et. al. op. cit.*

[125] Vinton G. Cerf, Robert E. Kahn, "A Protocol for Packet Network Intercommunication", IEEE Transactions on Communications, Vol. 22, No. 5, May 1974 pp. 637-648

A central control component of this model was the *"Transmission Control Protocol (TCP)* that incorporated both connection-oriented links and datagram♠ services between hosts. The monolithic Transmission Control Program was later divided into a modular architecture consisting of the Transmission Control Protocol at the connection-oriented layer and the *Internet Protocol (IP)* at the internetworking (datagram) layer. The model became known informally as *TCP/IP*, although formally referenced as the *Internet Protocol Suite."*[126]

From this came the concept of the *IP Address*. This is a unique number that identifies each node on the network (computer, printer, or other piece of equipment). Initially (in the version called "IPv4") the address was 32 bits long, providing or the ability to address approximately 4 billion (actually 4.3×10^9) nodes. With the explosive growth of the World Wide Web, this is not enough. Currently, a new version, IPv6 will use 128 bits, which will provide for 3.4×10^{38} nodes.♣

During the 1970s, numerous networks were developed by various government agencies and universities. On January 1, 1983, however, all hosts were required to simultaneously convert from NCP to TCP/IP "or be left having to communicate via rather ad-hoc mechanisms". This transition was carefully planned within the community over several years before it actually took place and went surprisingly smoothly.♠

"Thus, by 1985, the Internet was already well established as a technology supporting a broad community of researchers and developers, and was beginning to be used by other communities for daily computer communications. Electronic mail was being used broadly across several communities, often with different systems, but interconnection between

---

♠ "The term packet applies to any message formatted as a packet, while the term datagram is generally reserved for packets of an "unreliable" service. An "unreliable" service does not notify the user if delivery fails." [Wikipedia, "Datagram"]

[126] Wikipedia. 2011. "Internet Protocol". Retrieved 7/29/2011 from http://en.wikipedia.org/wiki/Internet_Protocol#Version_history

♣ As of 2011, this is still being implemented.

♠ It but resulted in a large distribution of buttons saying "I survived the TCP/IP transition".

different mail systems was demonstrating the utility of broad based electronic communications between people."[127]

By 1990 when the ARPANET itself was finally decommissioned, TCP/IP had supplanted or marginalized most other wide-area computer network protocols worldwide, and IP was well on its way to becoming *the* bearer service for the global information infrastructure.

The World Wide Web

In 1980, Tim Berners-Lee took a software consulting job with CERN, the Swiss/French nuclear research center. Among other things, he wrote a program for his own purposes to help him keep track of connections among various people, computers, and projects in the lab. He called it "Enquire", short for *Enquire Within upon Everything,* a musty old book of Victorian advice he noticed as a child in his parents' house outside London.

This got him to thinking.

"Suppose all the information stored on computers everywhere were linked. Suppose I could program my computer to create a space in which anything could be linked to anything. All the bits of information in every computer at CERN, and on the planet would be available to me and to anyone else. There would be a single, global information space.

"Once a bit of information in that space was labeled with an address, I could tell my computer to get it. By being able to reference anything with equal ease, a computer could represent associations between things that might seem unrelated but did, in fact share a relationship. A web of information would form."[128]

This was at about the same time that the Internet had come into existence, making such a "web" possible. But the network alone was not sufficient. What was needed was a way to label and refer to each of those pieces of information. If you were reading something and wanted to refer to something else, mechanisms were required to make that possible.

As time went on, his requirements for improvement to "Enquire" became clearer. "In addition to keeping track of relationships between all

---

[127]   Barry M. Leiner *et. al. op. cit.*

[128]   Berners-Lee, Tim. 2000. *Weaving the Web: The original Design and Ultimate Destiny of the World Wide Web.* (New York: HarperCollins). 4.

the people, experiments, and machines, I wanted to access different kinds of information, such as a researcher's technical papers, the manuals for different software modules, minutes of meetings, hastily scribbled notes, and so on…

"What I was looking for fell under the general category of *documentation systems*–software that allows documents to be stored and later retrieved." Until now, however, examples of products in that category didn't work well, because the software that provided the facility required researchers to fit their work to the system. "I would have to create a system with common rules that would be acceptable to everyone. This meant as close as possible to no rules at all.

"This notion seemed impossible until I realized that the diversity of different computer systems and networks could be a rich resource– something to be represented, not a problem to be eradicated. The model I chose for my minimalist system was **hypertext**."[129]

This had in fact already been described fifteen years earlier. At the same time that **ARPANET** was being developed, visionaries were imagining just what life with these networked computers might look like. All major histories of what we now call hypertext start in 1945, when Vannevar Bush wrote an article in *The Atlantic* magazine called "As We May Think", about a futuristic device he called a "Memex".[130] Starting in 1963, Ted Nelson developed a model for creating and using linked content he called "hypertext" and "hypermedia". (The first published reference to it was in 1965.[131]) He later worked with Andries van Dam to develop the Hypertext Editing System in 1967 at Brown University.

"I happened to come along," wrote Mr. Berners-Lee, "with time and the right interest and inclination, after hypertext and the Internet had come of age. The task left to me was to marry them together."[132]

---

[129]   *Ibid.* 15.

[130]   Vannevar Bush. 1945. "As We May Think". *The Atlantic.* July, 1945. Retrieved 8/2/2011 from http://www.theatlantic.com/magazine/archive/1945/07/as-we-may-think/3881/.

[131]   Lauren Wedeles. 1965. "Professor Nelson Talk: Analyzes P.R.I.D.E." *Vassar Miscellany News.* Retrieved 8/2/2011 from http://faculty.vassar.edu/mijoyce/MiscNews_Feb65.html

[132]   *Ibid.,* 5-6.

The system had to have one other characteristic. It had to be decentralized. "That would be the only way a new person somewhere could start to use it without asking for access from anyone else."[133]

Thus, the **World Wide Web** became a network of interconnected *documents*, each of which is located at a uniquely identifiable **web site**, consisting of one or more **web pages**.

A Web page is made available to the World Wide Web via the **hypertext markup language**, otherwise known as **HTML.** This is the publishing *language* of the World Wide Web, and contains the commands necessary to retrieve a desired document, transmit it and present it on the recipient's computer. The first version of this was invented by Mr. Berners-Lee in 1991.

Web pages are maintained on computers that each play the role of **web server.** That is, the documents are stored there, and the HTML code required to retrieve and send them is also maintained there. Someone looking to retrieve a document has computer software called a **web browser.** A requestor specifies the desired web site via such a web browser, whereupon that browser uses the Internet to 1) locate the Web Server where the desired web pages are stored, 2) retrieve the pages, and 3) (under the control of the included HTML code and other any bits of program code that may have been included) display it on the requestor's machine. That is, the HTML code may imbedded with be some small programs that enhance the display process and make possible interactions with the user.

Indeed the development of the Java object-oriented language by Sun Microsystems in 1995 made the kinds of code required to enhance a web page much easier than was possible before, largely because it has fewer implementation-specific dependencies.

In his original vision, Mr. Berners-Lee stipulated, "Once a bit of information in that space was labeled with an address…" The question now was what should that address look like?

To refer to a location on the Internet required knowing that location's **IP (Internet Protocol) address.** As described above, this is the number that uniquely identifies a node. For hypertext to retrieve something from a node, its IP address is required.

---

[133] *Ibid.* 16.

To make the address more meaningful to the humans who are looking for information there, however, Mr. Berners-Lee imagined a *Universal Resource Identifier* (*URI*) that would identify each web site. This is also referred to as a *domain name*. This would be a meaningful set of words that would provide a human readable label as a synonym for that IP address. The group of his colleagues that he gathered together to manage the World Wide Web (the *World Wide Web Consortium* or the **W3C**) vetoed that term for it and the label has been known ever since as the *Uniform Resource Locater (URL)*. This is how the hypertext-equipped *World Wide Web* refers to other "documents" to be retrieved as part of this document.♥

Mapping of a URL to an IP address is done via the *Domain Name System* (*DNS*). Note that the requested URL consists of four components. For example, the URL, *http://henriettahay.com/women/99mar12.htm* consists of:

- *http://* - "tells your PC what protocol (what language so to speak) to use talking with this site. In this case, you are using HTTP (HyperText Transfer Protocol)."[134]

- *henriettahay.com* - the *domain name.* This is the "name" of the site, a unique name, understandable to humans, and ending with ".com", ".edu", ".gov", etc. This is what the Domain Name System maps to an IP address. In this case, Henrietta Hay is a columnist for the Grand Junction, Colorado *Daily Sentinel.* This is the web site where the columns she has written are kept.

- */women* - one or more directories on the web site. The web request directs the web server to go to this directory to find the page. In this example "/women" is the directory on Henrietta Hay's site where you will find her columns on the subject of women's politics.

♥ Mr. Berners-Lee kept the idea behind the Universal Resource Identifier to use when the Semantic Web was developed. See the next section, below.

[134] Scott Meyer. 2011. "DNS Tutorial". *GNC Web Creations.* Retrieved 8/11/2011 from http://www.gnc-web-creations.com/dns-tutorial.htm. (This is a particularly good description of the entire process of locating web sites via the DNS.)

- ***99mar12.htm*** - the name of the file being retrieved. In this case, it was Ms. Hay's March 12, 1999 column on the subject of "Uppity Women's History Month". ♥

This "translates domain names meaningful to humans into the numerical identifiers associated with networking equipment for the purpose of locating and addressing these devices worldwide." [135]

An often-used analogy to explain the Domain Name System is that it serves as the "phone book" for the Internet by translating human-friendly computer hostnames into IP addresses. For example, the domain name www.henriettahay.com translates to the IP address 72.167.204.90.

"The Domain Name System (DNS) makes it possible to assign domain names to groups of Internet resources and users in a meaningful way, independent of each entity's physical location. Because of this, World Wide Web (WWW) hyperlinks and Internet contact information can remain consistent and constant even if the current Internet routing arrangements change or the participant uses a mobile device." [136] The site for http://henriettahay.com could be moved to another provider. This would change its IP Address. The URL would remain the same, however, and visitors would not be able to tell the difference.

At the request of Jon Postel, Paul Mockapetris invented the Domain Name System in 1983 and wrote the first implementation. In 1984, four Berkeley students—Douglas Terry, Mark Painter, David Riggle, and

---

♥   Yes, as you may have guessed, your author is related to Henrietta Hay. She's his mother. She was 85 years old when she wrote that column in 1999. She finally decided to stop writing in 2011, when she was almost 97 years old. Her eyes were going bad, so it was becoming hard to use her computer. And yes, you can read nearly all of her columns at http://davehay.com/henrietta. (From 1988 until about 1995, they were typed onto pieces of paper and mailed to the newspaper. From 1995, though, they were also recorded on her web site.)

[135]   Wikipedia. 2011. "Domain Name Service". Retrieved 8/9/211 from http://en.wikipedia.org/wiki/Domain_Name_System.

[136]   Wikipedia. 2011. "Domain Name Service". Retrieved 8/9/211 from http://en.wikipedia.org/wiki/Domain_Name_System.

Songnian Zhou—wrote the first Unix implementation, called The Berkeley Internet Name Domain (BIND) Server."[137]

BIND was widely distributed, especially on Unix systems, and is the dominant DNS software in use on the Internet.[138]

The TCP/IP protocol describes the "packets" transmitted across the internet. On top of that is required a protocol that understands the HTML that is requested and returned across the Web. "The Hypertext Transfer Protocol (HTTP) is an application-level protocol for distributed, collaborative, hypermedia information systems. HTTP has been in use by the World-Wide Web global information initiative since 1990."[139]

The Semantic Web

In recent years companies have discovered that one reason it is hard to bring the data from disparate systems together is that they use terms differently. They were developed from different projects, each with priority being to get the particular system working, and little concern for how it interacted with other systems. The underlying problem was only partly technical. It went to the fact that different departments themselves didn't communicate very well.

Different departments used the same words to mean different things and different words to mean the same things. *Semantics*, a term that goes back to the mid-19th century, means the study of *meaning* in language. This has now become a hot new buzzword. If they are to resolve the problems of connecting their computers, companies and government agencies must come to terms with the semantics of the people who run

---

[137] Douglas Brian Terry, Mark Painter, David W. Riggle and Songnian Zhou. 1984. *The Berkeley Internet Name Domain Server*, Proceedings USENIX Summer Conference, Salt Lake City, Utah. June 1984. 23–31.   Retrieved   8/10/2011   from http://www.eecs.berkeley.edu/Pubs/TechRpts/1984/5957.html.

[138] Don Moor. 2004. "DNS Survey". Retrieved 8/9/2011 from http://mydns.bboy.net/survey/

[139] World Wide Web Consortium. *1999. Hypertext Transfer Protocol -- HTTP/1.1*. Retrieved 7/29/2011 from http://www.w3.org/Protocols/rfc2616/rfc2616-sec1.html#sec1.1,

their business. Moreover, this is at the heart of learning how to manage corporate data as an asset.

To address the problem it became evident that what was needed was an *ontology*. This second hot new buzzword actually goes back about 2500 years to ancient Greece. Ontology was the branch of philosophy that concerned understanding *what exists*. Aristotle in particular wrote a lot on this subject. In modern times, the definition of the word has been modified to mean a structured description of what exists in a company. This could be as simple as a glossary or something as sophisticated as a conceptual data model. This is where it is possible to provide the definitive definition for each term.

Yes, a conceptual entity/relationship model is a kind of ontology.

Mr. Berners-Lee, while he was pleased with the success of the World Wide Web in managing documents, realized quickly that it didn't really address what he was after: He wanted to use the computer as a repository of knowledge itself, with enough intelligence in the technology to allow the computer to deal with the meaning (semantics) of the language involved. Out of this came the Semantic Web. Where the World Wide Web manages *pages*, the Semantic Web manages *concepts*.

What is remarkable about the Semantic Web is that each of the concepts being managed is pre-defined and labeled with a *Universal Resource Identifier* (*URI*). Where the *Uniform Resource Locator* (*URL*) returned an IP Address to locate a document, the *Universal Resource Identifier* makes it possible to locate a single *term*. This in turn makes it possible to define an entire vocabulary on the Web, so that anyone can refer to the term and assume that it has a single meaning.

The semantic web is embodied in three new modeling languages:[140]

Resource Definition Framework (RDF) – "the basic framework that the rest of the Semantic Web is based on. RDF provides a mechanism for allowing anyone to make a basic statement about anything and layering these statements into a single model."[141] The statements are assembled from Universal Resource Identifiers in the form <subject><predicate><object>. For example, an RDF statement can

---

[140] Dean Allemang and Jim Hendler. 2011. *Semantic Web for the Working Ontologist: Effective Modeling in RDFS and OWL*. (Boston: Morgan Kaufmann).

[141] Dean Allemang and Jim Hendler. 2011. *Op cit*. 23-24

assert that "Dave" "owns" "an Acura". This captures the underlying simple semantics of the sentences. Each of the components is either a literal ("Dave"), a description of a relationship ("owns") or the identifier of a concept located somewhere on the web.("Acura"). Note that both predicates ("owns") and subjects and objects are defined somewhere on the Web.

RDF Schema – an enhanced version of RDF that includes language constructs to recognize that some words describe classes, sub-classes, and properties. For example: "Person / is a / class." "Dave / is a member of / Person." "Person / may own / car."

Web Ontology Language (OWL)   brings the expressivity of logic to the Semantic Web. It allows modelers to express detailed constraints between classes, entities, and properties. Thus, given the RDF Schema sentences above, OWL allows the computer to infer that "Dave / may own / car."

The underlying language beneath the three of these is XML.

Note that as companies began compiling even basic glossaries, it turned out that simply imposing a single definition for each word wasn't going to work. The accounts receivable department has a different definition for "customer" than does the marketing department. What was required was a scheme that not only captured each definition but it did so in context.

The structure of a Universal Resource Identifier begins with a web address. This makes it possible to define its context. Because the web address begins with the identification of organization that sponsors it, the definition of the word described in the context of that address can be presumed to be in the context of that organization. For example, if URIs described both http://www.bigcompany.com/Marketing/#customer and http://www.bigcompany.com/AccountsReceivable/#customer, anyone, anywhere in the world, can retrieve a single definition for each context. For convenience, http://www.bigcompany.com/Marketing would be abbreviated "bcmk", so all references to the Big Company, Inc's Marketing Department term for customer would be to "bcmk:customer". Similarly, all references to Big Company's Acounts Receivable Department's definition of "customer" would be represented as "bcar:customer".

Even the languages of RDF Schema and OWL are themselves in terms of reserved words that are URIs: "subClassOf", "subPropertyOf", "label", "unionOf", etc. These are respectively "rdfs:subClassOf", "rdfs:subPropertyOf", and "owl:unionOf".

While the semantic web is very closely related to the conceptual entity/relationship diagram, there are two very significant differences (ok, "impedance mismatches", if you will) between the outlooks represented by the conceptual data modeling approach to describing the world and the semantic web approach:

First of all, data modeling (and its cousin, database design) operates under what is called the *closed world assumption*. Given that practitioners are concerned with the quality of the data managed, it is assumed that if incoming data do not conform to what is known to be true, they must be false.

The Semantic Web, on the other hand, is based on the *open world assumption*. This is valuable when analyzing a large body of previously unstructured (and relatively undocumented) data. Here it is assumed that if we have not explicitly said that something is false, it could be true.

For example:

> Assume that a database is created according to the model assertion: "Each **City** must be *located in* one and only one **State**".

> Now imagine that a record arrives that has a **City** (say "Portland") with no **State** specified.

> The database would reject it because it violates the requirement that a *state* must be specified.

> The Semantic Web, on the other hand, would accept it as something we know. Something that calls itself a **City** with the name "Portland" exists. That there is information that is missing is of no consequence in this world view.

> Now imagine that a record arrives that specifies a **City** of "Portland" and a **State** of "Maine".

> In both views of the world, this is fine. It follows the rules.

> But now imagine that a second record arrives that specifies a **City** of "Portland" and a **State** of "Oregon".

> Oops! This violates our rule that says a **City** can be in one and only one **State**. The problem is, both of these

statements are true statements. The database will bounce the second record, causing considerable problems further down the road.

The Semantic Web simply comes back and asks:

Does the name "Maine" refer to the same **State** as the name "Oregon", or

Is the **City** named "Portland" that is in "Maine" a different **City** than the **City** named "Portland" that is in "Oregon"?

Note that the Semantic Web is semantically much richer than any of the data modeling approaches described thus far in this book.

A second difference between an entity relationship diagram and a semantic web ontology is the relationship between entity classes and relationships. In the former case, entity classes are defined first and then relationships and attributes are defined as properties of them. This has the effect that, for example, if each city must be *located in* one state, and each state must be *located in* one country, there are here two relationships that happen to have the same name ("located in"), each of which is a property of its respective entity class.

In the case of a semantic web ontology, properties (both attributes and relationships) are defined first and only then are the classes defined that have those properties. In the example, that means that there is only one relationship called "located in" which happens to be applied between city and state, and again between state and country.

If you assume the rule that all relationships must be named uniquely, you can name the relationships "located in state" and "located in country", but that isn't elegant. It does mean that they can be described in a straightforward way, however. If, on the other hand, you want to permit duplicate relationship names, you have to say something like:

Both **City** and **State** are members of the class of things that happen to be "located in" something. In the first case, all values of the **State** a **City** may be *located in* are from the class **State**. In the second case, all values of the

Country a **State** may be *located in* are from the class
Country.*

Up until now, we have been concerned with the differing world views
between the object-oriented designers and developers and the conceptual
entity/relationship analysts. The semantic web is introducing a third
world-view altogether.

Summary – The "Reconciliation"

The history of modern information technology started with the invention
of the computer in the 1940's, followed by its use as a complex, research-
oriented electronic device throughout the 1950's. Programming was
originally in machine language (in zeros and ones), until Assembly
Language provided alphanumeric mnemonics for the instructions. Only
in the late 1950s did more sophisticated programming languages
(specifically Fortran and COBOL) make it possible for people with
problems to use its computing power and its power for abstraction. This
led to the development of the data processing industry throughout the
1960s.

Structured programming and design provided a more systematic way to
pursue what remained a procedural approach to programming.

Meanwhile, Ole-Johan Dahl and Kristen Nygaard invented Simula-67
with a completely different approach to programming—organizing
programs around the data manipulated and the objects they described,
instead of around the processes.

In the late 1960s, computer time-sharing introduced people to the idea of
interacting directly with computers in order to perform business tasks.
Starting in 1980, the personal computer placed that computer power
right on people's desks. Business people could now use computers
directly, which meant that the approach to programming had to change.
As it happens, programming user interfaces is very difficult with
procedural languages, but relatively easy using object-oriented ones. The
era of object-orientation applications began in about 1985. Toward the
end of the 1980s, using graphics to present object structures became
popular, culminating in the introduction of UML in the mid-1990s.

---

*   You may think this is a *very strange* way of looking at the world. If so,
     you are right. But that's how it is…

Meanwhile, the people responsible for managing that data struggled through the 1960s. Charles Bachman invented the original database management systems, IDS, and eventually IDMS. CODASYL created a standard for organizing database management systems, but that organization—into hierarchies—was too complex to manage reasonably. Then, in 1970, Dr. Edward Codd presented his views of how to organize data: use simple two dimensional tables—a disciplined approach derived from relational theory in mathematics..

This was not accepted immediately, but within ten years, relational database management systems were on the market. It took another ten years after that, however, before they were economically viable.

In 1976, Philip Chen introduced the world to data modeling—using graphics to represent the inherent structure of data. This went through several generations, with information-engineering and the Harry Ellis-Richard Barker method being thoroughly in place by 1990.

Ever since the advent of manufacturing planning systems in the late 1970s, companies have realized that managing a modern, automated business relies heavily on having high quality data. This recognition resulted in the evolution of data management as a discipline, and "data quality" as a movement.

Now, there are two communities, populated by people who are each largely unfamiliar with the disciplines of the other. On one side, you have people who are charged with designing and building systems. The body of knowledge they have mastered is concerned with design and construction using object-oriented technology. The other consists of business people who are responsible for the management of data as a corporate resource, along with the systems analysts, data administrators, and database administrators who support those business people. There are at least two bodies of knowledge here: The business dimensions of data management, including the semantics of human communications, and the technology of systems development.

It is incumbent upon both groups to understand each other better. This book is an attempt to bridge that gap. Figure B-14 shows this.

And just to make things interesting, that thread squeezed in between the two streams—showing the development of the Internet and the World Wide Web, and leading to the Semantic Web—this is going to be bigger than both of them. But that is yet to come.

That will be the subject of another book.

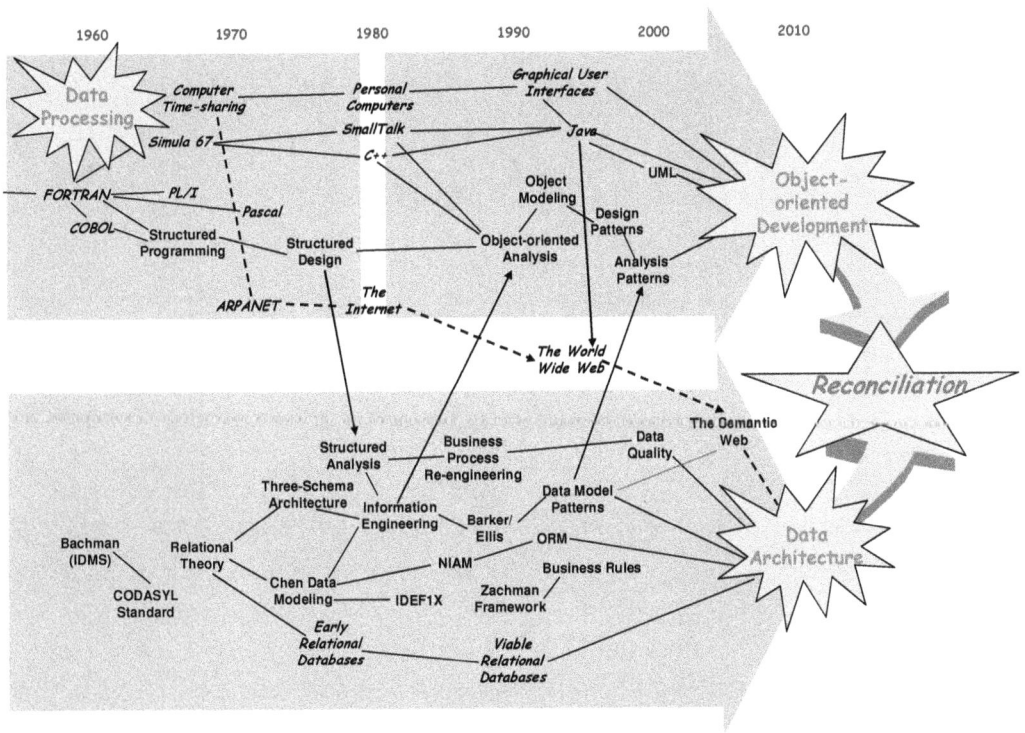

Figure B-14: Reconciliation

Glossary

The following pages contain definitions of both the specialized words highlighted in the text of this book, and of each entity class present in its models. In the definitions, other defined words are also highlighted. Note that this includes not only terms directly associated with UML and data modeling, but words from adjacent disciplines as well.

To the right of each definition is a list of the chapters in which the term is discussed. The first occurrence is listed first.

Term	Definition	Chapter
{isId}	In UML, a property of an attribute or an association to designate that it is part of the unique identifier for a class. (New in 2011)	3
<<ID>>	A **stereotype** that can be used instead of {isId} to designate that an attribute or an association is a unique identifier for a class.	3
aesthetics	A pleasing appearance or effect, based on a branch of philosophy dealing with the nature of beauty, art, and taste and with the creation and appreciation of beauty.[142]	1
algorithmic programming	(See procedural programming)	Appendix B
annotation	UML allows notes to be added to a drawing, linked to a drawing object. This is one of those notes.	2
architect's view	In the *architecture framework*, this is the third row representing the view of those who are concerned with the underlying fundamental structure of an enterprise's data. This is as opposed to the *business owner's view*, the perspective of those carrying out the business's activities, or the *designer's view*, the perspective of those setting about to specify how to use technology to meet the enterprise's information processing requirements.	1
essential data model	A representation of the entity classes that describe the underlying structure of an organization. The entity classes, attributes, and relationships are a portion of the semantics that could describe the organization, but these focus on fundamental concepts.	1

---

[142] Merriam-Webster Online Dictionary. "aesthetics". Retrieved 7/19/2011 from http://www.merriam-webster.com/dictionary/aesthetics.

Term	Definition	Chapter
architecture framework	David Hay's variation on the **Zachman Framework**. His rows describe the views of: planners, business owners, architects, designers, builders, and the production system.	2
ARPANET	the world's first operational packet switching network and the core network of a set that came to compose the global Internet. The network was funded by the Defense Advanced Research Projects Agency (DARPA) of the United States Department of Defense for use by its projects at universities and research laboratories in the US. The packet switching of the ARPANET was based on designs by Lawrence Roberts of the Lincoln Laboratory.	Appendix B
assembly language	"A low-level programming language for computers, microprocessors, microcontrollers, and other integrated circuits. It implements a symbolic representation of the binary machine codes and other constants needed to program a given CPU architecture. This representation is usually defined by the hardware manufacturer, and is based on mnemonics that symbolize processing steps (instructions), processor registers, memory locations, and other language features. An assembly language is thus specific to a certain physical (or virtual) computer architecture."[143]	Appendix B

---

[143] Wikipedia, 2010, "Assembly Language". Retrieved October 10, 2010 from *http://en.wikipedia.org/wiki/Assembly_language*.

Term	Definition	Chapter
association	The fact that one class Is in some way related to another. This may be an inheritance relationship (one is a sub-type of the other) or an associative relationship (instances of one are in some way associated with specific instances of the other.) This is analogous (but not equivalent) to the entity/relationship concept *relationship*)	2
association class	In UML design, this is a class attached to an association as a means to describe attributes of the association. This constrains the relationship, however, such that there can be no duplicate instances of a particular combination of the two entity classes. It is preferable to define a full-blown *intersect entity class*.	3
attribute	Relational theory: In Dr. Codd's constraints, the definition of a value given to a tuple (row). Data modeling and UML: definition of a characteristic evaluated for or describing instances of an entity class.	Appendix B, 3
basic entity class	An entity class specified directly in an entity/relationship model, as opposed to a *virtual entity class* that is defined from a combination of *basic entity classes* and *relationships.*	2
behavior	How an object acts and reacts, in terms of its state changes and message passing. [Booch, 1994, p. 86]	3
builder's view	In the *architecture framework*, this is the second row representing the view of those who carry out the activities of the enterprise. This is as opposed to the *planner's view,* the perspective of those laying out the basic terms of the business, or the *architect's view,* the perspective of those identifying the underlying structure of the enterprise's data.	1

Term	Definition	Chapter
business concept modeler	A person who creates models to represent the concepts of interest to the people who run a business, without regard for technology that might be used to carry out that business.	1
business owner's view	(See Owner's View.)	1
business process model	A graphic representation of *business processes* and the flow of data among them.	1
business process	An activity carried out in the course of conducting the enterprise's mission, described in terms of sequence and the transformation of inputs to outputs.	1
business rule	A constraint that affects either the data that can be captured, an activity that can be performed, or both.	2, Appendix B
cardinality	A constraint on an attribute or a relationship end determining how many of something can be associated with something else. Also used interchangeably with *maximum cardinality*.	2, Appendix B
child relation	In a relational structure, where there is a "one-to-many" relationship (one instance in one relation related to many instances in the other relation), this is the relation on the "many" side.	Appendix B
class	"the descriptor for a set of objects that share the same attributes, operations, methods, relationship, and behavior." [Rumbaugh, *et. al.* 1999, p. 185]	2

Term	Definition	Chapter
COBOL	"One of the oldest programming languages. Its name is an acronym for **CO**mmon **B**usiness-**O**riented **L**anguage, defining its primary domain in business, finance, and administrative systems for companies and governments."[144]	Appendix B
code set	A set of legal values for a column in a database. Compare with *"value set"*.	2
completeness rule	In the entity/relationship modeling, a constraint dictating that each instance of a super-type must be an instance of one of its sub-types.	4
composition	In a UML association, a symbol describing that instances of one class are components of instances of the other class.	3
communications protocol	a formal description of digital message formats and the rules for exchanging those messages in or between computing systems and in telecommunications. Protocols may include signaling, authentication and error detection and correction capabilities. A protocol defines the syntax, semantics, and synchronization of communication, and the specified behavior is typically independent of how it is to be implemented. A protocol can therefore be implemented as hardware or software or both.	Appendix B
conceptual data model	A kind of entity/relationship data model that describes things of significance to the business, their attributes, and relationships among them.	2

---

[144] Wikipedia, 2010, "Cobol". Retrieved October 10, 2010 from http://en.wikipedia.org/wiki/Cobol.

Term	Definition	Chapter
conceptual schema	An arrangement of the elements of a conceptual schema that consists of fundamental things of significance to the business, their attributes, and relationships among them.	*Appendix B*
cohesion	*Program Design:* "How tightly bound or related its internal elements are to one another."[145]	*Appendix B*
computer time-sharing	A technology invented in 1961, where by multiple people interact with a single computer, with each imagining exclusive use. The processing is sliced so that each person's work is interspersed with everyone else's work, but a controller keeps the streams all separated and correctly reassembling the results. This is as opposed to **batch processing** whereby individual jobs are submitted as units of work and processed sequentially.	Appendix B
construction	The phase of the **system development life cycle** concerned with actually creating the designed system or other artifacts.	Appendix B
copula	In the field of logic, what remains of the predicate: the *copula*. This is "a part of the verb *be* connecting a subject and predicate".[146] That is, this is the "must be" or "may be" in relationship role sentences.	2
coupling	The amount of information that must be passed from one module to another. As Messrs. Yourdon and Constantine put it, this is "the degree of interdependence between modules".[147]	Appendix B

---

[145] Edward Yourdon and Larry L. Constantine, 1979, *Op. cit.* 106.

[146] *DK Illustrated Oxford Dictionary.* 1998, *Op. cit.* 187.

[147] C. Finkelstein, 1992, Information Engineering: Strategic Systems Development (Sydney: Addison-Wesley) 85.

Term	Definition	Chapter
CRUD matrix	A matrix correlating a set of business processes or functions with the entity classes that each (c)reates, (r)etreives, (u)pdates, or (d)eletes.	2
cultural impedance mismatch	The divergence of attitudes between the object-oriented community and the data community.[148] This includes both the "architects" and "designers" in the data world, vs. the "designers" in the object-oriented world. A metaphor derived from *impedance matching* in the electrical engineering industry.	2
DARPA	The Defense Advanced Research Projects Agency (also known as ARPA), that is, among other things, the source of **ARPANET**, the precursor to the Internet.	Appendix B
data administration	(See data management)	Appendix B
data architecture	The discipline of defining the things of significance to an enterprise, the characteristics of each, and how they are related together. In this book, the term refers to the historical thread leading to the consensus that data represent an important corporate asset.	Appendix B
database administration	The management of database management systems, including ensuring that versions are current, training, and sometimes, database design.	Appendix B
database modeler	A person who develops data models to support the tasks associated with designing a database.	1
data flow	In a *data flow diagram,* the fact that a specified kind of data may flow between two *processes* or between an *external entity* and a *process*.	Appendix B

---

[148] S. Ambler, 2009, *Op. cit.*

Term	Definition	Chapter
data flow diagram	A graphic representation of a set of processes, outside sources of data, stores of data, and the data flows connecting them all together.	2, Appendix B
data governance	The exercise of authority and control (planning, monitoring, and enforcement) over the management of data assets. The data governance function guides how all other data management functions are performed.[149]	Appendix B
data management	An effort by an enterprise or government agency to manage its data and information as an asset. This involves programs for improving data quality, data stewardship, and others.	Appendix B
data model	(See entity/relationship data model)	2
data processing	The original term used to describe the information technology industry. This highlighted the fact that it concerned the computers that processed data, more than other associated technologies.	1. Appendix B
data store	In a *data flow diagram*, the fact that a particular kind of data is stored somewhere temporarily. It is created by one *process* for potential use by another *process*.	Appendix B
data type	A characteristic of an *attribute* that describes the kind of symbols (characters, digits, etc.) used to describe the values of that attribute. This can be expanded in UML to describe templates for the values, such as for a social security number or for a US telephone number. It does not go so far as to describe lists of values or validation algorithms.	2

---

[149] DAMA International, 2009, The DAMA Guide to the Data Management Body of Knowledge (Bradley Beach, NJ: Technics Publications, LLC).

Term	Definition	Chapter
declarative language	A language that describes what it wants to accomplish rather than focusing on how to achieve its goal. Writing a declarative program is not about specifying a sequence of statements to run one after another to create an application, but to write declarative statements that show a relationship between each other.[150]	Appendix B
derived attribute	An attribute whose value is not fixed upon entry for storage, but which is derived from other attribute values. This is an architectural concept. The physical design of a database may call for it to be derived before input, rather than being derived when it is retrieved.	2
designer's view	In the *architecture framework*, this is the fourth row representing the view of those who are concerned with applying technology to meet the requirements of the enterprise—especially for information processing. This is as opposed to the *architect's view*, the perspective of those analyzing the fundamental structure of an enterprise's information, or the *builder's view*, the perspective of those who apply technology to create the products designed by the designers.	1
detailed representation	(See builder's view.)	1
Domain Name	Text describing a particular **Uniform Resource Locator** on the **World Wide Web**. This also is used for routing **Electronic Mail**.	Appendix B
Domain Name System	The set of software distributed throughout the Internet to map **domain names** (**Uniform Resource Locators**) to **IP Addresses**.	Appendix B

---

[150] Paul Leahy. 2011. "Declarative Language". *About.com*. Retrieved 7/19/2011   from http://java.about.com/od/d/g/declarativelang.htm.

Term	Definition	Chapter
DNS	(See **Domain Name System**)	Appendix B
electronic mail	A system for posting messages on a computer network, so they can be read by designated recipients. While the makings of this came about in the early 1960s, the system as it is known today was invented in 1972 by Ray Tomlinson.	
enterprise model	(see ***business owner's view***.)	1
email, or e-mail	(See ***electronic mail***.)	
entity class	The definition of a set of similar things of significance to a business, or a *problem space*. A sub-set of all possible *classes*.	2
entity life history	A kind of model in which, for each entity class, it represents the behavior of that entity class in terms of the events in the world that affect the data described by the entity class. A simple event in the world is represented by a box. Strung across from left to right are events that cause instances to be created, cause them to change in some way, and cause them to be removed. A symbol could have boxes under it, representing components of the event. Annotations indicate whether the event is repeated, or whether it is optional. Separately, a more detailed model can add symbols to represent operations carried out in response to these events.[151]	2
entity/relation ship data model	A graphic representation of categories of data elements, their attributes, and relationships between them.	2

---

[151] Among other sources, see David C. Hay, 2003, *Op. cit.*

Term	Definition	Chapter
enumeration	"A user-definable data type. It has a name and an ordered list of enumeration literal names, each of which is a value in the range of the data type—that is, it is a predefined instance of the data type."[152] It is represented in this book by a class box with the *stereotype* <<enumeration>>.	3
essential data flow diagram	A *data flow diagram* whose processes are described without reference to any mechanisms that might carry them out. The processes are organized so that any *external event* causes only one to be carried out. Any fragments of flows or processes that might be triggered by this event are subsumed under this *essential process*. This is a more rigorous definition of a *logical data flow diagram*.	Appendix B
event	In a *state/transition diagram*, something that happens to cause a *transition* from one *state* to another *state.*	2
exclusivity rule	A constraint that can be applied in entity/relationship modeling that asserts that any instance of a super-type entity class can be an instance of *no more than one* sub-type entity classes.	Appendix B
exclusive or constraint	A constraint that can be described in a model between two or more relationships. This asserts that one entity class may (or must) be related to one or another second class, but not more than one. In UML, this is the "XOR" constraint and can only be between two relationships. In the Barker/Ellis notation, it can be across any number of relationships.	Appendix B

---

[152] James Rumbaugh, *et. al.* 1999. *Op. cit.*

Term	Definition	Chapter
external entity	A person or organization outside the scope of a *date flow diagram* that is the ultimate source and/or destination of all data described by the diagram.	Appendix B
external schema	An arrangement of the elements in a subject area that consists of things seen and known by the viewer, their characteristics, and relationships among them.	Appendix B
external event	An *event* which is caused by something outside the organization's control, such as "receipt of a sales order", or "hurricane".	Appendix B
event	Something that happens in the world that causes an activity or a process to take place.	Appendix B
first normal form	*Relational Theory:* the first of Dr. Codd's constraints on a relational design: Every *tuple* (row) may have only one value for an *attribute* (column) in a *relation* (table).[153]	Appendix B
fifth normal form	*Relational Theory:* the fifth of Dr. Codd's constraints on a relational design: A three-way (or more) relationship is redundant if all its occurrences may be derived from combinations of two-way occurrences.	Appendix B
foreign key	*Data base design:* A column in a relational database table that corresponds to a column in a *primary key* in a different database table, for the purpose of retrieving instances of that second table. *Relational theory:* an attribute in a relation that is logically associated with an attribute that is part of a *primary key* in another relation, for the purpose of associating instances of the two relations.	2

---

[153] David C. Hay, 2003, *Op. cit.* 413.

Term	Definition	Chapter
Fortran	"A general-purpose, procedural, imperative programming language that is especially suited to numeric computation and scientific computing."[154]	Appendix B
fourth normal form	*Relational Theory:* the fourth of Dr. Codd's constraints on a relational design: there may be no independent sets of dependencies within a *primary key.* [155]	Appendix B
function	An activity or set of activities performed by an enterprise in order to carry out its mission, or in support of such activities. This is without regard either to sequence or to any mechanisms required to carry it out.	?
function hierarchy	A graphic description of the hierarchy that represents what an enterprise does, beginning with its *mission* and the 6 or 7 or 8 functions required to support that mission. Each of these is then described in terms of 6 or 6 or 8 sub-functions, and so forth until the most atomic functions are revealed.	2
fundamental concepts, model of	(See architect's view.)	1
functioning system	In the *architecture framework*, this is the fourth row representing the view of a completed system in a particular location or set of locations.	1
http	(See *hypertext transfer protocol.*)	Appendix B
http	(See *hypertext transfer protocol.*)	Appendix B
HTML	See *Hypertext Markup Language*.	Appendix B

---

[154] Wikipedia, 2010, "Fortran". Retrieved October 10, 2010 from http://en.wikipedia.org/wiki/Fortran

[155] David C. Hay, 2003, *Op. cit.* 413.

Term	Definition	Chapter
hypertext	The fact that a bit of text on one *Web Page* can be used to automatically retrieve text from some other *Web Page*, anywhere on the *Internet*.	Appendix B
hyperlink	The path through the *Internet* by which *hypertext* is retrieved.	Appendix B
Hypertext Markup Language	The publishing language of the *World Wide Web* and contains the commands necessary to retrieve a desired document, transmit it and present it on the recipient's computer. It may also contain pieces of program code to present animation and accept input data.	Appendix B
hypertext transfer protocol (http)	A networking protocol for distributed, collaborative, hypermedia information systems. HTTP is the foundation of data communication for the *World Wide Web*. HTTP functions as a request-response protocol in the client-server computing model. In HTTP, a *web browser*, for example, acts as a *client*, while an application running on a computer hosting a *web site* functions as a *server*. The client submits an HTTP *request* message to the server. The server, which stores content, or provides *resources*, such as HTML files, or performs other functions on behalf of the client, returns a response message to the client. A response contains completion status information about the request and may contain any content requested by the client in its message body.[156]	Appendix B

---

[156] Wikipedia. 2011. "HTTP". Retrieved 7/28/2011 from http://en.wikipedia.org/wiki/Hypertext_Transfer_Protocol

Term	Definition	Chapter
impedance matching	*In electrical engineering:* the requirement for a transformer (or other device) to make the load (impedance) required on a target device (such as a loudspeaker) match the load produced on a source device (such as an amplifier). *In information technology:* the problems associated with making objects in an object-oriented program *persistent*, by saving them in a relational data base. The underlying structure of a relational database is vastly different from the underlying structure of object-oriented code, and the problems associated with translating one to the other have led to the adoption of this term to describe those problems.	2
inheritance	The fact that each instance of a sub-type has as properties all of the attributes and relationships of its super-type.	Appendix B
internal event	An *event* that is the completion of an activity under the control of the enterprise.	Appendix B
internal schema	An arrangement of the elements in a subject area that consists of data elements as they are stored in a particular computer storage device, along with relationships among them. Variations include the *logical schema* and the *physical schema*.	Appendix B
The Internet	A global system of interconnected computer networks that use the standard *Internet Protocol Suite* (TCP/IP) to serve billions of users worldwide. It is a *network of networks* that consists of millions of private, public, academic, business, and government networks, of local to global scope, that are linked by a broad array of electronic, wireless and optical networking technologies. The Internet can also be defined as a worldwide interconnection of computers and computer networks that facilitate the sharing or exchange of information among users.	Appendix B

Term	Definition	Chapter
Internet Protocol Suite	The formal name for **Transmission Control Protocol / Internet Protocol**.)	Appendix B
intersect entity class	An entity class with two many-to-one relationships between it and one or two other entity classes. It is defined to be the fact that a particular instance of an entity class is associated with a particular instance of another entity class.	3
logical data flow diagram	A *data flow diagram* that is not in terms of any physical mechanisms. It simply describes the processes (in non-technical terms) and the flows of data from one to another. Also more precisely defined as an *essential data flow diagram*.	Appendix B
logical data model	A kind of entity/relationship data model that describes things of significance and their relationships, in terms compatible with a particular data management technology.	2
logical schema	An arrangement of the elements of a subject area that consists of the things of significance in the *conceptual schema*, but organized in accordance with a particular database technology, such as relational, object-oriented classes, etc. Part of an *internal schema*.	Appendix B
maximum cardinality	*Attributes:* How many values an attribute may take. In fact, this number can never be more than 1. *Relationships:* How many instances of a second entity class may be associated with an instance of the first entity class. Typically is "1" or "*" (meaning "unlimited")	2, Appendix B
message	A communication from one object to another, triggering an *operation*.	3

Term	Definition	Chapter
minimum cardinality	*Attributes:* If an attribute must have a value, this is "1". If it may or may not have a value, this is "0". *Relationship:* If an instance of one entity class must be associated with at least one instance of another entity class, this is "1". If it may or may not be associated with anything, this is "0".	2, Appendix B
mission	The ongoing operational activity of the enterprise. The mission describes what the business is or will be doing on a day-to-day basis.[157]	2
multiple inheritance	A situation where an entity class is a sub-type of more than one other entity class.	2
multiple type hierarchy	A violation of the *exclusivity rule* for sub-types. That is, an instance of a super-type may be an instance of *more than one* sub-types.	2
namespace	*Object-oriented design*: "A part of the model in which the names may be defined and used. Within a namespace, each name has a unique meaning. All named elements are declared in a namespace, and their names have scope within it. The top-level namespaces are packages whose purpose is to group elements primarily for human access and understandability, and also to organize models for computer storage and manipulation during development."[158]	3
NCP	(See *Network Controlled Protocol*)	Appendix B
Network Controlled Protocol	The first packet-switching *protocol* to be used in *ARPANET*.	Appendix B

---

[157] The Business Rules Group. 2005. "The Business Motivation Model: Business Governance in a Volatile World".

[158] James Rumbaugh, *et. al.* 1999. *Op. cit.*

Term	Definition	Chapter
object	*Logic:* The class of things that are operated on by a *subject*, as part of a *predicate*. *Grammar:* "A noun or noun equivalent (as a pronoun, gerund, or clause) denoting the goal or result of the action of a verb."[159] *Object orientation:* "Discrete entity with a well-defined boundary and identity that encapsulates state and behavior; an instance of a class."[160]	2
object class model	A graphic representation of the structure of a set of classes and associations among them.	1
object model	A graphic representation of the structure of a set of object instances and associations among them.	2
object-oriented analysis	A method for analyzing system requirements that produces object class models as its principal result.	2
object-oriented approach	(...to systems development) This views the task of designing a system in terms of *objects* that are described by bits of software to be manipulated by programs.	2
object-oriented design model	A description of the artifacts of specifying a design for one or more object-oriented programs. UML is commonly used to represent this.	Appendix B
object-oriented development	An approach to systems development that presumes the technology to be used for implementation will be object-oriented programming.	1-4, Appendix B

---

[159] Merriam Webster, 2010, "object". Merriam-Webster On-line Dictionary. Retrieved on October 1, 2010. from http://www.merriam-webster.com/dictionary/object.

[160] James Rumbaugh, *et. al.* 1999. *Op. cit.*

Term	Definition	Chapter
Object Role Modeling (ORM)	A modeling technique that—rather than representing entity classes as analogues of relational tables—shows *relationships* (that contain one or more "roles" in ORM parlance) to be such analogs. Like Mr. Barker's notation, it makes extensive use of language in making the models accessible to the public, but unlike any of the other modeling techniques, it has much greater capacity to describe business rules and constraints.	Appendix B
operation	An action that one object performs on another, triggered by receipt of a ***message***.	3
optionality	(See minimum cardinality.)	3
ORM	(See object role modeling.)	Appendix B
ordered (relationship)	A property of an association that asserts the instances of the related class will appear in a particular sequence.	3
OWL	(See Web Ontology Language)	Appendix B
owner's view	In the ***architecture framework***, this is the second row representing the view of those who carry out the activities of operating the business. This is as opposed to the **planner's view**, the perspective of the top executives, defining the enterprise's direction and business purpose., or ***architect's view,*** the perspective of those who are concerned with the underlying fundamental structure of an enterprise's data.	1
package	A UML symbol used to describe a general-purpose for organizing elements into groups. Packages may be nested within other packages.[161]	Appendix B

[161] James Rumbaugh, *et. al.* 1999. *Op. cit.* 379

Term	Definition	Chapter
packet switched network	A network technology that moves data in separate, small blocks -- packets -- based on the destination address in each packet. When received, packets are reassembled in the proper sequence to make up the message. This approach does not require a continuous connection between the sender and the receiver. This is as opposed to circuit-switched networks that are used for telephone calls. Circuit-switched networks require dedicated point-to-point connections during calls.[162]	Appendix B
parent relation	In a relational structure, where there is a "one-to-many" relationship (one instance in one relation related to many instances in the other relation), this is the relation on the "one" side.	Appendix B
persistent data (persistence)	Data processed by a program that must be kept after the program has completed its work and been removed from memory.	2
physical data flow diagram	A *data flow diagram* in which processes are defined in terms of the mechanisms (forms, systems, communications mechanism) required to carry them out.	Appendix B
physical design	Based on the requirements identified in the previous phase of the *systems development life cycle*, design of the database structure, the applications program structure, and the organizational structure that will support the world to be created.	Appendix B

---

[162] Lee Copland. 2000. "QuickStudy: Packet-Switched vs. Circuit-Switched Networks" *Computerworld*. March 20, 2000.

Term	Definition	Chapter
physical schema	An arrangement of the things in a subject area that consists of physical elements of data storage technology and the relationships among them. Part of an *internal schema*.	Appendix B
planner's view	In the *architecture framework*, this is the first row representing the perspective of the top executives, defining the enterprise's direction and business purpose. This is as opposed to the *owner's view*, the perspective of those who carry out the activities of operating the business.	1
predicate	What is affirmed or denied about the subject".[163] That is, the preposition that describes the content of an assertion being made.	3,4
primary key	*Relational design:* a set of columns, the value of which distinguishes between instances of a table. *Relational theory:* a set of attributes, the value of which distinguishes between instances of a relation.	Appendix B
problem space	A domain of interest that is the reason for and object of an effort to solve problems. This consists of the real-world (concrete or abstract) things that are of interest.	2
procedural programming	An approach to creating computer programs that is organized in terms of the steps required to carry out a programming task (a "procedure"). Also called an *algorithmic* approach.	Appendix B

---

[163] *DK Illustrated Oxford Dictionary*, 1998, *Op. cit.* 642.

Term	Definition	Chapter
procedural language	A programming language that requires programming discipline, such as C/C++, Java, COBOL, FORTRAN, Perl and JavaScript. Also called an "imperative language," programmers writing in such languages must develop a proper order of actions in order to solve the problem, based on a knowledge of data processing and programming.[164]	Appendix B
production	The phase of the *system development life cycle* concerned with the ongoing process of monitoring the new system, fixing errors, and anticipating future improvements.	Appendix B
RDF	(See Resource Description Framework.)	Appendix B
RDF Schema	A vocabulary for describing properties and classes of RDF resources, with a semantics for generalization-hierarchies of such properties and classes.	Appendix B
relation	In Dr. Codd's relational theory, this is equivalent to a *table*. That is, it is a collection of attributes, populated by a series of *tuples* that each has a value for each of the specified attributes.	Appendix B
relational database approach	This views the task of designing a system in terms of first defining the structure of a repository that will hold the data involved, plus programs to populate, manipulate, and retrieve those data.	2

---

[164] The Free Dictionary. "Procedural Programming". Retrieved 7/19/2011 from http://encyclopedia2.thefreedictionary.com/procedural+language

Term	Definition	Chapter
relationship	The fact that one entity class is in some way associated with another. This may be an inheritance relationship (one is a sub-type of the other) or an associative relationship (instances of one are in some way associated with specific instances of the other.) (see also *association*)	2
requirements analysis	A phase of the **system development life cycle** that entails (for a particular part of the company) determination of the nature of a significant part of the company, and its information processing shortcomings. From this comes a vision of what future systems should accomplish	Appendix B
resource description framework	A data model[ling language] for objects ("resources") and relations between them, provides a simple semantics for this data model, and these data models can be represented in an XML syntax.[165] Resource Description Framework (RDF) is a foundation for processing metadata; it provides interoperability between applications that exchange machine-understandable information on the Web. The broad goal of RDF is to define a mechanism for describing resources that makes no assumptions about a particular application domain, nor defines (a priori) the semantics of any application domain. The definition of the mechanism should be domain neutral, yet the mechanism should be suitable for describing information about any domain.	Appendix B

---

[165] World Wide Web Consortium. 2004. *OWL Web Ontology Language Overview.* Retrieved 7/20/2011 from http://www.w3.org/TR/2004/REC-owl-features-20040210/#s1.2.

Term	Definition	Chapter
solution space	A domain of interest that includes the various technological mechanisms that are being brought to bear on the problems in a particular problem space.	1
state diagram	(See *state/transition diagram*.)	2
state / transition diagram	A diagram to describe the "behavior" of either a part of the business or a particular entity class. This model portrays each *state* (the particular condition that someone or something is in at a specific time) and each *event* (something that happens) that moves the part of the business or entity class from one state to another. Note that the *transition* described refers to the event that caused it, rather than the process.	2
state	In a *state/transition diagram*, the particular condition that someone or something is in at a specific time. This either precedes or follows a *transition*.	2
stored procedure	A piece of code that is imbedded into a relational database that does provide some behavior associated with database transactions.	2
strategy	The part of the *system development life cycle* concerned with determining the mission, vision, goals, and objectives, first of the company as a whole, and then of this particular effort. This is actually composed of "Corporate Strategic Planning" and "Business Unit Strategic Planning".[166]	Appendix B

---

[166] Clive Finkelstein, 1992, Information Engineering: Strategic Systems Development (Sydney: Addison Wesley).

Term	Definition	Chapter
rim shot	For a stand-up comedian's routine, this is the drum roll telling the audience that something humorous has just been said. (In case they missed it.) (Think ☺.)	3
row	An instance of a *table*, with a value for each *attribute* in the *table*. (Known in relational theory as a *tuple*.)	Appendix B
scope	(See planner's view.)	1
second normal form	Relational theory: the second of Dr. Codd's constraints on a relational design: Each attribute must be dependent on the entire *primary key*.[167]	Appendix B
semantic web	Derived from the World Wide Web, which is an infrastructure that supports a web of *pages*, the semantic web supports a web at the level of data.	Appendix B
structured programming	An approach to programming requiring all system logic to be expressed in terms of "IF/THEN/ELSE" statements. Doing so creates programs that are provably correct. Among other things, this approach eliminated the "GOTO" statements that were a significant contributor to program complexity.	Appendix B
structured design	Provided guidance for organizing programs into coherent modules. The approach addressed the problem of how to divide a large program design into digestible modules. [168]	Appendix B

---

[167] David C. Hay, 2003, Requirements Analysis: From Business Views to Architecture. (Englewood Cliffs, NJ: Prentice Hall PTR). 432.

[168] Edward Yourdon and Larry L. Constantine, 1979, Structured Design: Fundamentals of a Discipline of Computer Program and Systems Design (Englewood Cliffs, NJ: Prentice Hall). (Widely circulated as an unpublished manuscript in 1976.)

Term	Definition	Chapter
subject	The term of a logical proposition that denotes the entity of which something is affirmed or denied.[169]	2
system development life cycle	An approach to developing systems developed by Clive Finkelstein and James Martin (and refined by the Oracle Corporation), that starts with *strategic planning*, then progresses through *requirements analysis*, *physical design*, *construction*, *transition*, and *production*.	Appendix B
table	In a relational database management system, this is a collection of data, organized in terms of a set of attributes, and populated by one or more rows (called *tuples* by Dr. Codd).	Appendix B
TCP/IP	(See *Transmission Control Protocol / Internet Protocol*.)	Appendix B
technology model	(see designer's view.)	1
third normal form	Relational theory: the third of Dr. Codd's constraints on relational design: Each *attribute* must be dependent *only* on the *primary key*.	Appendix B
transition	In a *state/transition diagram*, the action of moving from one *state* to another.	2

---

[169] Merriam Webster, 2010, "object". Merriam-Webster On-line
        Dictionary. Retrieved on October 1, 2010. from
        http://www.merriam-
        webster.com/dictionary/subject?show=0&t=1285963736

Term	Definition	Chapter
Transmission Control Protocol / Internet Protocol	Two computer network protocols created in the 1970s by DARPA, an agency of the United States Department of Defense. These evolved from ARPANET, which was the world's first wide area network and a predecessor of the Internet. The TCP/IP model, or Internet Protocol Suite, describes a set of general design guidelines and implementations of specific networking protocols to enable computers to communicate over a network. TCP/IP provides end-to-end connectivity specifying how data should be formatted, addressed, transmitted, routed and received at the destination. Protocols exist for a variety of different types of communication services between computers.170 There are actually two protocols: "the simple IP which provided only for addressing and forwarding of individual packets, and the separate TCP, which was concerned with service features such as flow control and recovery from lost packets."[171]	Appendix B
transition	The phase in the **system development life cycle** concerned with the task of enterprise management to understand the implications of the new technology and to manage its implementation. This includes educating the enterprise as a whole as to the implications of the new system, training the people who will use it, and populating the initial stage of the database, either through data entry or through conversion of legacy data.	Appendix B

---

[170] Wikipedia. 2011. "TCP/IP Model". Retrieved 7/27/2011 from http://en.wikipedia.org/wiki/TCP/IP_model.

[171] Barry M. Leiner, *et. al.* 2011. *Op. cit.*

Term	Definition	Chapter
tuple	Dr. Codd's term (derived from relational algebra) for a *row* in a *table* (in a *relation*).	Appendix B
UML class model	A kind of UML static model that describes categories of objects, attributes of them, and associations between them. One of several kinds of UML models.	2
Uniform Resource Locator	A text label that is a synonym for an *IP Code* that locates a node on the *Internet*. The label is in natural language so that a human being can understand the nature of the node and the kinds of things to be found there.	Appendix B
Universal Resource Identifier	An extended *URL* that identifies the location of a term on the *Internet*. It is of the form <URL>#<term>.	Appendix B
URI	(See *Universal Resource Identifier*)	Appendix B
URL	(See *Uniform Resource Locator*)	Appendix B
value set	A list of legal values for an attribute in an architectural model. This is as opposed to a *"code set"*, that is a more specific list of values for a column in a data base. For example, a *value set* might be "States in the United States", without respect to how each would be represented. One of several corresponding *code sets* would be the list of state codes, or postal abbreviations, or official names.	2
verbal auxiliary	*Grammar:* "Accompanying another verb and typically expressing person, number, mood, or tense."[172] "Must" and "may" in the expressions "must be" and "may be" are verbal auxiliaries.	2

---

[172] Merriam Webster. "auxiliary". Retrieved on September 28, 2010 from http://www.merriam-webster.com/dictionary/auxiliary.

Term	Definition	Chapter
virtual entity class	A derived entity, based on a specified combination of **basic entity classes** and relationships.	2
visibility	An annotation of attributes in UML that describes the extent to which the values of an attribute can be used outsider reference to the class in which the attribute is found.	3
Web Ontology Language	A vocabulary that adds more vocabulary to **RDF** and **RDF Schema** for describing properties and classes: among others, relations between classes (e.g. disjointness), cardinality (e.g. "exactly one"), equality, richer typing of properties, characteristics of properties (e.g. symmetry), and enumerated classes.	Appendix B
web browser	A piece of software that uses a file written in the a web language such as **html, XML,** or **Cascading Style Sheets** to formulate requests for and process responses from another **web site**.	Appendix B
web site	An identified site on the **World Wide Web** that provides to anyone asking documents, pictures, or any other resources that can be translated into binary form for electronic transmission. It may also include programs that can be invoked from long distance. The web site is uniquely identified by a text label called a **uniform resource locator**. It is also identified to the internet by an **IP Address.**	Appendix B
World Wide Web	a system of interlinked **hypertext** documents accessed via **the Internet**. With a **web browser**, one can view web pages that may contain text, images, videos, and other multimedia and navigate between them via **hyperlinks**.[173]	Appendix B

[173] Wikipedia. 2011. "World Wide Web". Retrieved 8/4/2011 from http://en.wikipedia.org/wiki/World_wide_web.

Term	Definition	Chapter
Zachman Framework	The original *architecture framework* in which the world of enterprise system development was laid out in a matrix. Each row represents a particular perspective on the world (scope, business owner, designer, builder, sub-contractor, and production system). Each column represents one of the interrogatives: data ("what"), processes ("how"), location ("where"), people and organizations ("who") timing and events ("when"), and motivation ("why"). The idea is that every artifact of systems development fits into one of the cells.	2

Bibliography

Adams, D. 1982. *The Restaurant at the End of the Universe.* New York:Pocket Books, pp. 37-38.

Allemang, D., Jim Hendler. 2011. *Semantic Web for the Working Ontologist: Effective Modeling in RDFS and OWL.* (Boston: Morgan Kaufmann).

Ambler, S. 2009. "The Cultural Impedance Mismatch", *The Data Administration Newsletter.* August 1, 2009. http://www.tdan.com/view-articles/11066.

American National Standards Institute. 1975. "ANSI/X3/SPARC Study Group on Data Base Management Systems; Interim Report". *FDT*(Bulletin of ACM SIGMOD) 7:2.

American Radio Relay League, 1958. *The Radio Amateur's Handbook: The Standard Manual of Amateur Radio Communication.* (Concord, New Hampshire: The Rumford Press).

Barker, R. 1989. *CASE*Method: Entity Relationship Modeling.* Wokingham, England: Addison Wesley.

Bell, A.E. 2004. "Death by UML Fever", *ACMQueue.* Association for Computing Machinery. Available at: http://queue.acm.org/detail.cfm?id=984495.

Berners-Lee, T. 2000. *Weaving the Web.* (New York: HarperCollins)

Blazek, R. 2004. "Introducing the Linear Reference System in GRASS"., *GRASS User Conference. Proceedings* Bangkok. http://gisws.media.osaka-cu.ac.jp/grass04/ viewpaper.php?id=50.

Booch, G. 1994. *Object-oriented Analysis and Design with Applications.* Redwood City, California: The Benjamin/Cummings Publishing Company, Inc. Pp. 16-17.

Box, George E. P. and Norman R. Draper. 1987. *Empirical Model-Building and Response Surfaces*, Wiley. 424. Available at: http://en.wikiquote.org/wiki/Special:BookSources/0471810339

Brown, R. G. 1993. "Data Modeling Methodologies – Contrasts in Style". *Handbook of Data Management.* Boston: Auerbach.

Bruce, T. 1992. Designing Quality Databases with IDEF1X Information Models. New York: Dorset House.

The Business Rules Group. 2000. "Defining Business Rules ~ What Are They Really?" 4th ed., formerly known as the "GUIDE Business Rules Project Report," (1995). Available at http://businessrulesgroup.org/first_paper/br01c0.htm.

Chen, P. 1977. "The Entity-Relationship Approach to Logical Data Base Design". *The Q.E.D. Monograph Series: Data Management.* Wellesley, MA: Q.E.D. Information Sciences, Inc. This is based on his articles, "The Entity-Relationship Model: Towards a Unified View of Data", ACM Transactions on Database Systems, Vol. 1, No 1, (March 1976), pages 9-36.

Coad, P. and Edward Yourdon. 1990. *Object-oriented Analysis.* Englewood Cliffs, NJ: Yourdon Press/Prentice Hall.

Codd, E. F. 1970. "A Relational Model of Data for Large Shared Data Banks". *Communications of the ACM* Vol. 13, No. 6 (June).

Copland, L., 2000. "QuickStudy: Packet-Switched vs. Circuit-Switched Networks" *Computerworld.* March 20, 2000.

New Jersey: Technics Publications, LLC.

DeMarco, T. 1978. *Structured Analysis and System Specification.* Englewood Cliffs, NJ: Prentice-Hall.

Dikstra, E.W., 1976. *A Discipline of Programming.* Englewood Cliffs, NJ: Prentice-Hall.

DK Illustrated Oxford Dictionary. 1998. New York: Oxford University Press.

Embly, D.W., Barry D. Kurtz, and Scott N. Woodfield. 1992. *Object-oriented Systems Analysis: A Model-driven Approach.* Englewood Cliffs, New Jersey: Prentice-Hall.

Eriksson, H-E, Magnus Penker, Brian Lyons, and David Fado. 2004. *UML 2 Toolkit.* Indianapolis, Indiana: Wiley Publishing, Inc.

Finkelstein, C. 1989. An Introduction to Information Engineering: From Strategic Planning to Information Systems. Sydney: Addison-Wesley.

_____. 1992. Information Engineering: Strategic Systems Development. Sydney: Addison-Wesley.

Flavin, Mathew. 1981. *Fundamental Concepts of Information Modeling.* New York: Yourdon Press.

Formark, B. 1976. "The ANSI/X3/SPARC/SGDBMS Architecture". *The ANSI/SPARC DBMS Model: Proceedings of the Second* SHARE Working Conference on Data Base Management Systems. [Jardine, D. A., Ed.] New York: North-Holland Publishing Company.

Fowler, M. 1997. *Analysis Patterns.* (Reading, MA: Addison-Wesley).

Gamma, E., Richard Helm, Ralph Johnson, and John Vlissides. 1995. *Design Patterns: Elements of Reusable Object-Oriented Software.* Reading, MA: Addison-Wesley Publishing Company.

Gane, C., and Trish Sarson. 1979. *Structured Systems Analysis: Tools and Techniques.* Englewood Cliffs, NJ: Prentice Hall.

Halpin, T. 1995. *Conceptual Schema & Relational Database Design,* Second Edition. Sydney: Prentice Hall.

_____. 2001. *Information Modeling and Relational Databases.* San Francisco: Morgan Kaufman Publishers.

_____. 2008 Information Modeling and Relational Databases, Second Edition. Boston: Morgan Kaufman Publishers.

Hammer, Michael (1990), "Reengineering Work: Don't automate, obliterate", *Harvard Business Review,* Jul/Aug 1990, pp 104–112

Hammer, Michael and Champy, James (1993), *Reengineering the Corporation: A Manifesto for Business Revolution,* Harper Business.

Hay, D. 1995. *Data Model Patterns: Conventions of Thought.* New York: Dorset House

_____. 1999. "UML Misses the Boat" *East Coast Oracle Users' Group: ECO 99* (Conference Proceedings / HTML File). Apr 1, 1999 Available at *http://essentialstrategies.com/publications/objects/umleco.htm*

_____, 1999a. "There is no Object-oriented Analysis" *Data to Knowledge Newsletter.* January 15, 1999. http://articles.davehay.com/public_pages/article_library/7?article_id=92

_____. 2003. *Requirements Analysis: From Business Views to Architecture.* Englewood Cliffs, NJ: Prentice Hall PTR.

_____. 2006. *Data Model Patterns: A Metadata Map.* Boston: Morgan Kaufmann.

_____. 2008. "Semantics, Ontology, and Data Modeling", *Cutter Report on Business Intelligence*, Vol. 6, No. 7. June 1, 2008

_____. 2010. "Prepositions, Not Verbs or Nouns". *The Data Administration Newsletter*. May 1, 2010.

Leiner, B. M., V. G. Cerf, D. D. Clark, R. E. Kahn, L. Kleinrock, D. C. Lynch,
Jon Postel, L. G. Roberts, S. Wolff. "Histories of the Internet". *Internet Society*. Retrieved 7/24/2011 from
http://www.isoc.org/internet/history/brief.shtml.

Lo, Lawrence. "Cuneiform". *http://www.ancientscripts.com/cuneiform.html* (5/11/2010).

McGilvray, D. 2008. "Data Model Comparison" in McGilvray, D., *Executing Data Quality Projects: Ten Steps to Quality Data and Trusted Information*. Boston: Morgan Kaufmann Publishers.

McMenamin, S., and John Palmer. 1984. *Essential Systems Analysis*. Englewood Cliffs, NJ: Yourdon Press.

Martin, J. 1977. *Computer Data-Base Organization*. (Englewood Cliffs, NJ: Prentice Hall).

Martin, J. and Clive Finkelstein. Nov. 1981. "Information Engineering", *Technical Report,* two volumes, Lancs, UK : Savant Institute, Carnforth.

Martin, J. and Carma McClure. 1985. *Diagramming Techniques for Analysts and Programmers*. Englewood Cliffs, NJ: Prentice Hall.

Martin, J. and James Odell. 1995. *Object-Oriented Methods*. Englewood Cliffs, NJ: Prentice Hall.

Merriam Webster. 2010. *Merriam-Webster Online*. Retrieved 2011 from http://merriam-webster.com.

Miller, G. A. 1956. "The Magical Number Seven, Plus or Minus Two: Some Limits on Our Capacity for Processing Information", *The Psychological Review*, Vol. 63, No. 2 (March, 1956). Available at http://www.musanim.com/miller1956/.

Mitchell, J., ed. 1977. *The Random House Encyclopedia*. New York: Random House.

Monash, C. 2005. "Is Ingres a Serious Player? First Some History…". Computerworld. June 2, 2005.

Morris, E. 2011. "Did My Brother Invent E-Mail With Tom Van Vleck?". *The New York Times*. Five articles, June 19-23, 2011.

Neward, T. 2006. "The Vietnam of Computer Science". *The Blog Ried: Ted Neward's Technical Blog*. June 26, 2006. Retreived 8/10/2011 from blogs.tedneward.com/2006/06/26/The+Vietnam+of+Computer+Science.aspx.

Object Management Group (OMG). 2010. "The Business Motivation Model Version 1.1". (OMG Document formal/2010-05-01). Available at http://www.omg.org/spec/BMM/1.1/PDF/.

_____. 1997. "UML Specification version 1.1" (OMG document ad/97-08-11). Available at http://www.omg.org/cgi-bin/doc?ad/97-08-11.

_____. 2005a. "UML 2.0:Infrastructure (OMG document 05-07-05)". Available at http://www.omg.org/docs/formal/05-07-05.pdf.

_____. 2005b. "UML 2.0:Superstructure (OMG document 05-07-04)". Available at http://www.omg.org/docs/formal/05-07-04.pdf.

_____. 2008. "Semantics of Business Vocabulary and Business Rules". (OMG Specification formal/2008-01-02). Available at http://www.omg.org/spec/SBVR/1.0/.

Oracle Corporation. 1986. "Strategic Planning Course", SQL*Development Method. Belmont, CA: Oracle Corporation.

Oracle Corporation. 1996. *Custom Development Method*. Redwood Shores, CA: Oracle Corporation.

Page-Jones, M. 2000. *Fundamentals of Object-Oriented Design in UML*. New York: Dorset House).

Peter, I. 2011"The History of Email". *Net History*. Retrieved 7/27/2011 from http://www.nethistory.info/History of the Internet/email.html.

Random House. 1977. *The Random House Encyclopedia*. New York: Random House, Inc.

Rumbaugh, J., Ivar Jacobson, and Grady Booch. 1999. *The Unified Modeling Language Reference Manual*. Reading, Massachusetts: Addison-Wesley.

_____, Michael Blaha, William Premerlani, Frederick Eddy, and William Lorensen. 1991. *Object-Oriented Modeling and Design.* Boca Raton, Florida: CRC Press.

Segaller, S. 1998. *Nerds 2.0.1: A Brief History of the Internet.* (New York: TV Books).

Shlaer, S. and Stephen J. Mellor. 1988. *Object-oriented Systems Analysis: Modeling the World in Data.* Englewood Heights, NJ: Yourdon Press.

Shlaer, S. and Stephen J. Mellor. 1992. *Object Lifecycles: Modeling the World in States.* Englewood Heights, NJ: Yourdon Press.

Silverston, L. 2001. *The Data Model Resource Book, Volume 1: A library of Universal Data Models for All Enterprises.* New York: John Wiley & Sons.

_____. 2001. *The Data Model Resource Book, Volume 2: A library of Universal Data Models by Industry Types.* New York: John Wiley & Sons.

_____, W.H Inmon, and K. Graziano. 1997. *The Data Model Resource Book: A Library of Logical Data Models and Data Warehouse Designs.* New York: John Wiley & Sons.

_____ and Paul Agnew. 2009. *The Data Model Resource Book, Volume 3.* Indianapolis, IN: Wiley Publishing, Inc.

Simsion, G.C, and Graham C. Witt. 2005. *Data Modeling Essentials. Third Edition.* Boston: Morgan Kaufmann.

Simsion, Graeme. 2007. *Data Modeling Theory and Practice.* Bradley Beach, NJ: Technics Publications.

Sowa, John. F. and John A. Zachman. 1992. "Extending and Formalizing the Framework for Information Systems Architecture", *IBM Systems Journal*, Vol. 31, No. 3. IBM Publication G321-5488.

Van Vleck, T. "The History of Electronic Mail". Undated manuscript reproduced at http://www.multicians.org/thvv/mail-history.html.

Webster's New World Dictionary of the American Language. 1964. Cleveland: World Publishing Company.

Weiner, Norbert. 1948, 1961. *Cybernetics: or Control and Communication in the Animal and the Machine, second edition.* (Cambridge, MA: MIT Press).

Wikipedia. 2008. "Composite Structure Diagram".
     http://en.wikipedia.org/wiki/Composite_structure_diagram
     (11/13/2008).

Wikipedia.   2009.   "Fortran".   http://en.wikipedia.org/wiki/Fortran
     (9/5/2009).

Wikipedia.   2009.   "COBOL".   http://en.wikipedia.org/wiki/COBOL
     (9/5/2009).

Yourdon, E. and Larry L.Constantine. 1979. *Structured Design:
     Fundamentals of a Discipline of Computer Program and Systems Design.*
     Englewood Cliffs, NJ: Prentice Hall. (Widely circulated as a
     manuscript in 1976.)

Zachman, John. 1987. "A framework for information systems
     architecture", *IBM Systems Journal*, Vol. 26, No. 3. (IBM
     Publication G321-5298)

Index

www.ingramcontent.com/pod-product-compliance
Lightning Source LLC
Chambersburg PA
CBHW081809200326
41597CB00023B/4199